DATE			

Doodlebug Country

Doodlebug Country

The Rail Motorcar on the Class I Railroads of the United States

By Edmund Keilty

Interurbans Special 77

Interurban Press • Glendale, California • 1982

DUST JACKET PAINTING BY HARLAN HINEY

Although the streamliner M-10000 would have hardly been called a doodlebug by the Union Pacific, it did represent the UP's final effort in the rail motor car field, coming as it did in 1934 at the dawn of the streamlined age. Running as the **City of Salina**, the M-10000 is depicted at the UP's Topeka, Kansas, station circa 1936 across the platform from an example of the earliest Union Pacific motorcar era — the McKeen. Thus were brought together the cars that opened and closed the doodlebug era on one major American railroad.

FRONT ENDPAPER: Across the lonely prairie (could it have been Montana or some lonely reach of North Dakota?) growls the B-22, an Electro-Motive product of 1929, and its combo-RPO coach. Passengers were few in the wide open spaces, but then, the crew of the railcar didn't expect very many. **M. D. McCarter Collection**.

REAR ENDPAPER: An unusual train, to say the least. At Maunch Chunk, Pa., on April 18, 1948, appears Lehigh Valley Electro-Motive car 11 with a lightweight "American Flyer" coach and an outside-braced boxcar. Such mixed consists were sometimes seen in doodlebug operation. **R. R. Wallin Collection**.

REAR DUST JACKET: For years the Santa Fe ran doodlebugs from Los Angeles to San Bernardino over two different routes. Electro-Motive car 181 pauses at Arcadia tower on the route via Pasadena in May of 1953. **Donald Duke**.

DOODLEBUG COUNTRY

©1982 by Edmund Keilty   First Printing 1982

Keilty, Edmund
    Doodlebug Country.

    Bibliography: p. 000
    Includes index.
    1. Railroad motorcars — United States.
I. Title.
TP494.K44   1982   625.2'6   82-10053
ISBN 0-916374-50-5

This book was manufactured in the United States of America.

Table of Contents

Someone pencilled on the back of this photograph the observation: "Can't see car 351 doing anything but spinning its wheels with this consist." Those seven heavyweights do look a bit much for Gulf, Mobile & Northern's Brill-built motorcar, location unknown but doubtless taken shortly after its delivery in 1930. *Robert G. Foley Collection*

Introduction

I
T HAS BEEN SAID that the placement of the railroad
lines, and the towns along them, in the great heartland
of this country—known variously as the Mississippi
Valley, the Great Plains, or the Midwest—was dictated by
how far a farmer could drive a team of horses and a wagon
during daylight hours.

This was reckoned at about 20 miles so that the towns and
rail lines were laid out with this figure in mind. In other
words, stations were located so that no farmer had to travel
more than 10 miles to deliver his crops to a shipping point.
And the railroad lines were built in a great mesh, or grid, all
over the Midwest.

Of course, many of these branch lines were busy only during the harvest season. Still, regular, year-around service had
to be operated to serve the small towns that grew up around
the railroad stations. From this set of circumstances evolved
the branch line "local" train, that uncomfortable, slow, not-
always-reliable, but absolutely essential fixture of rural
railroading from roughly 1880 until the 1920s.

Even in the days before the automobile and good roads, the
"local" was almost always a money loser. Many railroads
called these trains "accommodations," which just about sums
up their place in the overall railroad scheme of things. For
many years the railroads could afford to lose money on the
locals, write them off as a necessary public service and still
make a profit on freight and mainline passenger trains.

The local passenger train needed a locomotive, tender, and
one or more passenger and baggage cars. The locomotive

used up a lot of coal, and required the attentions of a vast
army of maintenance men between runs. The road crew consisted of at least four, sometimes five or more, men.

The railroads were keenly anxious to cut these losses, but
the early internal combustion replacements that were
offered—the McKeen car and the General Electric gas-
electric— represented a first generation experiment with a
new means of propulsion and proved expensive and unreliable
in service. In fact, the cars presented a welter of technological
problems that the average railroad was not prepared to deal
with, since most railroad mechanics were trained only to fix
the less sophisticated steam locomotive.

So, with a few notable exceptions, purchases of gas cars
were limited to a small number of units. Most of the roads,
therefore, entered the 1920s with a few cranky rail motorcars
and thousands of the same cars and locomotives they had
been using for 50 years.

By this time the spread of the paved roads and the mass
acquisition of automobiles by the public had made the local
train even more of an anachronism. Had the railroad industry
been equipped with a clear crystal ball, the end of the local
train might have occurred then and there. Instead, a man
named Harold Hamilton came along with a vastly improved
rail motorcar and the course of railroad history was bent for
another generation.

Hamilton's Electro-Motive Corporation followed shortly by
J. G. Brill, the giant streetcar and railcar builder, began to
offer a larger and much more reliable self-propelled car than

had been available. These cars promised to cut costs dramatically, and the railroad industry was ready to try them in a big way.

Even if many passengers had deserted the branch line local, the carriage of express and packages, and U.S. mail, was still heavy, so the trains had to stay. In any event, state regulatory bodies almost universally refused to recognize changing times and continued to mandate retention of the locals. So the market existed for a good self-propelled railcar, and slowly at first but with rapid acceleration as the 1920s wore on, the roads purchased the new cars.

The pages of *Railway Age* of the late 1920s are replete with advertised testimonials to the cost saving and reliability of these new cars. Nowhere was this more true than on the rail lines that served mid-America. From the Canadian border to the Gulf of Mexico, from the Appalachians to the Rockies, the burble of the gas-electric car was heard across the land. Doodlebug Country!

A pattern of doodlebug operation evolved, particularly in the Midwest, in which the self-propelled car replaced a standard steam train on the "local." This train was hardly scheduled for passenger convenience. Crack-of-dawn (or earlier) departures were common, the time often dictated by connections with certain main line schedules. Speeds were slow, stops frequent and lengthy. A bus or auto on a parallel highway could make a round trip or two in the time it took the doodlebug to cover the run.

And the runs were frequently long, covering an entire division, perhaps a good part of a state or even two states. The main business of the train was mail and express, hence the usual division of the railcar into baggage and passenger sections. And frequently the baggage/express section took up more room than the passenger section.

Among the roads that closely followed the standard railcar pattern were the Burlington, Great Northern, Northern Pacific, The Milwaukee Road, Chicago & North Western, Santa Fe, Alton, Rock Island, Missouri Pacific, Chicago Great Western, Mobile & Ohio, Gulf, Mobile & Northern, Minneapolis & St. Louis, Texas & New Orleans, and the western portions of the Pennsylvania, New York Central, and Baltimore & Ohio.

The Union Pacific system used the McKeen car which it to a large degree built and financed, but otherwise followed the pattern—or more accurately, helped to set the pattern since the McKeen came some 15 or so years earlier than the EMC and Brill gas-electrics. A few roads which resisted this general plan of doodlebugs on the branches included the Soo Line, Wabash and Katy, although each had a few cars.

The Cotton Belt stuck with its General Electric cars until some used standard cars were purchased in the early 1940s. The Midland Valley-Kansas Oklahoma & Gulf combination started with General Electrics and continued to operate them (albeit much rebuilt) until the very end of all passenger service. By the 1940s they were a bit on the quaint side.

Outside of doodlebug country, probably only one railroad operated its rail motorcars in the typical branch line pattern and that was the Seaboard. In Doodlebug Country and on the Seaboard the long run of more than 100 miles was the rule; in the rest of the country it was the exception and the runs were more oriented toward passengers. Some were actual commuter-type trains.

In the Boston area, the Boston & Maine and the New Haven operated this type of service, and in the New York district the New York Central, Susquehanna and Erie. Out of Philadelphia there was the Reading, the Pennsylvania, and their jointly-owned subsidiary the Pennsylvania-Reading-Seashore Lines. These frequently connected with electrified commuter trains. At Baltimore the Pennsy had a rather unique commute line to Parkton that was operated completely with railcars. The B&O also had a couple of routes.

Out of Washington, D. C., the Richmond, Fredericksburg & Potomac and the Washington & Old Dominion operated commuter doodlebugs for a short time. Outside of this east coast corridor the railcar commuter runs were rather scarce. The Southern Pacific tried it on its San Francisco-San Jose line, but only in non rush hours and even then the self-propelled cars could not maintain the tight schedules and were withdrawn after a short time. For a period a Port Costa-Oakland Pier run was made by a railcar in commuter hours, but it didn't last long.

A third type of railcar operation was the short line car. Probably this is the type that most people would think of when doodlebugs are mentioned: the little, dilapidated car meeting a main line train, either operated by a small, independent railroad or on a short and obscure branch of a trunk line. The equipment was generally lightweight, had a mechanical drive, and was often second-hand (or third or fourth).

Trying to categorize this kind of operation, though, is next to impossible. Such roads as the Chesapeake & Ohio and the Lehigh Valley used the same type of heavy-duty equipment that was used on the long distance runs of the Midwest. Other roads used anything from spiffy EMC gas cars to slightly-modified Model T Fords equipped with flanged wheels. Some of the home-built contraptions were literally beyond description; they had to be seen to be believed.

But the most common type used in short line service was the Brill Model 55 and the Edwards Model 10, both of which were lightweight, direct-drive cars equipped with gasoline engines. The fact that these cars had a great deal in common with motor trucks was no doubt a factor in their popularity on short lines which often lacked the facilities to maintain the more sophisticated equipment. If a mechanic could fix a Ford Model T, he could do a pretty good job keeping one of these small railcars going.

It is perhaps ironic—but all the more understandable—to note that many of these simple cars outlived by many years their more glamorous and complicated cousins, the gas-electric car.

There were, inevitably, a few major railroads which did not purchase any railcars at all. Prominent among these carriers were the Norfolk & Western, Lackawanna, Atlantic Coast Line, Nickel Plate and (until the advent of the RDC car) the Jersey Central. One might wonder, too, why some roads had only one or two units (the Louisville & Nashville, for example) but operated them for such a long period of time.

This book is the second in a series of volumes dedicated to the rail motorcar. The first, *Interurbans Without Wires*, profiled the manufacturers—major and minor—of the motorcar and traced the technological development of the mode, stopping short of the postwar super doodlebug—the Budd RDC car. Special 66 also carried complete builders' lists of the major and some minor manufacturers.

Now we tackle the subject from a new direction. This volume has a section covering each of the Class I railroads of the 1900-1960 period complete with photos, maps, rosters, a sampling of schedules, and, where the story is sufficiently complex, a short text on how the cars were employed.

A major departure is the inclusion of the Budd RDC car in the system coverage. The development of the RDC will well merit a book of its own. However, it was felt that in presenting a roster of each railroad's motorcars, the RDCs should be listed to give a complete picture, and this we have done.

As we did in the first book, we have covered some of the early mid-1930 articulated streamliners, since they qualified as close kin to the traditional doodlebug and even resembled some of the later motorcars in their streamlining.

In a future book we plan to cover doodlebugs on the short lines, in some ways our stiffest challenge due to the bewildering complexity of the rosters and unending variety in the type of equipment operated.

As of 1982, the doodlebug was still not quite dead. Still alive, if you count the RDC cars still operating on certain Amtrak and commuter authority routes. But for all practical purposes, the rail motorcar today is but a memory. Its tracks in Doodlebug Country lingered longer but even now they, too, are disappearing in some places with the demise of the Rock Island and parts of the Milwaukee Road, and thinning-out pro-grams now being carried out by Burlington Northern and other prosperous railroads.

Today's farmer is hardly limited to his 20-mile trek, and probably wouldn't know where the railroad station is located—if it still exists. He may still use the railroad to haul his grain, but times have changed. As for the doodlebug in Doodlebug Country—it is an extinct species.

The doodlebug did the local work, and that truck backed up to Chesapeake & Ohio Brill car 9051 means there's some express business to be transacted here at Whitesville, WV on this overcast July 14, 1948.   *C. A. Brown*

The Columbia Falls-Kalispell MT doodlebug met the main line trains at Columbia Falls. Under threatening skies, RPO-baggage unit 2301 and trailer, having discharged passengers and cargo, patiently await the highball of engine 2505 and a train of heavyweights. *Railway Negative Exchange*

This diminutive McKeen single-truck trailer was built for the Southern Pacific.

James H. Harrison Collection

Never having operated any doodlebugs, ordinarily the Monon wouldn't have a place in this book. But a new Budd RDC car did demonstrate on the Hoosier line and here passes the depot at Monon in 1950. So, here it is.

M. D. McCarter Collection

Inbound to Los Angeles from Pasadena, this Santa Fe motorcar crosses the Pasadena Freeway on the Arroyo Seco Viaduct in July of 1953. *Donald Duke*

The 5925-5934 series of motors appeared thusly after being rebuilt by the Milwaukee Road from baggage-passenger cars. Car 5930 takes the sharp turn out of the Old Milwaukee depot circa 1940. See the title page for a photo of this car as originally built.
Gordon Lloyd

New York, Susquehanna & Western streamlined unit 1001 passes the local freight at Swatswoord Jct., NJ, on June 23, 1940.
Stephen D. Maguire Collection

One of the very distinctive Stover cars belonging to the Panama Canal Commission rides the rails of the Panama Railroad circa 1910.
Author's Collection

There's mail and express aplenty for McKeen M-16 at the Union Pacific depot at Solomon, KS, circa mid-1930s.
W. C. Whittaker Collection

The Santa Fe's "Surf Line" between Los Angeles and San Diego was aptly named. And for several years two daily roundtrips of the SAN DIEGANS were handled by the ATSF's pair of RDCs. Here's the train at San Clemente in April of 1953. *Donald Duke*

The face of the Baltimore & Ohio's car 6500 looks rather menacing, especially amid the Victorian surroundings of Baltimore, circa 1927. *Author's Collection*

ROAD NO.	BUILDER	DATE	BLDR. NO.	ENGINE & DRIVE	BODY TYPE	LGTH.	WT.	DISPOSITION	REMARKS
M-98	EMC St. Louis	1928	242 1454	Wint. 120 275hp GE	7win RPO Bag. 20p	72'	52½t	Ret. 1961	To work service, 1949
M-99	EMC St. Louis	1927	190 1414	Wint. 120 275hp GE	13win Bag. 36p	72'	48t	Ret. 1946	Pass. sect. eliminated

Oregon Short Line

ROAD NO.	BUILDER	DATE	BLDR. NO.	ENGINE & DRIVE	BODY TYPE	LGTH.	WT.	DISPOSITION	REMARKS
M-60 (470)	McKeen	1909	51	McKeen A 200hp GM	10win RPO Bag.	70'	37½t	To Pac. & Idaho Nor., 1928	Reacq. from PIN, 8/30. Ret. 1944
M-61 (480)	McKeen	1909	52	McKeen A 200hp GM	10win RPO Bag.	70'	37½t	Ret. 12/42	—
M-62[1] (491)	McKeen	1911	116	McKeen A 200hp GM	16win CE Bag. 50p	70'	40½t	To UP M-15, 10/17	—
M-62[2]	McKeen	1905	3	Riotti 100hp GM	10win Bag.-Pass.	55'	35t	Rblt. tlr. T-52, 1924	Ex-UP M-3, acq. 9/24
M-63 (492)	McKeen	1911	117	McKeen A 200hp GM	16win CE Bag. 50p	70'	43½t	To UP M-16, 10/17	—

Notes on Reading the Tables

THIS SAMPLE was taken from the Oregon Short Line and the Oregon-Washington Ry. and Navigation Co. tables. For the most part, the table is self-explanatory but a few notes may be in order.

ROAD NO.—The principal number of the car during most of its life is given. A small number elevated and to the right (see car M-62) indicates that it was the first car to bear that number, and that a second car later bore the same number. Usually, the second car follows in sequence in the listing. If another number appears in parenthesis below the main number (again see car M-62) that is a previous number assigned the same car. Some railroads renumbered cars one or more times.

BUILDER—If a single builder is mentioned, that builder built the entire car. If more than one builder is mentioned, one was usually the prime contractor (see car M-98) with the other builder responsible for the carbody.

DATE—Almost always the year the car was delivered.

BLDR. NO.—If more than one builder, each builder's number is given in the same sequence.

ENGINE & DRIVE—If the number 2 appears first, there were 2 engines. Number or letter appearing right after builder of engine (such as McKeen A or Wint. 120) indicates the model number of the power plant. The horsepower is given next followed by type of engine: GE—gas electric; GM—gas mechanical. DE—diesel electric. DH—diesel hydraulic. DM—diesel mechanical. Key to builder abbreviations: Alco—American Locomotive Co. Bal.—Baldwin. Cont.—Continental. FM—Fairbanks-Morse. GE—General Electric. H-S—Hall-Scott. Ham.—Hamilton. Her.—Hercules. Sterl.—Sterling. Wauk.—Waukesha. WH or West.—Westinghouse. Wint.—Winton.

BODY TYPE—Car M-60 listing means: 10 window, Railway Post Office compartment, Baggage section. Where seating capacity is known, it is given next (such as 50p for passengers). Often cars had no seating capaity, being used only for baggage, mail and express.

LENGTH—given in feet, rounded off to the nearest even foot.

WEIGHT—given in tons, rounded off to the nearest half-ton.

DISPOSITION—Retirement or sale dates given where known, or dates rebuilt to other use. Roster number or car under new owner given if known.

REMARKS—Deals primarily with former owners or additional information on disposition. Major rebuilding information also supplied where known.

Alaska Railroad

THE ALASKA RAILROAD—serving our 50th state—has been isolated over the years not only geographically but philosophically. Unlike the other major U. S. roads, which are privately-owned, the Alaska was built by the government because private capital was unwilling to venture into the northern wilderness.

One result of government ownership has been the railroad's need to battle the far-off bureaucrats in Washington for needed improvements. The railroad has had to buy its equipment where and when it could—that certainly has been the case in the Alaska's experience with self-propelled railcars.

It is certain that the Alaska's collection of doodlebugs was one of the most varied of any American railroad of comparable size.

Two small railroads, the Alaska Northern in the Kenai Peninsula, and the Tanana Valley in the Fairbanks area, were taken over by the ARR and incorporated into its construction. The Alaska Northern had two Fairbanks-

The front end of Brill-built car 214 has been extensively modified, probably to aid in snow-fighting. All of the Alaska Railroad's doodlebugs either were converted to trailers or off the roster by the mid-1950s.
Author's Collection

Morse model 24 cars, and possibly also an open F-M car, but there is no record that they were ever used on the ARR.

The Tanana Valley, which was three-foot gauge, had two cars, one of them an Edison battery-electric, and the other a rather curious-appearing open car of unknown manufacture. These cars were used on the Alaska until the TV lines were converted to standard gauge, which was delayed until the early 1930s.

In 1925 the AAR purchased the first car of its own, a Brill model 75 gas-mechanical unit. It was in that year also that one of the more interesting cars in doodlebug history was acquired. This car, built in 1907, was one of the earliest of the McKeen cars and was built for the San Diego, Cuyamaca & Eastern and was named the "Cuyamaca."

After a few years on this road, it was sold to the Yuma Valley of Arizona, a line built by the U. S. Department of Reclamation for use in building the early irrigation projects in the lower Colorado River valley.

After its need was over in Arizona, the U. S. Department of the Interior, which controlled both the Reclamation Department and the Alaska Railroad, sent the car up to the ARR. Thus the car went from one of the hottest areas in the U. S. to one of the coldest. When the car arrived in Alaska in run-down condition, the ARR had to rebuild it but unaccountably failed to make it fit for the rigors of the Alaskan climate.

The Oneida Co. provided parts to convert the car to gasoline engine drive. Normally Oneida kits were used to change old steam coaches to self-propulsion and this may have been the only instance in which the drive was applied to an already-powered car. In any case, the engines were mounted under the McKeen car in a very exposed position.

In another twist of logic, the pointed front (A McKeen trademark), which might have come in handy for fighting snow drifts, was rounded off. Once in service the car proved a failure, and soon was demotorized for use as a combine behind steam locomotives.

A Brill model 250 gas-electric car was purchased new in 1927; two more 250s were bought second-hand, one from the Lehigh Valley in 1938 and a larger unit with a Railway Post Office section came from the New York Central in 1944. During World War II, two streamlined cars, an Edwards model 20 and an ACF "Motorailer" (both gas-mechanical), were requisitioned from the U.S. Navy.

During the time railcars were used on the ARR, nine were acquired from six builders, plus an open-end observation trailer. Apparently only two regular Alaska Railroad runs were operated by self-propelled units; one between Fairbanks and what became the campus of the University of Alaska up until about 1931, and an Anchorage-Palmer service, to serve the Mantanuska Valley Colony, founded in 1935. Otherwise, the units were used mostly in special tourist service.

Alaska Railroad

ROAD NO.	BUILDER	DATE	BLDR. NO.	ENGINE & DRIVE	BODY TYPE	LGTH.	WT.	DISPOSITION	REMARKS
—	Fed. Stor. Btry.	1912	—	Edison Btry-Elec	5win 4wh Bag. 20p	28'	—	OS 1931	3' gauge, ex-Tanana Valley
80	—	—	—	Pierce GM	Open 4wh 15p	—	—	—	3' gauge, ex-Tanana Valley
107	Brill	1925	22285	Brill 75 175hp GM	13win Bag. 50p	55'	26½t	Rblt. to tlr. 304	—
108	McKeen (Oneida-Co. Shops)	1907 (1925)	—	2 Cont. 104hp GM	11win CE Bag. p	55'	34t	Rblt. to comb. 83	Ex-San Diego Cuyumaca & East "Cuyumaca" then Yuma Vy. No. 1, rblt. to dbl. end by AAR, acq. 1925
212	Edwards	—	—	Buda 125hp GM	11 win Bag. 40p	50'	25t	Ret. 4/54	Ex-US Navy (Demo. 200?)
213	ACF	1942	2514	Waukesha GM	9win Bag. p	75'	40t	Ret. 4/54	Ex-US Navy
214 (114)	Brill	1927	22539	Brill-West 250hp GE	13win Bag. 26p	60'	46t	Ret. 4/54	Re-eng. with 250hp Cummins D
215 (115)	Brill	1927	22563	Brill-West 250hp GE	13win Bag. 53p	60'	45t	Ret. 4/54	Ex-Lehigh Valley 5, acq. 1938. Re-eng. 250hp Cummins D
216 (116)	Brill	1927	22544	Brill-West 250hp GE	7win DE-RPO Bag. 40p	75'	62t	Ret. 4/54	Ex-NYC. M-400, acq. 1944. Re-eng. 250hp Cummins D. Named "Tanana"

Trailers

ROAD NO.	BUILDER	DATE	BLDR. NO.	ENGINE & DRIVE	BODY TYPE	LGTH.	WT.	DISPOSITION	REMARKS
303	Brill	1927	22540	—	16win Obs. 60p	50'	27t	Ret. 2/51	Open obs. platform
304	Brill (Co. Shops)	1925 (1931)	22285	—	16win 50p	55'	—	Ret. 2/51	Ex-motor 107

ACF-built car 213 was a World War II purchase from the U. S. Navy and it is shown in service (above) early in its Alaska Railroad career. McKeen No. 4 (below) is shown in service on the Ann Arbor in 1914. *Both: Author's Collection*

Ann Arbor

ROAD NO.	BUILDER	DATE	BLDR. NO.	ENGINE & DRIVE	BODY TYPE	LGTH.	WT.	DISPOSITION	REMARKS
1-5	McKeen	1911	—	McKeen 200hp GM	15win CE Bag. 83p	70'	35t	OS by 1931	Arch windows

Santa Fe

ATSF Rail Motorcar Runs—1933

Route	Train No.	Mileage
Chicago-Pekin IL	13-12	159.6
Streator IL-Shopton IA	25-26	145
Hutchinson-Kinsley KS	61-68	94
Corcoran-Fresno CA	25-30	71.4
Fresno-Calwa CA	15-26	3
San Bernardino-Los Angeles CA	53-54	71.2
San Bernardino-Redlands loop	101	27.4
Emporia-Moline, KS	66-65	84.4
Lawrence-Ottawa KS	53-54	27.1
Lawrence-Emporia KS	55-56	82
St Joseph MO-Topeka KS	57-58	71.4
Florence-Ellinwood KS	57-58 (cq)	99
Florence-Winfield KS	53-54	74
Strong City-Concordia KS	51-52	117.7
Hutchinson KS-Ponca City OK	49-50	146
Blackwell-Ponca City OK	63-64	16
Arkansas City KS-Shawnee OK	51-52	143.5
Shawnee-Lindsay OK	305-306	76
Wichita KS-Okla City OK	17-18	172
Wichita-Mulvane KS	47-48	15
Newton-Wichita KS	13	27
Guthrie-Skedee OK	58-57	82
Skedee-Ripley OK	51-52	52.6
Guthrie-Kiowa OK via Enid	54-53	117
Attica-Belvedere KS	73-74	52
Kansas City-Chanute KS	51-52	126
Chanute-Emporia KS	61-62	84
Chanute KS-Joplin MO	57-58	85
Wichita KS-San Angelo TX	45-46	511.5
Independence-Wellington KS	75-74	104
Tonkawa OK-Wellington KS	75-74	104
Cleburne-Paris TX	67-68	154
Coleman-San Angelo TX	75-76	76
Beaumont-Longview TX	202-201	117
Port Bolivar-Beaumont TX	242-241	70
Kirbyville TX-Oakdale LA	292-291	83
Somerville-Beaumont TX	205-206	175
Shattuck OK-Etter TX	49-50	134
Amarillo TX-Carlsbad NM	93-96	287
Pampa TX-Clinton OK	62-63	138
San Angelo-Alpine TX	45-46	226

THE SANTA FE, famed for its mighty transcontinental main-line streamliners, was a railroad of branch lines. They formed a dense spiderweb in the nation's heartland, particularly in states like Kansas, Oklahoma and Texas, extended as well to the remote mesas of New Mexico and Arizona, and criss-crossed the lush San Joaquin Valley of California.

To serve the passenger and express needs of the branches, the Santa Fe was a doodlebug operator in a big way. Railcar service on the far-flung Santa Fe system operated from terminals all the way from Chicago to Oakland, and Kansas City to Beaumont. In its usual conservative way, the Santa Fe got into railcar operation cautiously, trying only a few of the early, temperamental types of car.

But the Santa Fe stuck to railcars long after most other railroads had given up passenger service on branch-lines, and it even toyed with the idea of a superdoodlebug for the main lines.

Starting in 1909 with a pair of McKeen cars, the ATSF was slow to make widespread use of the railcar until the late 1920s. Early operation saw three McKeens, which were gone by 1922, two General Electric cars which lasted into the 1940s, an experimental Ganz steam-powered car which was rebuilt into a coach in a very short time, and one Hall Scott car which was scrapped in 1933.

After this, except for a few cars picked up from lines merged into the system, the Santa Fe did not buy another car until 1928, when two Electro-Motive/St. Louis units and one Brill car were acquired.

Upon determining that these cars were more reliable than their predecessors, the company embarked on a wide-scale program which saw 21 cars bought in 1929, two in 1930, 14 in 1931 and two more in 1932, including the articulated M-190 built by EMC/Pullman.

The Santa Fe therefore entered the Great Depression with a fleet of 40 modern cars which took over most of the branchline and some secondary mainline passenger, mail and express

Santa Fe rail motorcars ranged over the entire system. Car M186, an EMC-Pullman, is shown halted at Lockport, Ill., in the 1950s on its run from Chicago to Pekin. *Author's Collection*

Mission Tower was the entrance to the Los Angeles Union Passenger Terminal. EMC-Pullman unit 181 is actually on a backing move to position itself for its departure to Pasadena, circa early 1950s. *Donald Duke*

runs. These routes included the longest pre-RDC railcar run in the nation, Wichita, Kan., to San Angelo, Tex. some 543 miles.

Compared to most other railroads, the Santa Fe's withdrawal from doodlebug operation was slow. Many of the prairie runs lasted all through the 1950s, and the last such run not using RDC cars was the Clovis to Carlsbad route in New Mexico. It lasted until 1967, and featured a railcar towing a round-end observation coach.

The Santa Fe did not become heavily involved with the RDC car, and it was to rue the day that it ever heard of the Budd-built unit which was so popular with most of the other passenger-carrying roads.

In 1952 ATSF purchased two 85-foot RDC-1 cars and assigned them to the busy and extremely popular Los Angeles-to-San Diego Surf Line, practically a commuter run. Their introduction was accompanied by much fanfare,

and train service was stepped up from five to seven round trips a day. One of the RDC trains ran non-stop, making the trip 45 minutes faster than present-day Amtrak trains.

Then, on January 23, 1956, the two

A rare bird on the Santa Fe was its lone Hall-Scott motor, originally a demonstrator leased in 1919 and purchased in 1921. *Bert Ward Collection.*

23

Santa Fe

Table 79—WICHITA AND PRESIDIO.

No. 47	23-45	Mls.	January 14, 1940.	Elev.	46-24	No. 48
......	*1030 A M	0	lve. +Chicago(C.T.) arr.	......	8 50 P M	......
......	1055 P M	451.1	lve.+Kansas City..arr.	......	7 50 A M	......
......	3 35 A M	663.4	arr....+Wichita....lve.	......	1 40 A M	......
			(Union Station.)			
Motor.	Motor.		LEAVE[51,52,62,73] ARRIVE (C.T.)		No. 46 Motor.	Motor.
*7 30 A M	*5 00 A M	0	+Wichita[51,52,62,73](C.T.)	1315	11 50 P M	7 15 P M
f7 47 »	f5 15 »	7.2	Prospect	1330	f11 30	f6 55 »
f7 51 »	f5 20 »	9.6	Schulte	1345	f11 25	f6 49 »
f8 03 »	f5 29 »	15.8	Clonmel	1387	f11 14	f6 38 »
8 16 A M	5 40 »	23.2	+..Viola[52]	1359	11 00	*6 25 P M
......	f5 47 »	27.6	Alloway	1400	f10 51	......
......	5 54 »	31.4	+..Milton	1490	10 43	......
......	f6 05 »	38.6	Hamner	1373	f10 29	......
......	6 14 »	42.0	Runnymede	1400	10 23	......
......	6 23 »	49.1	+Harper[48,73]	1432	10 08	......
......	6 42 »	58.4	+Anthony[48,60]a	1356	9 48	......
......	......	63.4	Hayter	1363	......	......
......	7 05 »	72.5	+Waldron, Kan	1263	9 21 »	......
......	7 20 »	81.6	+..Byron	1208	9 03 »	......
......	7 36 »	92.3	+Cherokee[68]	1199	8 33 »	......
......	7 53 »	98.1	Yewed	1270	8 24 »	......
......	8 08 »	106.5	+..Carmen	1358	8 07 »	......
......	8 18 »	111.3	+..Aline	1309	7 58 »	......
......	8 30 »	118.6	West Cleo	1204	7 44 »	......
......	8 37 »	121.8	+..Orienta	1264	7 37 »	......
......	8 55 »	128.0	+..Fairview	1317	7 25 »	......
......	9 18 »	139.6	+..Longdale	1675	6 57 »	......
......	9 29 »	146.0	+..Canton	1610	6 44 »	......
......	9 50 »	157.0	+..Oakwood	1854	6 22 »	......
......	f1000 »	163.3	Nobscott	1590	f6 09 »	......
......	10 13 »	170.8	+..Thomas	1749	5 54 »	......
......	10 35 »	180.0	+Custer City	1800	5 34 »	......
......	10 45 »	187.2	+..Arapaho	1568	5 21 »	......
......	11 06 »	192.8	+..Clinton	1600	5 09 »	......
......	f1130 »	203.8	Braithwaite	1579	f4 38 »	......
......	11 44 »	211.9	Dill City	1850	4 23 »	......
......	11 50 A M	220.7	+..Sentinel	1611	4 07 »	......
......	f1210 P M	226.8	+..Cambridge	1590	f3 56 »	......
......	12 20 »	232.9	+Lone Wolf	1573	3 45 »	......
......	12 33 »	240.3	+..Lugert	1540	3 30 »	......
......	12 49 »	249.5	+..Blair	1460	3 13 »	......
......	#1 05 »	259.3	arr. +Altus lve.	1384	2 55 »	......
......	1 20 »	259.3	lve. ..Altus ..arr.	1384	#2 45 »	......
......	1 41 P M	270.2	Elmer, Okla	1271	2 21 P M	......
			Okla.-Texas State Line (P.&S.F.)			
......	2 01 »	280.3	+..Odell, Tex	1340	2 01 P M	......
......	2 19 »	289.5	+..Chillicothe	1387	1 45 »	......
......	2 32 »	296.3	Medicine Mound	1489	1 33 »	......
......	2 51 »	306.6	+..Margaret	1370	1 13 »	......
......	3 03 »	313.3	+..Crowell	1456	1 03 »	......
......	3 17 »	321.1	+..Foard City	1485	12 49 »	......
......	3 33 »	330.4	+..Truscott	1522	12 32 »	......
......	3 57 »	343.1	+..Benjamin	1468	12 08 P M	......
......	4 16 »	355.1	+..Knox City	1530	11 45 A M	......
......	4 22 »	357.7	O'Brien	1575	11 40 »	......
......	4 31 »	362.5	+..Rochester	1592	11 31 »	......
......	4 49 »	372.1	+..Rule	1687	11 13 »	......
......	5 03 »	380.4	+..Sagerton	1636	10 58 »	......
......	5 39 »	397.8	+..Hamlin	1726	10 25 »	......
......	5 56 »	406.3	McCaulley	1882	10 05 »	......
......	6 05 »	411.1	+..Sylvester	1856	9 56 »	......
......	6 18 »	418.5	Longworth	1963	9 42 »	......
......	6 50 »	432.1	arr.+Sweetwater lve.	2138	9 15 »	......
......	7 05 »	432.1	lve.+Sweetwater..arr.	2138	9 10 »	......
......	f7 14 »	437.4	Shauffler	2175	f8 59 »	......
......	7 33 »	449.3	+..Maryneal	2564	8 40 »	......
......	7 58 »	463.0	+..Blackwell	2100	8 17 »	......
......	8 09 »	469.5	Ft. Chadbourne	1960	8 07 »	......
......	8 22 »	477.3	+..Bronte	1893	7 55 »	......
No. 45 Motor	8 38 »	487.5	+..Tennyson	1872	7 39 »	No. 46 Motor
*7 15 A M	9 20 P M	509.4	arr.+San Angelo lve.	1835	*7 00 A M	
7 42 »	......	509.4	lve.+San Angelo..arr.	1835	5 30 »	
8 03 »		524.4	+..Tankersly	2002	5 03 »	
8 41 »		537.7	+..Mertzon	2184	4 42 »	
9 12 »		563.6	+..Barnhart	2548	3 58 »	
9 20 »		582.6	+..Big Lake	2677	3 30 »	
9 30 »		588.1	Landmark		f3 20 »	
f9 35 »		592.7	+..Best	2744	3 12 »	
9 40 »		594.8	Rita Santa		f3 07 »	
10 06 »		596.8	+..Texon		3 02 »	
10 36 »		611.9	+..Rankin	2494	2 37 »	
10 55 »		630.6	+..McCamey		2 05 »	
No. 129 Mixed.		641.6	+..Girvin	2267	1 47 »	No. 130 Mixed.
f1105 »		648.9	+..Owego	2277	f1 35 »	
11 45 A M	b115 P M	673.7	+Fort Stockton	2951	1 00 P M	*1 00 P M
......	f1 42 »	684.9	Belding	3188	f1034 »	
......	f2 10 »	696.3	Chancellor	3385	f1007 »	
......	f2 40 »	709.2	Hovey	3530	f9 37 »	
......	f3 02 »	720.4	Leoncita	3875	f9 14 »	
......	f3 20 »	726.4	Titley	4068	f8 56 »	
......	3 45 »	736.3	arr.+Alpine lve.	4469	8 35 »	
......	5 30 »	736.3	lve.+Alpine..arr.	4469	7 50 »	
......	f6 10 »	748.9	+..Paisano		f7 10 »	
......	9 00 P M	818.7	arr....Presidio..lve.		a4 30 P M	

See To Table 52. / From Englewood See Table 52.

Motor Car Trains operate between Wichita and Fort Stockton.

Table 80—INDEPENDENCE AND WELLINGTON.

No. 13 Motor	Mls.	LVE.] (Central time.) [ARR. January 14, 1940.	No. 14 Motor
*2 40 A M	0	+...Independence[74]...	8 15 P M
f2 50 »	6.1	+....Crane....	8 00 »
3 00 »	12.7	+...Elk City..	7 47 »
f3 09 »	19.1	+..Oak Valley..	7 35 »
3 18 »	24.4	+....Longton..	7 25 »
3 27 »	30.2	+...Elk Falls..	7 15 »
3 41 »	36.9	+....Moline[28]	7 03 »
3 55 »	45.3	+...Grenola..	6 48 »
f4 10 »	51.7	+..Grand Summit..	f6 35 »
4 22 »	60.2	+..Cambridge..	6 18 »
4 32 »	65.3	+...Burden..	6 08 »
f4 44 »	73.2	+..New Salem..	5 56 »
4 44 »	81.6	+Winfield (Main St.)..	5 40 »
4 59 »		+Winfield[44,62]..	5 30 »
5 18 »	87.9	+...Kellogg..	f5 04 »
5 41 »	91.4	+...Oxford..	4 58 »
f5 52 »	97.1	+....Dalton..	4 45 »
6 10 A M	104.1	arr. +Wellington[73,83] lve.	*4 30 P M

Table 81—CHERRYVALE AND COFFEYVILLE.

⊙73 A M	Mls.	LVE.] (Central time.) [ARR. January 14, 1940.	⊙74 P M	⊙84 P M
*3 05 »	0	+...Cherryvale[74]..	8 15	5 45
3 30 »	8.3	+....Liberty..	7 50	5 20
3 50 »	16.6	+..Coffeyville..	†7 30	§5 00
ARRIVE			LEAVE P M	P M

Table 82—OTTAWA AND GRIDLEY.

⊙No. 79	Ms	January 14, 1940.	⊙No. 80
†1015 A M	0	lv.+Ottawa[2,34,38,74](C.T.) ar.	6 10 P M
11 05 »	16.6	+..Williamsburg....	5 25 »
11 20 »	22.8	+..Agricola....	5 00 »
11 35 A M	27.0	+..Waverly..	4 40 »
12 05 P M	37.3	+..Sharpe..	4 00 »
12 50 »	45.6	+..Burlington..	3 35 »
1 20 P M	56.0	arr.+Gridley lve.	†3 00 »

Table 83—WELLINGTON, TONKAWA AND PONCA CITY.

Bus. A M	Bus.	Mls.	LVE.] (Central time.) [ARR. January 14, 1940.	Bus.	Bus.	Bus. P M
*6 15		0	+..Wellington[73,80]..			11 45
6 29		7.0	+...Rome..			11 30
6 50		15.2	+..South Haven[60]a..			11 14
6 57		18.5	+..Hunnewell..			11 02
P M		25.8	+..Braman..	P M	P M	10 37
*1 45	7 40	35.2	+..Blackwell[48]..	1 25	4 15	10 17
2 15	8 10	43.7	+..Tonkawa..	12 58	3 55	9 40
2 50	10 15		arr.+Ponca City[48,62] lve.	*1230	*3 05	*9 00

Table 84. SATANTA AND PRITCHETT.

⊙85	Mls.	LEAVE] January 14, 1940. [ARRIVE	⊙86
a1240	0	+..Satanta[85](C.T.)..	11 15
f1 35	16.0	+...Hickok..	f1000
2 05	23.9	+...Ulysses..	9 35
3 25	45.7	+...Johnson..	8 35
3 52	53.5	+...Manter..	8 15
f4 50	67.0	+...Bartlett..	f7 35
5 20	77.0	+....Walsh..	7 15
6 30	90.9	+..Springfield[87]..	6 15
f7 10	103.4	+....McCall..	f5 45
7 45	109.6	+..Pritchett..	b5 30
P M ARRIVE			LEAVE A M

Table 85. DODGE CITY AND BOISE CITY.

⊙73	Mls.	February 12, 1940.	⊙74
*1000	0	+Dodge City[2,3](C.T.)..	3 15
11 10	26.5	+..Montezuma..	1 45
12 20	49.8	+...Sublette..	12 20
12 50	58.2	+...Satanta[84]..	12 01
2 05	87.0	+...Hugoton..	10 15
3 45	119.9	+...Elkhart..	8 50
f4 05	126.2	+...Libbey..	f8 28
f4 45	138.4	+.McCullough..	f8 02
5 10	143.8	+....Keyes..	7 50
6 00	159.5	+..Boise City[86,87]..	*7 15
P M ARRIVE			LEAVE P M

Table 86—BOISE CITY AND FARLEY.

97 A M	73 A M	Mls.	LEAVE] (C.T.) [ARRIVE January 14, 1940.	74 A M	98 A M
......	*6 30	0	+Boise City[85,87]..	4 00	......
......	f6 50	9.5	+...Harmer..	f3 30	......
Mix.	7 10	19.2	+....Felt..	3 00	Mix.
P M	f7 35	30.5	+....Nieto..	f2 25	A M
■8 30	800	42.5	+...Clayton..	*2 00	1 35
f9 00	f9 00	58.5	+.Mount Dora..	A M	f1258
f9 10	f9 10	64.8	+..Cernada..		f1245
f9 30	f9 30	71.9	+...Vargas..		f1223
f1000	f1000	81.0	+....Sofia..		f1159
10 45	10 45	95.5	+....Farley..		■1120
P M	P M		ARRIVE] [LEAVE		P M

Table 87—AMARILLO, BOISE CITY AND LA JUNTA.

53 Mix.	Mls.	LVE.] (P. & S. F.) (C.T.) [ARR. Jan. 14, 1940.	54 Mix.
A M			P M
*8 15	0	+..Amarillo..	9 30
1 30	124.0	ar. Boise City lv.	3 45
P M		*(Central time.) (A. T. & S. F.) (Mountain time.)*	P M
*1 00	124.0	lv Boise City[85,86] ar	2 30
f1 30	136.3	+..Castaneda..	1 30
2 00	152.8	+....Campo..	12 55
f2 20	163.5	+...Bisonte..	f1230
2 47	174.1	+.Springfield[84]..	12 05
f3 10	187.0	+...Harbord..	f1130
f3 30	197.6	+....Frick..	f1105
3 58	213.9	+...Ruxton..	f1027
f4 20	227.6	+...Gilpin..	9 53
4 40	238.9	+Las Animas[3,66]..	f9 30
5 15	257.8	+La Junta[3,66,66]...	*9 00
P M ARR.] (M.T.) [LVE.			A M

*Daily.
† Daily, except Sunday.
§ Sunday only.
a Monday, Wednesday and Friday.
b Tuesday, Thursday and Saturday.
f Flag stop.
■ Friday only.
⊙ Mixed train.
● Fred Harvey meal stop.
Lunch room (not Fred Harvey service).
+ Coupon stations.
ᵭ Telegraph stations.

The Santa Fe's two RDC cars charge the Pacific Electric crossing at Los Nietos, October 1952.
Donald Duke

RDCs, coupled together, rocketed from the track at Redondo Jct. (just south of Los Angeles Union Station) after having accelerated to 70MPH on a 15MPH curve. The disaster cost 30 lives and injured 131 more; it was the worst passenger train wreck in the history of California.

Though heavily damaged, the cars were rebuilt at the Topeka shops of the Santa Fe, and after use in Kansas were assigned to the Albuquerque-El Paso train. On this run, which the Santa Fe dubbed the *El Pasoan*, they ended ATSF railcar service on April 10, 1968.

After departure of the RDC cars, the Los Angeles-San Diego service was never quite the same, either. The number of trains was cut, and the Santa Fe abandoned earlier plans to replace all *San Diegan* service with RDC cars, and it also gave up the ideas of investigating a super-RDC transcontinental service.

Pasadena, CA, was where the movie stars got off the SUPER CHIEF, but certainly not Santa Fe motorcar 181, July 1953.
Donald Duke.

Atchison, Topeka & Santa Fe

ROAD NO.	BUILDER	DATE	BLDR. NO.	ENGINE & DRIVE	BODY TYPE	LGTH.	WT.	DISPOSITION	REMARKS

Motors

ROAD NO.	BUILDER	DATE	BLDR. NO.	ENGINE & DRIVE	BODY TYPE	LGTH.	WT.	DISPOSITION	REMARKS
M 100[1]	McKeen	1909	—	McKeon 200hp GM	11win CE 75p	55'	31½t	Scr. 8/21	—
M 100[2]	Brill	1924	21994	Midwest 68hp GM	10win Bag. 29p	43'	14½t	To Va. Central 5/27	Ex-Clinton & Okla. Cen. 100, acq. 1926
M 101[1]	McKeen	1909	—	McKeen 200hp GM	11win CE 75p	55'	31½t	Scr. 10/21	—
M 101[2]	Mack-Brill	1921	70010 21372	Mack AB 45hp GM	8win hood Frt. 25p	29'	5½t	To SW Lumber	Ex-N.M. Central 101, acq. 1926
M 102[1]	McKeen	1910	105	McKeen 200hp	16win CE Bag. 85p	70'	42t	To UPRR 10/22	Became UP M-25
M 102[2]	Brill	1925	22241	Brill 75 175hp GM	13win Bag. 38p	55'	28t	Rblt. tlr. 4/35	Ex-KCM&O, M-1, acq. 1929; became T-102
M 103[1]	McKeen	1910	104	McKeen 200hp GM	16win CE Bag. 77p	70'	42t	To SA & AP 3/22	Became San Ant. & Ar. Pass 501, then T&NO 1007
M 103[2]	Brill	1925	22241	Brill 75 175hp GM	13win Bag. 38p	55'	28t	Scr. 8/40	Ex-KCM&O M-2; acq. 1929; re-eng. 250hp Win. 1929
M 104[1]	Ganz. Bald. ACF	1911	—	Ganz steam 448hp	9win Bag. 100p	71'	—	Rblt. to coach 1356, 10/17	Re-no. 2543. 1926; Donated Orange Empire Ry. Museum, 1972
M 105	GE-Wason	1913	3761 13505	GE 16C1 175hp GE	14win CE Bag. 89p	68'	53½t	Wrecked 2/43	Re-eng. 275hp Winton 120, 6/28; pass. cap. 62
M 106	GE-Wason	1913	3762 13505	GE 16C1 175hp GE	14win CE Bag. 89p	68'	53½t	Scr. 6/42	—
M 107	Hall Scott	1917	20	H-S 80hp GM	14win Bag. 43p	56'	33½t	Scr. 5/33	Demo 300, leased 1919, pur. 1921
M 108	EMC-St. Louis	1928	244 1456	Wint. 120 275hp GE	14win Bag. 77p	74½'	55t	Rblt. tlr. 6/52	Became T-105. Seating reduced to 37, 1938
M 109	EMC-St. Louis	1928	245 1456	Wint. 120 275hp GE	17win Bag. 77p	74½'	55t	Rblt. tlr. 6/52	Became T-106. Seating reduced to 37, 1938
M 110	Brill	1928	22595	H-S 150 275hp GE	17win Bag. 76p	76'	55t	Rblt. tlr. 6/52	Became T-107. Seating reduced to 54 1938
M 115	EMC-Pullman	1929	372 6259	Wint. 148D 400hp GE	12win RPO 57p	75'	75t	Ret. 3/65	Re-eng. Cat. D397 D, 1951
M 116	EMC-Pullman	1929	373 6259	Wint. 148D 400hp GE	12win RPO 57p	75'	76t	Scr. 2/60	Re-eng. Cat. D397 D, 1951
M 117	EMC-Pullman	1929	374 6259	Wint. 148D 400hp GE	12win RPO 57p	75'	75t	Scr. 10/58	Re-eng. Cat. D397 D, 1951
M 118	EMC-Pullman	1929	375 6259	Wint. 148D 400hp GE	12win RPO 57p	75'	74t	Ret. 2/65	Re-eng. Cat. D397 D, 1951
M 119	EMC-Pullman	1929	376 6259	Wint. 148D 400hp GE	12win RPO 57p	75'	75t	Ret. 11/63	Re-eng. Cat. D397 D, 1951
M 120	EMC-Pullman	1929	377 6259	Wint. 148D 400hp GE	12win RPO 57p	75'	74½t	Scr. 2/60	Re-eng. Cat. D397 D, 1951. Conv. to RPO-Bag.
M 121	EMC-Pullman	1929	378 6259	Wint. 148D 400hp GE	12win RPO 57p	75'	74½t	Scr. 10/58	Re-eng. Cat. D397 D, 1951
M 122	EMC-WH Pullman	1929	389 6259	Wint. 148D 400hp GE	12win RPO 57p	75'	73t	Ret. 10/63	Re-eng. Cat. D397 D, 1951. Conv. to RPO-Bag.
M 123	EMC-WH Pullman	1929	390 6259	Wint. 148D 400hp GE	12win RPO 57p	75'	75t	Scr. 9/58	Re-eng. Cat. D397 D., 1950. Conv. to RPO-Bag.
M 124	EMC-WH Pullman	1929	391 6259	Wint. 148D 400hp GE	12win RPO 57p	75'	73t	Scr. 9/58	Re-eng. Cat. D397 D, 1949. Conv. to RPO-Bag.
M 125	EMC-WH Pullman	1929	392 6259	Wint. 148D 400hp GE	12win RPO 57p	75'	71t	Ret. 9/58	—

ROAD NO.	BUILDER	DATE	BLDR. NO.	ENGINE & DRIVE	BODY TYPE	LGTH.	WT.	DISPOSITION	REMARKS
M 126	EMC-Pullman	1930	441 6259	Wint. 148D 400hp GE	12win RPO 57p	75'	74½t	Scr. 2/65	Re-eng. Cat. D397 D, 1952
M 130	EMC-Pullman	1929	384 6259	Wint. 148D 400hp GE	8win RPO-Bag. 35p	80'	67t	Scr. 9/58	RPO section not installed
M 131	EMC-Pullman	1929	385 6259	Wint. 148D 400hp GE	8win RPO-Bag. 35p	80'	72t	Scr. 9/58	RPO section not installed. Re-eng. Cat. D397 D, 1952
M 150	EMC-WH Pullman	1931	484 6401	Wint. 148D 400hp GE	RPO-Bag. 2 Bag. doors	75'	73t	Scr. 2/60	Re-eng. Cat. D397 D, 1951
M 151	EMC-WH Pullman	1931	485 6401	Wint. 148D 400hp GE	RPO-Bag. 2 Bag. doors	75'	73t	Scr. 2/50	Re-eng. Cat. D397 D, 1950
M 152	EMC-WH Pullman	1931	486 6401	Wint. 148D 400hp GE	RPO-Bag. 2 Bag. doors	75'	72t	Scr. 9/58	Re-eng. Cat. D397 D, 1950
M 153	EMC-WH Pullman	1931	487 6401	Wint. 148D 400hp GE	RPO-Bag. 2 Bag. doors	75'	72t	Scr. 9/58	Re-eng., Cat. D397 D, 1950
M 154	EMC-WH Pullman	1931	488 6401	Wint. 148D 400hp GE	RPO-Bag. 2 Bag. doors	75'	69½t	Scr. 9/58	Re-eng. Hamilton 685 D, 1948
M 155	EMC-Pullman	1931	477 6401	Wint. 148D 400hp GE	RPO-Bag. 2 Bag. Doors	75'	79t	Scr. 9/58	Re-eng. Cat. D397 D, 1950. Power truck moved to rear
M 156	EMC-Pullman	1931	478 6401	Wint. 148D 400hp GE	RPO-Bag. 2 Bag. doors	75'	75½t	Scr. 10/58	Re-eng. Cat. D397 D, 1950

Not actually on the Santa Fe roster was Hall Scott inspection motor 151, but it was employed in revenue service for a time between Riverbank and Oakdale, CA. Car 151 on the ATSF roster was an EMC-Pullman built in 1931.
James Harrison Collection

The Santa Fe had a number of lightweight trailers that it teamed with rail motorcars. The T-102 was photographed at Topeka, KS, on October 21, 1948; it was used on trains 55-56 from Topeka to St. Joseph, MO.
A. C. Phelps

ROAD NO.	BUILDER	DATE	BLDR. NO.	ENGINE & DRIVE	BODY TYPE	LGTH.	WT.	DISPOSITION	REMARKS
M 157	EMC-Pullman	1931	479 6401	Wint. 148D 400hp GE	RPO-Bag. 2 Bag. doors	75'	70t	Scr. 9/58	Re-eng. Hamilton 685 D, 1948. RPO section removed
M 160	Brill	1931	22919	Brill 860 535hp GE	RPO-Bag. 2 Bag. doors	80'	83t	To Texas St. Fair, Dallas, 1969	Re-eng. Sterling VDS-8 D, 1946, and GM 6-567 D, 1952. Boiler installed 1962
M 161	Brill	1931	22919	Brill 860 535hp GE	RPO-Bag. 2 Bag. doors	80'	84t	Scr. 2/60	Re-eng. Hamilton T685A D, 1948, and GM 6-567 D, 1952
M 162	Brill	1932	22959	Brill 860 535hp GE	RPO-Bag. 2 Bag. doors	80'	83t	Scr. 2/60	Re-eng. Sterling VDS-8 D, 1947, and GM 6-567 D, 1952
M 175	EMC-Pullman	1929	379 6259	Wint. 148D 400hp GE	10win RPO Bag. 35p	80'	74t	Scr. 9/58	Re-eng. Cat. D397 D, 1950. Conv. to RPO-Bag. 1946
M 176	EMC-Pullman	1929	380 6259	Wint. 148D 400hp GE	8win RPO Bag. 35p	80'	75t	Scr. 7/52	Re-eng. Cat. D397 D, 1952. RPO section removed 1938
M 177	EMC-Pullman	1929	381 6259	Wint. 148D 400hp GE	8win RPO Bag. 35p	80'	68t	To Travel Town, L.A., 1958.	RPO section removed, 1938
M 178	EMC-Pullman	1929	382 6259	Wint. 148D 400hp GE	8win RPO Bag. 35p	80'	76t	Scr. 9/58	Re-eng. Cat. D397 D, 1952. RPO section removed, 1938
M 179	EMC-Pullman	1929	383 6259	Wint. 148D 400hp GE	8win RPO Bag. 35p	80'	77t	Scr. 2/60	Re-eng. Cat. D397 D, 1951
M 180	EMC-Pullman	1929	387 6259	Wint. 148D 400hp GE	8win RPO Bag. 35p	80'	74t	Scr. 9/58	Re-eng. Cat. D397 D, 1951
M 181	EMC-Pullman	1929	388 6259	Wint. 148D 400hp GE	8win RPO Bag. 35p	80'	77½t	Scr. 9/58	Re-eng. Cat. D397 D, 1951. RPO section removed, 1938, then reinstalled
M 182	EMC-Pullman	1929	386 6259	Wint. 148D 400hp GE	8win RPO Bag. 35p	80'	70t	Scr. 9/58	Re-eng. Hamilton 685A D, 1946. Wrecked 1945, reblt. as RPO-Bag.
M 183	EMC-Pullman	1930	442 6342	Wint. 148D 400hp GE	8win RPO Bag. 35p	80'	78t	Scr. 3/60	Re-eng. Cat. D397 D, 1950, seating reduced to 28
M 184	EMC-Pullman	1931	481 6401	Wint. 148D 400hp GE	8win RPO Bag. 35p	80'	77t	Scr. 2/60	Re-eng. Cat. D397 D, 1951
M 185	EMC-Pullman	1931	482 6401	Wint. 148D 400hp GE	8win RPO Bag. 35p	80'	77t	Wrecked 8/45, Chicago	Rear section used to rbld. M-182
M 186	EMC-Pullman	1931	483 6401	Wint. 148D 400hp GE	8win RPO Bag. 35p	80'	76½t	Ret. 11/63	Re-eng. Cat. D397 D, 1950
M 187	EMC-Pullman	1931	480 6401	Wint. 148D 400hp GE	8win RPO Bag. 35p	80'	70t	Scr. 9/58	—
M 190	EMC-Pullman	1932	499 6407	Wint. 12-194 900hp DE	Artic. RPO Bag.	30' 50'	126t	Stored at Albuquerque, NM	Re-eng. GM 12-567 D, 1949
DC 191	Budd	1952	5603	2-GM6-280 275hp DH	RDC-1 86p	85'	63t	To C&O, 2/70	Became C&O 1913 then B&O 9918
DC 192	Budd	1952	5604	2-GM6-280 275hp DH	RDC-1 86p	85'	63t	To Downtown Area R.T. (Indianapolis), not used. Sold to SEPTA for parts.	Rblt. after wreck to Bag. 36 Pass, 1958

Trailers

ROAD NO.	BUILDER	DATE	BLDR. NO.	ENGINE & DRIVE	BODY TYPE	LGTH.	WT.	DISPOSITION	REMARKS
T-100,1	Brill	1925	22242	—	RPO-Bag.	53'	—	T-100 Scr. 10/56; 101, 1/60	Ex-KCM&O T-1, T-2, acq. 1929
T-102	Brill	1925	22241	—	RPO-Bag.	57'	—	Scr. 12/64	Ex-KCM&O M-1, then M-102[2]
T-103[1]	Brill	1925	22241	—	RPO-Bag.	57'	—	Scr. 8/40	Ex-KCM&O M-3, then M-104[2]
T-103[2]	Penn RR	—	—	—	16win 46p	64½'	—	Ret. 12/61	Ex-PRR elec. tlr. 381, acq. 1950
T-104	Penn RR	—	—	—	16win 46p	64½'	—	Ret. 7/61	Ex-PRR elec. tlr. 386, acq. 1950
T-105,6	St. Louis	1928	1456	—	14win 52p	74½'	—	Ret. 12/61	Ex-motor M-108, 109. Had bag. section
T-107	Brill	1928	22595	—	16win 38p	76'	—	Scr. 7/61	Ex-motor M-110. Had bag. section

Note: many passenger cars used as trailers.

Atlanta, Birmingham & Atlantic

ROAD NO.	BUILDER	DATE	BLDR. NO.	ENGINE & DRIVE	BODY TYPE	LGTH.	WT.	DISPOSITION	REMARKS
99	Ry. Stor. Btry. Brill	1917	— 20375	Btry-Elec	11win Bag. p	50'	—	—	Ex-Demo

Baltimore & Ohio

MAYBE the Baltimore & Ohio nursed a grudge. But for whatever reason, it is a fact that after buying some of the earliest St. Louis-Electro-Motive gas-electrics and returning them as unsatisfactory, the B&O never bought another EMC-designed car.

Probably more to the point is the fact that the J. G. Brill Co. of Philadelphia was an "on line" manufacturer. Brill was the B&O's favorite railcar builder, and except for a small Edwards car and trailer, purchased in 1922, and a rather unusual three-car train built by Standard Steel Car Co. in 1928, everything else up to the RDC era acquired by the B&O was built by Brill.

And, except for two gas-mechanical cars, all of the Brill units were of the type 250, the smallest of that builder's gas-electric models.

This type of unit seems to have suited the B&O's needs pretty well, and they were used in commuter service in the Baltimore area, on short branch lines in Maryland, Pennsylvania and West Virginia, and on relatively long runs in Ohio, Indiana and Illinois.

Most of them were in the all-passenger configuration, and they pulled an amazing variety of trailers, most rebuilt from old open-platform wooden cars going back as far as 1881.

After World War II, several of the Brill cars were rebuilt to what the railroad termed "Little Royal Blues," after the B&O's premier Washington-New York full-size streamliner of that name. The self-propelled cars were given an attractive blue and grey paint scheme, equipped with reclining seats and re-engined with Cummins Diesel power plants.

The Baltimore & Ohio was a major user of the Budd RDC. Here is car 6516 (later 9916) at Ft. Meade, Jct., MD, on Oct. 22, 1953.

George E. Votava

B&O Rail Motorcar Runs—1928

Route	Train No.	Mileage
Harrisonburg-Lexington	55, 59-54, 56	62
Green Spring-Petersburg	65-62	54
Green Spring-Romney	63-68	16
Indianapolis-Tuscola	60-61	117
Springfield-Tuscola	62-63	80

1933

Route	Train No.	Mileage
Harpers Ferry-Strasburg	55-54	51
Baltimore-Frederick	47-48	58
Frederick-Point of Rocks	80, 370-81, 381	7
Clarksburg-New Martinsville	41, 45-42, 46	60
Grafton-Parkersburg	37	103
Tygart Jct-Pickens	54-53	51
Grafton-Belington-Elkins (Belington to Elkins on WM)	33-32	60
Parkersburg-Portsmouth	43-44	56
Cleveland-Valley Jct	32-31	74.2
Beardstown-Flora	40-41	154.1
Flora-Shawneetown	42-43	74
Punxsautawney-Indiana	115, 111-112, 116	36
Silver Lake Jc-Perry	15-16	7.5

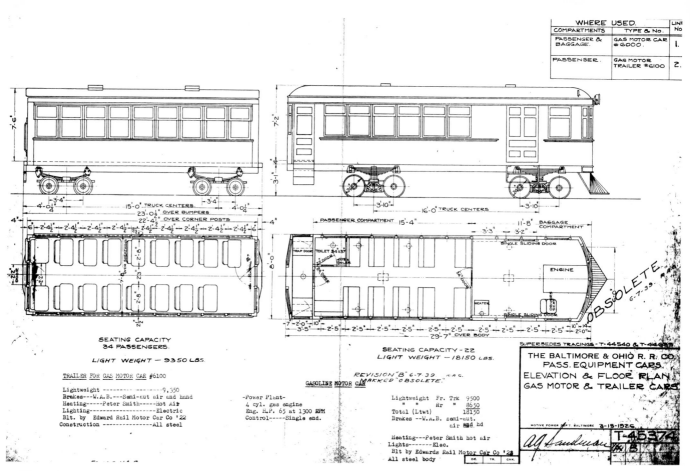

SEATING CAPACITY
34 PASSENGERS.

LIGHT WEIGHT - 9350 LBS.

TRAILER FOR GAS MOTOR CAR #6100

Lightweight ---------- -------9,350
Brakes---W.A.B.---Semi-cut air and hand
Heating-----Peter Smith-----Hot Air
Lighting--------------------Electric
Blt. by Edward Rail Motor Car Co '22
Construction --------------All steel

SEATING CAPACITY - 22
LIGHT WEIGHT - 18150 LBS.

REVISION "B" 6-7.39 K.A.G.
MARKED "OBSOLETE."

GASOLINE MOTOR CAR

-Power Plant-
4 cyl. gas engine
Eng. H.P. 65 at 1300 RPM
Control----Single end.

Lightweight Fr. Trk 9500
      "   "   Rr " 8650
Total (Ltwt)   18150
Brakes--W.A.B. semi-cut.
               air and hd

Heating---Peter Smith hot air
Lights------Elec.
Blt by Edwards Rail Motor Car Co '2
All steel body

SUPERSEDES TRACINGS - T-44540 & T-44932

THE BALTIMORE & OHIO R. R. CO
PASS. EQUIPMENT CARS
ELEVATION & FLOOR PLAN
GAS MOTOR & TRAILER CARS

MOTIVE POWER DEPT. BALTIMORE 3-13-1926

T-45374

These drawings show the first B&O car and its bobtail trailer, along with the unsuccessful St. Louis-EMC "Standard" unit.
Author's Collection.

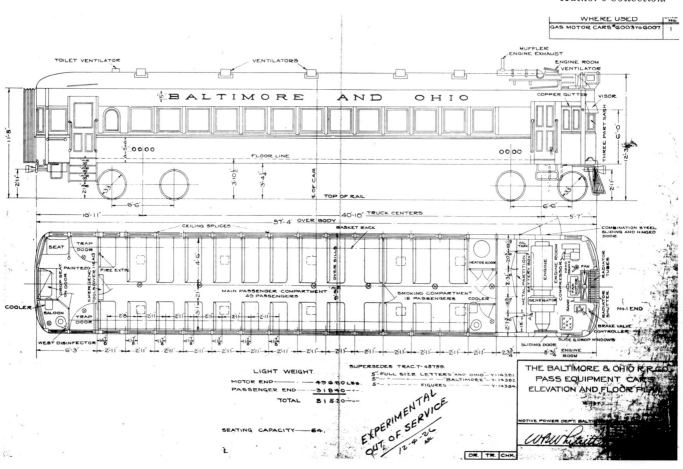

BALTIMORE AND OHIO

LIGHT WEIGHT.
MOTOR END -------- 49680 LBS.
PASSENGER END --- 31840---"
      TOTAL   81520 --"

SEATING CAPACITY ---- 64.

SUPERSEDES TRAC. T-45759.
5" FULL SIZE LETTERS "AND OHIO"--Y-14381
5"   "   "   "   "BALTIMORE"--Y-14382
5"   "   "   "   FIGURES ----Y-14384

EXPERIMENTAL
OUT OF SERVICE
12-4-2C

THE BALTIMORE & OHIO R.R.CO
PASS EQUIPMENT CARS
ELEVATION AND FLOOR PLAN

MOTIVE POWER DEPT. BALTI

Brill-built 6044 and its RPO-baggage trailer, 6144, stops at Beardstown, Ill., on June 3, 1950. The clean lines of these B&O units contrasted sharply with the cluttered look of many major roads' doodlebugs.

C. T. Felstead; Ray W. Buhrmaster Collection.

The three-car train built by Standard Steel (itself about to be taken over by Pullman) was made up of unusually heavy and large cars and was placed in Baltimore-Washington local service. But it was not successful on this short start-and-stop operation and was shunted about to various runs, appearing later on the Cumberland Valley line and the Indianapolis-Decatur run.

On these longer hops the Standard Steel train finally proved itself, and it was eventually upgraded with a diesel engine and air-conditioning, finally entering retirement in 1951. The last of the "Royal Blue" cars ran until 1954.

The unwanted EMC units, incidentally, were rebuilt and eventually wound up as Sperry rail detector cars where most, if not all, are ironically still in service.

The Baltimore & Ohio was an early advocate of Budd's RDC car, and has had good success with it. A train of three RDC units which included a food and beverage section ran for a time on the B&O main line between Philadelphia, Washington and Pittsburgh. Most service, however, was in the Washington-Baltimore and Pittsburgh suburban areas, and as of 1981 many of the RDCs were still operating though under the aegis of regional transportation authorities.

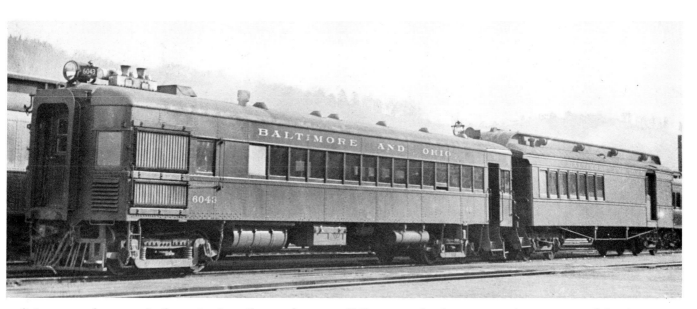

Only one number away in the roster from the car above, car 6043 presented quite a contrast in appearance. It has in tow a very ancient wooden combine.

Henry P. Stearns; Rail Photo Service

ROAD NO.	BUILDER	DATE	BLDR. NO.	ENGINE & DRIVE	BODY TYPE	LGTH.	WT.	DISPOSITION	REMARKS

Motors

ROAD NO.	BUILDER	DATE	BLDR. NO.	ENGINE & DRIVE	BODY TYPE	LGTH.	WT.	DISPOSITION	REMARKS
6000	Edwards Thomas	1922	115	Kelly-Spr. 60hp GM	7win Bag. 22p	30'	9t	Scr. 4/36	"Bonnet" front hood, removed later
6001[3]	Brill	1925	22173	Brill 190hp GM	13win Bag. 67p	55'	28t	Rblt. to tlr. 6173	G-2 model 75, ex-6002[1]
6002[2]	Brill	1925	22172	Brill 190hp GM	7win RPO-Bag. 25p	55'	37t	Rblt. to tlr. 6193	G-3 model 75, ex-6001[2] then 6070
6003[1]	St. Louis EMC	1926	1368c 171	Wint. 106A 220hp GE	14win 64p	57'	41t	Ret. to bldr., 12/26	Rblt. to Sperry 119, 10/33
6004[1]	St. Louis EMC	1926	1368c 172	Wint. 106A 220hp GE	14win 64p	56'	41t	Ret. to bldr., 12/26	Rblt. to Sperry 118, 10/33
6005[1]	St. Louis EMC	1926	1368c 173	Wint. 106A 220 hp GE	14win 64p	56'	41t	Ret. to bldr., 12/26	Rblt. to Sperry 117, 10/33
6006[1]	St. Louis EMC	1926	1368c 174	Wint. 106A 220hp GE	14win 64p	56'	41t	Ret. to bldr., 12/26	Rblt. to Lehigh Valley 14, 1/29, then Sperry 123, 1936
6007[1]	St. Louis EMC	1926	1368c 175	Wint. 106A 220hp GE	14win 64p	56'	41t	Ret. to bldr., 12/26	Rblt. to Lehigh Valley 15, 1/29, then Sperry 128, 1938
6008	Brill	1927	22525	Brill-West 250hp GE	16win 71p	60'	49t	Rblt. 7/27, Re No. 6030	GE-1, model 250, rblt. by Brill (see next line)
6030	Brill	1927	22604	Brill-West 250hp GE	16win 71p	60'	49t	—	GE-1, model 250, rbld. of 6008
6031	Brill	1927	22568	Brill-West 250hp GE	16win 71p	60'	47t	Ret. 5/51	GE-2, model 250, ex-6003[2]
6032	Brill	1927	22568	Brill-West 250hp GE	16win 71p	60'	47t	Ret. 1950	GE-2, model 250, ex-6004[2]
6033	Brill	1927	22568	Brill-West 250hp GE	16win 71p	60'	47t	Ret. 1950	GE-2, model 250, ex-6005[2]
6034	Brill	1927	22568	Brill-West 250hp GE	16win 71p	60'	47t	Ret. 8/54	GE-2, model 250, ex-6006[2] re-eng. 250hp Cummins D, 1949
6035	Brill	1927	22602	Brill-West 250hp GE	16win 71p	60'	47½t	Ret. 5/51	GE-3, model 250
6036	Brill	1927	22602	Brill-West 250hp GE	16win 71p	60'	47½t	Burned 1950	GE-3, model 250
6037	Brill	1927	22602	Brill-West 250hp GE	16win 71p	60'	47½t	Ret. 5/51	GE-3, model 250, rblt. to 50p
6038	Brill	1927	22602	Brill-West 250hp GE	16win 71p	60'	47½t	Ret. 8/54	GE-3, model 250, re-eng. 250hp Cummins D, 1949, rblt. to 50p, wt. 55t
6039	Brill	1927	22602	Brill-West 250hp GE	16win 71p	60'	47½t	Ret. 8/54	GE-3, model 250
6040	Brill	1927	22602	Brill-West 250hp GE	16win 71p	60'	47½t	Ret. 8/54	GE-3, model 250, re-eng. 250hp Cummins D, 1949, rblt. to 50p, wt. 55t
6041	Brill	1927	22602	Brill-West 250hp GE	16win 71p	60'	47½t	Ret. 8/54	GE-3, model 250
6042	Brill	1927	22602	Brill-West 250hp GE	16win 71p	60'	47½t	Ret. 1951	GE-3, model 250
6043	Brill	1927	22625	Brill-West 250hp GE	15win DE 48p	60'	49½t	Ret. 5/51	GE-6, model 250
6044	Brill	1927	22602	Brill-West 250hp GE	16win 71p	60'	47t	Ret. 1953	GE-3, model 250, re-eng. 250hp Cummins D, 1949, rblt. to 50p, wt. 55t
6045	Brill	1927	22602	Brill-West 250hp GE	16win 71p	60'	47t	Ret. 5/51	GE-3, model 250, ex-6007[2]

ROAD NO.	BUILDER	DATE	BLDR. NO.	ENGINE & DRIVE	BODY TYPE	LGTH.	WT.	DISPOSITION	REMARKS
6071	Brill	1927	22618	Brill-West 250hp GE	3win RPO Bag. 11p	60'	53½t	Ret. 8/54	GE-5, model 250
6500	Std. Steel	1928	324	2-Sterl. 300hp GE	12win Bag. 44p	75'	88½t	Ret. 5/51	GE-7, re-eng. 2/300hp Fair-Mor. D, A/C 1935
9910	Budd	1950	5004	2-GM6-280 275hp DH	RDC-1 89p	85'	58½t	—	DC-1, ex.-1912, orig. C&O 9062, acq. 11/67
9911	Budd	1950	5201	2-GM6-280 275hp DH	RDC-1 89p	85'	59t	To Md. DOT 9811, 1982	DC-1, ex-1900, then 6510
1901	Budd	1950	5202	2-GM6-280 275hp DH	RDC-1 89p	85'	59t	Destroyed by fire 1970	DC-1, ex-6511
9912	Budd	1953	5810	2-GM6-280 275hp DH	RDC-1 89p	85'	59t	To Md. DOT 9812, 1982	DC-1, ex-1902, then 6512
9913	Budd	1953	5811	2-GM6-280 275hp DH	RDC-1 89p	85'	59t	—	DC-1, ex-1903, then 6513
9914	Budd	1953	5812	2-GM6-280 275hp DH	RDC-1 89p	85'	59t	Wrecked 12/30/76	DC-1, ex-1904, then 6514
9915	Budd	1953	5813	2-GM6-280 275hp DH	RDC-1 89p	85'	59t	—	DC-1, ex-1905, then 6515
9916	Budd	1953	5814	2-GM6-280 275hp DH	RDC-1 89p	85'	59t	—	DC-1, ex-1906, then 6516
9917	Budd	1953	5815	2-GM6-280 275hp DH	RDC-1 89p	85'	59t	—	DC-1, ex-1907, then 6517
9918	Budd	1952	5603	2-GM6-280 275hp DH	RDC-1 89p	85'	59t	—	DC-1, orig. ATSF DC-191, acq. 2/70; ex-1913
9920	Budd	1956	6511	2-GM6-280 275hp DH	RDC-1 89p	85'	61½t	—	DC-2, ex-1908
9921	Budd	1956	6512	2-GM6-280 275hp DH	RDC-1 89p	85'	61½t	—	DC-2, ex-1909
9922	Budd	1956	6513	2-GM6-280 275hp DH	RDC-1 89p	85'	61½t	—	DC-2, ex-1910
1911	Budd	1956	6514	2-GM6-280 275hp DH	RDC-1 89p	85'	61½t	Burned 4/62	DC-2
9930	Budd	1950	5009	2-GM6-280 275hp DH	RDC-2 Bag. p	85'	59t	—	DC-2, orig. CNW 9935 then C&O 9060, acq. 3/63. Ex-1970
1971	Budd	1950	5003	2-GM6-280 275hp DH	RDC-1 89p	85'	58½t	Burned 2/66, to SEPTA 9/69	DC-2, orig. CNW 9933 then C&O 9061, acq. 9/65
9931	Budd	1955	6015	2-GM6-280 275hp DH	RDC-2 70p	85'	61½t	To Md. DOT 9831, 1982	DC-2, orig. LIRR 3121, acq. 8/68; ex-1972
1950	Budd	1953	5911	2-GM6-280 275hp DH	RDC-2 Bag. 70p	85'	59t	Burned 3/62	DC-3, ex-6550
9932	Budd	1953	5912	2-GM6-280 275hp DH	RDC-2 Bag. 70p	85'	59t	To Md. DOT 9832, 1982	DC-3, ex-1951, then 6551
9940	Budd	1956	6505	2-GM6-280 275hp DH	RDC-2 Food, 48p	85'	67t	—	DC-4, orig. dinette, rblt. to coach. Ex-1960
9941	Budd	1956	6506	2-GM6-280 275hp DH	RDC-2 Food, 48p	85'	67t	—	DC-4, orig. dinette, rblt. to coach Ex-1961

Trailers

ROAD NO.	BUILDER	DATE	BLDR. NO.	ENGINE & DRIVE	BODY TYPE	LGTH.	WT.	DISPOSITION	REMARKS
6100	Edwards	1922	—	—	9win 34p	23'	4½t	Ret. 4/36	No platforms, train doors only. Rblt. Perley Thomas
6125	Brill	1928	22621	—	16win 60p	51'	—	Returned to builder.	—
6172	Brill	1928	22662	—	RPO-Bag.	67'	38t	Ret. 1953	—
6173	Brill	1925	22173	—	13win Bag.	60'	—	Ret. 1953	Ex-motor 6001[2]
6193	Brill	1925	22172	—	7win 32p	55'	28½t	Ret. 1953	Ex-motor 6002, rblt. 1936

NOTE: Many passenger cars converted to trailers, all numbered into 6100 series.

Bangor & Aroostook

ROAD NO.	BUILDER	DATE	BLDR. NO.	ENGINE & DRIVE	BODY TYPE	LGTH.	WT.	DISPOSITION	REMARKS
5[1]	Wason GE	1911	3717	GEGM16 175hp GE	18win CE Bag. 97 pas	66'	47t	To AC&Y 6/20	Ex-GE Demo 5
5[2]	Std. Steel West.	1930	—	W-Beard 400hp DE	6win Mail Bag. 22 pas	76'	84t	Scr. 8/56	Ex-WH Demo 20, then GN 2341, acq. 1952
6	Wason GE	1912	3722	GE16A5 175hp GE	14win CE Bag. 91 pas	68'	48t	To AC&Y 6/20	—

Bessemer & Lake Erie

ROAD NO.	BUILDER	DATE	BLDR. NO.	ENGINE & DRIVE	BODY TYPE	LGTH.	WT.	DISPOSITION	REMARKS
1	McKeen	1913	—	McKeen 200hp GM	8win CE Bag. 48p	55'	35½t	Scr. 1927	Used until 1916
301	Twin Coach	1933	—	Hercules 22½hp GM	5win CE 12p	—	2½t	Sold to a dairy, 1939	"Milk wagon" style body

One of Ingersoll-Rand's pioneering efforts was this collaboration with St. Louis Car, shovelnose unit 1140 shown in June of 1935 at Boston.

George E. Votava

Now preserved at the National Railway Museum is B&M unit 1180, pictured in Boston on July 4, 1936. Behind it is trailer 1070.
George E. Votava

Boston & Maine

A FRIEND indeed of the rail motorcar was the Boston & Maine, which tried one of the early steam units, sampled the wares of a number of builders in the standard railcar era, and fielded the largest fleet ever of the post World War II Budd RDC car.

The B&M's first and only steam railcar was the pilot model of the Unit Railway Car Co., a hometown Boston firm organized by the Stanley brothers of steam automobile fame. This car with its vertical boiler was destroyed in a 1923 roundhouse fire, before the railroad began buying internal-combustion powered cars.

In 1924 and 1925 the B&M purchased a variety of self-propelled equipment including some Brill gas-mechanical cars, a Sykes gas mechanical, then Brill and EMC gas-electrics.

The Edward G. Budd Co., which was later to dominate the B&M's railcar fleet, was first heard from in 1935 when the Philadelphia builder supplied a near-duplicate of its famous Burlington "Zephyr" self-propelled train. On the B&M this became the "Flying Yankee," first operated in conjunction with the Maine Central on the Boston-Bangor run.

The B&M apparently couldn't find a niche for the Budd streamlined train because of its limited capacity; it built up the Bangor business smartly and thereby caused its own demise. Like its early Zephyr cousins on the Burlington, the "Flying Yankee" was reassigned several times. Unlike on the Burlington, every time it moved it got a new

A single hood-front Sykes car found its way to the Boston & Maine. Here is car 120 (later 1120) at the factory.
Author's Collection.

35

Type and Service Assignments of Boston & Maine Rail Motor Cars—April 7, 1927

Car No.	Builder	Design	Type of Engine	Type of Drive	Assigned Routes	Trips Per Day	Miles Per Day Except Sunday
150	St. Louis Car Co.	Electro Motive	Winton, 175 hp.	Electric	Spare Service	..	...
151	St. Louis Car Co.	Electro Motive	Winton, 175 hp.	Electric	Winchenden and Concord, N. H.	2	120
152	St. Louis Car Co.	Electro Motive	Winton, 175 hp.	Electric	Lincoln and Plymouth, N. H.	6	129
190	J. G. Brill Co.	Brill 250	Brill Westinghouse	Electric	Springfield and Northampton, Mass.	12	205
					Springfield and Northampton, Mass.	4	68*
185	Osgood Bradley Car Co.	Electro Motive	Winton, 275 hp.	Electric	Manchester, N. H., and Portland, Me., via Portsmouth and Dover	2	200
182	Osgood Bradley Car Co.	Electro Motive	Winton, 275 hp.	Electric	Boston and Fitchburg, Mass.	4	121
181	Osgood Bradley Car Co.	Electro Motive	Winton, 275 hp.	Electric	Laconia and Dover, N. H.	4	185
†184	Osgood Bradley Car Co.	Electro Motive	Winton, 275 hp.	Electric	Hillsboro, N. H., and Worcester, Mass.	3	192
187	Osgood Bradley Car Co.	Electro Motive	Winton, 275 hp.	Electric	Concord, N. H., and Worcester, Mass.	2	161
**186	Osgood Bradley Car Co.	Electro Motive	Winton, 275 hp.	Electric		..	...
†183	Osgood Bradley Car Co.	Electro Motive	Winton, 275 hp.	Electric	Worcester, Mass., and Elmwood, N. H.	3	163
195	Osgood Bradley Car Co.	Electro Motive	Winton, 275 hp.	Electric	Boston, Marlboro and Lancaster, Mass.	3	183
196	Osgood Bradley Car Co.	Electro Motive	Winton, 275 hp.	Electric	Boston, Lawrence, Mass., and Portsmouth, Me.	6	217
***120	St. Louis Car Co.	Sykes	Sterling, 225 hp.	Mechanical		..	...
101	J. G. Brill Co.	Brill 55	Midwest, 75 hp.	Mechanical	Milford, N. H., Ayer, Mass., and Greenville, N. H.	2	97
121	J. G. Brill Co.	Brill 75	Winton, 190 hp.	Mechanical	Salem, Lowell and Lawrence, Mass.	6	98
122	J. G. Brill Co.	Brill 75	Winton, 190 hp.	Mechanical	North Adams, Mass., and Troy, N. Y.	2	96
123	J. G. Brill Co.	Brill 75	Winton, 190 hp.	Mechanical	Lowell, Lowell Jct. and Ayer, Mass.	8	84
					Lowell and Lowell, Jct., Mass.	8	68*
124	J. G. Brill Co.	Brill 75	Winton, 190 hp.	Mechanical	Concord and White River Jct., Mass.	2	140
125	J. G. Brill Co.	Brill 75	Winton, 190 hp.	Mechanical	Wolfboro and Sanbornville, N. H.	8	96
126	J. G. Brill Co.	Brill 75	Winton, 190 hp.	Mechanical	Rochester, N. H., and Portland, Me.	2	106
170	J. G. Brill Co.	Brill 250	Brill Westinghouse 250 hp.	Electric	Hillsboro and Manchester, N. H.	2	108
††171	J. G. Brill Co.	Brill 250	Brill Westinghouse 250 hp.	Electric		..	...
180	Osgood Bradley Co.	Electro Motive	Winton, 275 hp.	Electric	Boston and Springfield, Mass.	2	244

* Sunday trains.　　** Not assigned; out of service since Nov. 19, account collision.　　*** Not assigned; awaiting transmission development.
† Alternate runs, daily.　　†† Not assigned; out of service since Nov. 11, account accidentally burned interior passenger compartment.

Budd built both the fluted-side FLYING YANKEE (above) and the RDC fleet (below) for the Boston & Maine. The RDCs are shown leaving Boston's North Station on July 21, 1952. *Author's Collection; George E. Votava*

name: "Mountaineer" and "Cheshire" are two.

Also included in the B&M tabulation is a pair of powered baggage-railway post office units built by St. Louis Car, one powered by Ingersoll-Rand (one of only two railcars sponsored by I-R) and the other powered by Westinghouse. These cars did not carry passengers and hence might be termed locomotives, but did carry revenue parcels, baggage and mail.

Most of the B&M cars survived into the 1940s and 1950, mostly in Boston commuter service, but about eight units were sold to other roads, mostly short lines. The "Flying Yankee" train is now preserved at Steamtown.

Starting in 1952 the Boston & Maine began acquiring Budd RDC cars in number, and ended up owning 102 of them in four configurations, including straight passenger, passenger-baggage, passenger-baggage-RPO and the only RDC-9s built, which were non-control, one engine "trailers." This was the largest such fleet on any railroad anywhere, and was unique also in that the cars were intended mainly for commuter service.

Some of the RDC cars, however, did hold down mainline runs, ultimately taking over all passenger service. In recent years the B&M's passenger service has been confined to the Boston commuter district, where many of the cars still operate, many of them having been demotorized for use behind locomotives.

Boston & Maine

ROAD NO.	BUILDER	DATE	BLDR. NO.	ENGINE & DRIVE	BODY TYPE	LGTH.	WT.	DISPOSITION	REMARKS
100	Unit Laconia	1917	—	Unit 60hp steam	11win Bag. 52p	51'	15t	Burned 10/23	Roundhouse fire
1101 (101)	Brill	1924	22011	Brill 68hp GM	10win Bag. 38p	43'	14½t	Scr. 1935	Model 55
1120 (120)	St. Louis Sykes	1925	1329A	Sterling 175hp GM	8win Bag. 30p	53'	20t	To West. Riv. Ry. 1934	Hood front; rblt. to GE, 1928 (Brill), wt. 33½t
1121-23 (121-23)	Brill	1925	22268	Brill-WH 175hp GM	13win Bag. 47p	57'	32t	To Cummins, 1937	Model 75
1124 (124)	Brill	1925	22268	Brill-WH 175hp GM	13win Bag. 47p	57'	32t	Sct. 1938	Model 75
1125-26 (125-26)	Brill	1925	22269	Brill-WH 175hp GM	13win Bag. 47p	57'	32t	To Cummins 1937	Model 75
1140	St. Louis Ing.-Rand	1935	1573	2-IR 400hp DE	RPO-Bag.	78'	110½t	Scr. 12/57	"Shovel Nose," re-eng. 800hp EMD-567 DE, 1951, wt. 117t
1141	St. Louis WH	1935	1575	WH 950hp DE	RPO-Bag.	78'	105½t	Ret. to bldr. 11/37	"Shovel Nose" to Tex-Mex RR 508, 8/40
1150 (150)	St. Louis EMC	1925	1368D 127	Wint. 106 175hp GE	12win Bag. 44p	60'	39t	To Lig. Val. 1943	Lig. Val. 1150
1151 (151)	St. Louis EMC	1925	1368D 128	Wint. 106 175hp GE	12win Bag. 44p	60'	39t	To Sperry Rail 8/39	Sperry 127
1152 (152)	St. Louis EMC	1295	1368D 129	Wint. 106 175hp GE	12win Bag. 44p	60'	39t	To Lig. Val. 1943	Lig. Val. 1152
1170 (170)	Brill	1926	22270	Brill-WH 250hp GE	12win Bag. 50p	62'	47t	Scr. 10/47	Model 250
1171 (171)	Brill	1926	22270	Brill-WH 250hp GE	12win Bag. 50p	62'	47t	To NYS&W 11/40	Susquehanna 3001
1180 (180)	Osgd Bdly EMC	1926	8795 163	Wint. 120 275hp GE	10win Bag. 54p	64'	47t	To St. Marys RR 1940	St. Marys 1180, now at National Railway Museum, St. Louis
1181 (181)	Osgd Bdly EMC	1926	8795 164	Wint. 120 275hp GE	10win Bag. 44p	64'	47t	To Clare. & Concord 1954	C&C 100
1182 (182)	Osgd Bdly EMC	1926	8795 165	Wint. 120 275hp GE	10 win Bag. 54p	64'	47t	Scr. 10/56	—
1183 (183)	Osgd Bdly EMC	1926	8795 166	Wint. 120 275hp GE	10win Bag. 54p	64'	47t	Burned 9/41	—
1184 (184)	Osgd Bdly EMC	1926	8795 167	Wint. 120 275hp GE	10win Bag. 28p	64'	47t	Scr. 12/47	—
1185 (185)	Osgd Bdly EMC	1926	8795 168	Wint. 120 275hp GE	10win Bag. 54p	64'	47t	Scr. 4/56	Re-no. back to 185
1186 (186)	Osgd Bdly EMC	1926	8795 169	Wint. 120 275hp GE	3win RPO Bag. 16p	64'	47t	Scr. 12/47	—
1187 (187)	Osgd Bdly EMC	1926	8795 170	Wint. 120 275hp GE	10win Bag. 54p	64'	47t	Scr. 10/56	Re-no. back to 187
1190 (190)	Brill	1926	22271	Brill-WH 250hp GE	19win DE 92p	73'	55½t	Scr. 12/47	Pass. doors front and rear
1195 (195)	Osgd Bdly EMC	1926	8690 161	Wint. 120 275hp GE	16win DE Bag. 84p	75'	52t	Scr. 4/56	Re-no. back to 195
1196 (196)	Osgd Bdly EMC	1926	8690 162	Wint. 120 275hp GE	16win DE Bag. 84p	75'	52t	To Int. Trade Co. 12/59	Re-no. back to 196
6000	Budd EMC	1935	— 529	Wint. 600hp DE	4win CE Bag.-Pas.	—	—	Donated to "Steamtown"	"Flying Yankee" artic-3 car train
6100-01	Budd	1952	5506-07	2-GM6-280 275hp DH	RDC-1 89p	85'	59t	—	All RDCs on roster being rblt. to tlrs, 1981, by MBTA and Morrison-Knudsen
6102-03	Budd	1953	5808-09	2-GM6-280 275hp DH	RDC-1 89p	85'	59t	—	

ROAD NO.	BUILDER	DATE	BLDR. NO.	ENGINE & DRIVE	BODY TYPE	LGTH.	WT.	DISPOSITION	REMARKS
6104-05	Budd	1953	5914-15	2-GM6-280 275hp DH	RDC-1 89p	85'	59t	—	—
6106-31	Budd	1955	6101-26	2-GM6-280 275hp DH	RDC-1 89p	85'	59t	In service 1981, except . . .	6106-08 to CN D118, 116, 117; 6109 to Reading 9165; 6110-11, 16, 19, 21 to CN D 112, 111, 115, 113, 114; 6130 wrecked
6132-48	Budd	1955	6201-17	2-GM6-280 275hp DH	RDC-1 89p	85'	59t	In service 1981, except . . .	6140 wrecked 1954, 6142 wrecked 1966
6149-51	Budd	1955	6224-26	2-GM6-280 275hp DH	RDC-1 89p	85'	59t	In service 1981, except . . .	6150 wrecked 1956
6152-53	Budd	1956	6315-16	2-GM6-280 275hp DH	RDC-1 89p	85'	59t	In service	—
6154-56	Budd	1957	6710-12	2-GM6-280 300hp DH	RDC-1 89p	85'	59t	In service	—
6200-10	Budd	1955	6003-13	2-GM6-280 275hp DH	RDC-2 Bag. 70p	85'	59½t	In service 1981, except . . .	6200 to CN D-206; 6205 to Reading 9165 (SEPTA)
6211	Budd	1955	6227	2-GM6-280 275hp DM	RDC-2 Bag. 70p	85'	59½t	In service	—
6212-13	Budd	1956	6501-02	2-GM6-280 275hp DH	RDC-2 Bag. 70p	85'	59½t	In service	—
6214	Budd	1958	6815	2-GM6-280 300hp DH	RDC-2 Bag. 70p	85'	59½t	In service	—
6300	Budd	1952	5610	2-GM6-280 275hp DH	RDC-3 RPO Bag. 48p	85'	61½t	Rblt. to steam heat car	—
6301	Budd	1953	5905	2-GM6-280 275hp DH	RDC-3 RPO Bag. 48p	85'	61½t	In service	—
6302	Budd	1953	5908	2-GM6-280 275hp DH	RDC-3 RPO Bag. 48p	85'	61½t	Rblt. to steam heat car	—
6303	Budd	1958	6705	2-GM6-280 300hp DH	RDC-3 RPO Bag. 48p	85'	61½t	In service	—
6304-06	Budd	1958	6818-20	2-GM6-280 300hp DH	RDC-3 RPO Bag. 48p	85'	61½t	In service, except . . .	6305 to Reading 9166 (SEPTA)
6900-29	Budd	1956	6401-30	1-GM6-280 300hp DH	RDC-9 94p	85'	53t	In service, except . . .	6900-02, 15, 19, 20, 25 to CN CN D500-506

NOTE: All remaining RDC's now operated by Massachusetts Bay Transit Authority.

Trailers

ROAD NO.	BUILDER	DATE	BLDR. NO.	ENGINE & DRIVE	BODY TYPE	LGTH.	WT.	DISPOSITION	REMARKS
1050	St.L.-Sykes	1924	1330A	—	52p	45½'	13½t	—	Ex-50. Tlr. for motor 1120
1070-1	Brill	1926	22272	—	16win 74p	—	21t	—	Ex-70, 71
1080-1	Brill	1926	22274	—	Bag. 50p	—	21t	—	Ex-80, 81
1090	Brill	1926	22273	—	20win 94p	—	26t	—	Ex-90

Buffalo, Rochester & Pittsburgh
(Merged into B&O)

ROAD NO.	BUILDER	DATE	BLDR. NO.	ENGINE & DRIVE	BODY TYPE	LGTH.	WT.	DISPOSITION	REMARKS
1001	McKeen	1910	90	McKeen 200ho GM	CE Bag.-Pass.	70'	37½t	To Deer River	"Rocket"
1002	Wason-GE	1911	— 3707	GE-GM16A4 175hp GE	14win CE Bag. 69p	66'	45t	To SD&AE 43, 1914	"Meteor"

Trinity & Brazos Valley
(Burlington-Rock Island)

ROAD NO.	BUILDER	DATE	BLDR. NO.	ENGINE & DRIVE	BODY TYPE	LGTH.	WT.	DISPOSITION	REMARKS
61-63	Pullman EMC	1928	6265 402-4	Winton 148 400hp GE	Mail-Bag.	75'	70t	Conv. to bunk cars, 1953. Scr. 1968-9	—
9901-02	Budd EMC	1935	— 530-1	EMD-Wint. 600hp DE	Bag.-Artic.	67'	50t	9901 wrecked 12/44 while on lease from CB&Q	9902 pur. from CB&Q, 11/38; returned to CB&Q in settlement for 9901

On one of the first runs of the SAM HOUSTON ZEPHYR on the Burlington-Rock Island, the 9901 prepares to leave Houston Union Station in October, 1936.

H. J. Heaney; G. C. Werner Collection.

Burlington-Rock Island

THE JOINTLY-OWNED Burlington-Rock Island in Texas (formerly the Trinity & Brazos Valley) operated a handful of both owned and leased rail motorcars. The owned units did just fine, but the leased equipment was jinxed.

The B-RI owned four motorcars; three conventional Pullman-EMC gas electrics and, for a period, Burlington Zephyr number 9902, one of the original *Twin City Zephyrs*. These cars all survived to be honorably retired, but the leased units all brought grief. First, there was the other Twin City Zephyr, number 9901. It was wrecked at Dacus, Texas, in December of 1944, never to run again.

Then the *Pioneer Zephyr*, on loan, was involved in a wreck near Houston in April of 1949; it was wrecked and immediately returned to the CB&Q for further service. Finally, in September of 1950, the Rock Island's much-travelled *Rocket Jr.*, number 9049, was destroyed by fire at Newby, Texas, apparently substituting for one of the B-RI gas-electrics.

These gas-electrics, known on the B-RI as *Red Heads*, held down the local schedules. Their southern terminal was always Houston, but the northern terminal varied over the years, sometimes Teague, sometimes Waxahachie (the end of the B-RI track; access to Dallas was over the MKT), sometimes Dallas.

The *Zephyr-Rocket* trains which used units 9901-9902 operated through

With a heavyweight coach for passengers, motor 63 prepares to leave Dallas in June of 1939 with the RED HEAD. *Harold K. Vollrath Collection*

to Fort Worth on Burlington (Fort Worth & Denver City) trackage and were really vest-pocket mainline streamliners. Their demise came in 1949 when the Rock Island began through operation of its *Twin Star Rocket* all the way from Minneapolis to Houston via the B-RI in Texas.

The Central of Georgia's entire doodlebug roster is captured in these two views; a head-on of Brill-built 10 and a side view of Edwards unit 11. Car 10 was photographed at Atlanta; 11 at Macon, GA, both in 1935. *Both: Harold K. Vollrath Collection*

Carolina, Clinchfield & Ohio
(Family Lines)

ROAD NO.	BUILDER	DATE	BLDR. NO.	ENGINE & DRIVE	BODY TYPE	LGTH.	WT.	DISPOSITION	REMARKS
75	Wason GE	1911	— 3721	GE-GM16A5 175hp GE	13win CE Bag. 91p	68'	46t	To GC&L then Apal. Nor. 75, 1942	Ex-D&H 2000, acq. 1917. Re-eng. Sterling Dolphin GE

Central of Georgia
(Merged into Southern Ry.)

ROAD NO.	BUILDER	DATE	BLDR. NO.	ENGINE & DRIVE	BODY TYPE	LGTH.	WT.	DISPOSITION	REMARKS
10	Brill	1928	22718	Brill 55 68hp GM	8win Bag. 29p	42'	16t	—	—
11	Edwards	1925	—	2-Buda 100hp GM	9win Bag. 52p	43'	22t	To Birm. SE, 1938	Type 25, ex-Marion & Rye. Val., acq. 1934

Central Railroad of New Jersey

ROAD NO.	BUILDER	DATE	BLDR. NO.	ENGINE & DRIVE	BODY TYPE	LGTH.	WT.	DISPOSITION	REMARKS
551-54	Budd	1953	5919-22	2-GM6-280 275hp GH	RDC-1	85'	56t	To NJ Dept. Trans., in service 5190-92	—
555-56	Budd	1956	6515-16	2-GM6-280 275hp GH	RDC-1	85'	56t	To NJ Dept. Trans., in service 5193-94	—
557	Budd	1957	6610	2-GM6-280 300hp GH	RDC-1	85'	56t	To NJ Dept. Trans., in service 5195	—
558-59	Budd	1950	5006-07	2-GM6-280 275hp GH	RDC-1	85'	56t	To NJ Dept. Trans., in service 5196-97	Ex-NY, Susq. & West M-1, M-2, acq. 4/58
560-61	Budd	1950	5107-08	2-GM6-280 275hp GH	RDC-1	85'	56t	To NJ Dept. Trans., in service 5198-99	Ex-NY, Susq. & West M-3, M-4, acq. 4/58

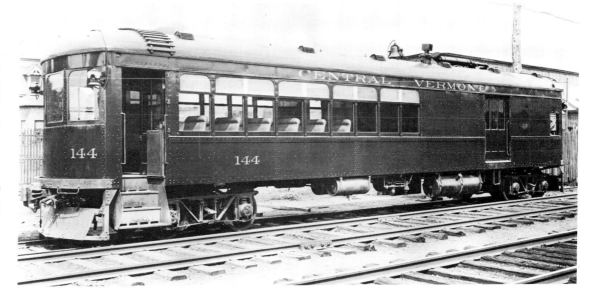

Central of Vermont 144 was built as a storage battery car but converted in 1927 to a gas-electric. This view was taken at Springfield, MA, after conversion.
George E. Votava Collection

One of four Brill units on the Central of Vermont, the 148 eventually went to parent Canadian National.

Author's Collection

Central of Vermont

ROAD NO.	BUILDER	DATE	BLDR. NO.	ENGINE & DRIVE	BODY TYPE	LGTH.	WT.	DISPOSITION	REMARKS
144	Wason Ry. Stor. Bty.	1924	—	Bty. Elec. 4-25hp	12win Bag. 24p	53'	32½t	Ret. 1932	Rblt. to gas-elec. by Brill (22518), 1927, 250 hp
145	Wason Ry. Stor. Bty.	1924	—	Bty. Elec. 4-25hp	12win Bag. 24p	53'	32½t	Rblt. to tlr. 153, 1929	—
146-147	Brill	1926	22410	Brill-WH 250hp GE	13win Bag. 59p	60'	46t	To CN, 1939	146 not used on CN, scr. 1948; 147 CN 15788
148	Brill	1927	22553	Brill-WH 250hp GE	13win Bag. 59p	60'	46t	To CN, 1954	CN 15845
149	Brill	1927	22554	Brill-WH 250hp GE	13win Bag. 59p	60'	46t	To Ga. Car., 1943	Became KC, Mex. & Orient (Mex.) 102

Trailers

ROAD NO.	BUILDER	DATE	BLDR. NO.	ENGINE & DRIVE	BODY TYPE	LGTH.	WT.	DISPOSITION	REMARKS
150	Brill	1926	22412	—	Bag.	51'	29t	—	—
151	Brill	1926	22411	—	Bag.	51'	29t	—	—
152	Brill	1927	22555	—	Bag.	51'	29t	—	—
153	Co. Shops	1929	—	—	12win 34p	53'	—	—	Rbld. of motor 145

Chesapeake & Ohio

Trio of RDCs (above) with the 9060 in front makes up the Chessieliner, pictured in 1958 at the Gordonsville, VA, station. Of a much earlier vintage (below) is 1920 Brill product 9054 at Durbin, WV, in 1957.

Gene Huddleston—C&O Historical Society Collection; Kenneth F. Coombs—P. Kutta Collection.

PERHAPS the most unique feature of Chessie railcar history was the railroad's entire fleet of Budd RDC cars was second-hand, and all but one was traded for, rather than purchased.

An earlier generation of railcars came in 1928 and the entire fleet was built (at least partially) by Brill.

In 1928 the Chesapeake & Ohio ordered a gas mechanical car, five gas-electrics, and three trailer combines. Other cars were acquired along with short lines that were purchased and incorporated into the system, and many of them wound up on the Nicholas, Fayette & Greenbriar, a jointly-owned (with the New York Central) coal-hauling line in West Virginia.

Chessie's earliest venture into self-propelled railcars came in 1912, when the road tried out a battery car. The trial was unsuccessful, and the car was soon sent back to its builder, the

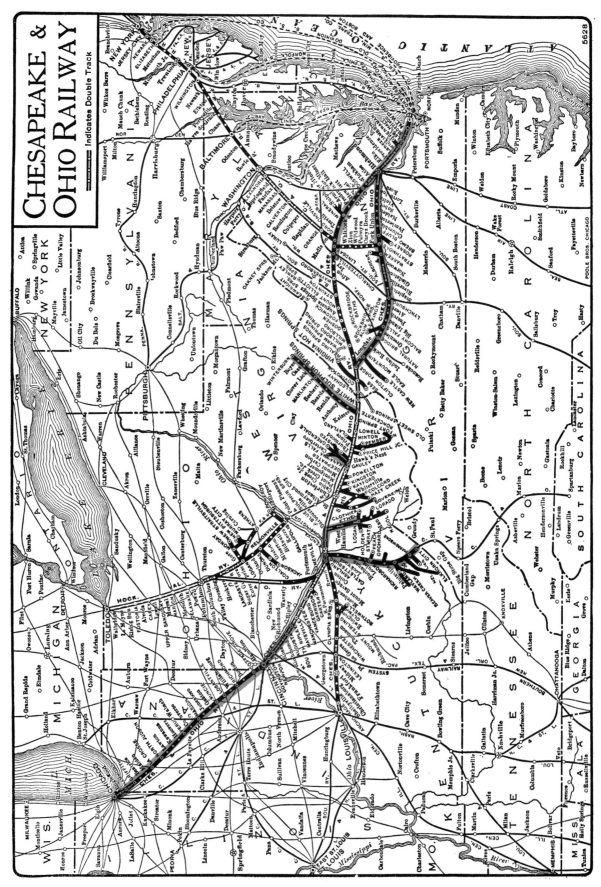

Heavy gray lines on this C&O company map indicate doodlebug runs.

Author's Collection

The 550 was one of three specially-built doodlebug trailers on the C&O. Here it is at Durbin, WV in May of 1955.

A. C. Phelps

C&O Brill 9025 became the 121 on the Nicholas, Fayette & Greenbriar. Here it passes Duo, WV.

G. Grabill Jr., Railway Negative Exchange.

The big Brill units survived well into the Budd RDC era. Here is the 9054 and an RPO-baggage car at an unknown location.

Author's Collection

Federal Storage Battery Car Co.

The fleet of 1928 Brills, except for a Model 55 that burned, served until 1959 when the accommodation runs they operated on were abandoned.

In 1957 the C&O received three Budd RDC cars from the Chicago & North Western Railway, exchanging them for three passenger coaches. The following year the C&O picked up two more RDCs from the Minneapolis & St. Louis Railway in exchange for 32 hopper cars. The last RDC was purchased from the Missouri-Kansas-Texas in 1962. This last car also contained baggage and RPO compartment.

The six-car RDC fleet was mainly used to replace locomotive-hauled passenger runs on parts of the main line. Ironically, the first route which was handed by a railcar, Richmond to Newport News (which started June 1, 1929) was also the last, closing out RDC operation on March 4, 1967.

Chesapeake & Ohio

ROAD NO.	BUILDER	DATE	BLDR. NO.	ENGINE & DRIVE	BODY TYPE	LGTH.	WT.	DISPOSITION	REMARKS
600 (15)	Federal	1912	—	Bty.-Elec.	10win Bag. 24p	38'	17t	Ret. to bldr.	—
124	Brill Mack	1921	21292 70005	Mack AB 30hp GM	8win hood Front bus	29'	5½t	To. E. Ky. Sou., 1929	Ex-Sewell Vy. 124
1000	Brill Mack	1921	21371 70009	Mack AB 30hp GM	8win hood front bus	29'	5½t	Sold?	Ex-Greenbriar & East. 100; road acq. by C&O. This car or the next one became C&O 1000
1000	Brill Service	1922	21524	Midwest 30hp GM	8win hood front bus	29'	5½t	Sold?	Ex-Pond Fork & Bald Knob 1; road acq. by C&O
9000	Brill	1923	21935	Cont. H-14 90hp GM	3win Bag.	43½'	16t	To NF&G	Ex-Sewell Vy 123, became Nicholas, Fayette & Greenbriar 123
9025-26	Brill	1923	21933-34	Cont. H-14 90hp GM	10win Bag. 39p	43½'	16t	To NF&G	Ex-Sewell Vy 121, 122; became NF&G 121, 122
9027	Brill	1928	22738	Cont. H-14 90hp GM	10win Bag 43p	43½'	16t	Burned 1941	—
9050-51	Brill	1928	22740	Hall Scott 300hp GE	8win RPO Bag. 24p	76'	65t	Scr. 1951	Re-eng. GM 268C 300hp D, 1949
9052	Brill	1928	22740	Hall Scott 300hp GE	8win RPO Bag. 40p	76'	65t	Scr. 6/55	—
9053	Brill	1928	22473	Hall Scott 300hp GE	9win RPO Bag. 16p	76'	65t	Scr. 1959	Re-eng. GM 268C 300hp D, 1949
9054-55	Brill	1928	22473	Hall Scott 300hp GE	6win RPO Bag. 16p	76'	65t	Scr. 1959	Re-eng. GM 268C 300hp D, 1949
9060	Budd	1950	5009	2-GM6-280 275hp DH	RDC-2 Bag. 66p	85'	59t	To B&O 1970, 3/63	Ex-C&NW 9935, acq. 9/57
9061	Budd	1950	5003	2-GM6-280 275hp DH	RDC-1 80p	85'	58½t	To B&O 1971, 6/65	Ex-C&NW 9933, acq. 9/57
9062	Budd	1950	5004	2-GM6-280 275hp DH	RDC-1 88p	85'	58½t	To B&O 1912, 11/76	Ex-C&NW 9934, acq. 9/57
9080-81	Budd	1957	6605-06	2-GM6-280 300hp DH	RDC-4 RPO Bag. 17p	74'	58t	To Kraut-Kramer Ultrasonic; then MBTA, Boston	Ex-M&St.L. 32, 33, acq. 12/58; bag. sect. mod. to seat 17
9082	Budd	1956	6301	2-GM6-280 275hp DH	RDC-3 RPO Bag. 49p	85'	62½t	To CN D-356, 8/65	Ex-MKT 20, acq. 6/62

Trailers

ROAD NO.	BUILDER	DATE	BLDR. NO.	ENGINE & DRIVE	BODY TYPE	LGTH.	WT.	DISPOSITION	REMARKS
550-52	Brill	1928	22742	—	12win 44p	73'	—	Scr. 1959	Had bag. sect.

Chicago Great Western

BY ALL THE RULES, the Chicago Great Western should never have been built. All of its main lines were paralleled by established roads with shorter routes. It managed to miss just about every important intermediate city. It was the new kid on the block in midwestern railroading.

In order to compete, the Great Western had to be innovative and open to new ideas, and with an idea to saving every dollar possible. For years the Great Western met the challenge, and its "can do" attitude was never more evident than in its railcar history.

Starting with some 1910 McKeen cars, the roster was to include such exotica as a battery-electric car, a Russell Car Co. set, some Sykes trainsets — and the very first Electro-Motive, St. Louis Car-built gas-electric car.

The crowning achievement was what the CGW claimed (with much justification) as the world's first streamlined train, the *Bluebird*. Rebuilt in 1929 at the Oelwein, Iowa, shops from McKeen carbodies, it incorporated all the facilities of a full-length passenger train in just three cars. The first car operated as a combination locomotive, express, baggage and railway post office car; the second was a coach, and the third car served as a combination diner, luxury coach, Pullman and solarium observation.

The Great Western was also to purchase some of the last gas-electric cars built by EMC, four baggage-RPOs, in the Depression year of 1932. These were used mostly on the Chicago-Oelwein passenger train up to 1955.

The *Bluebird's* locomotive, cut down a couple of times, was used as a switch engine until fairly recent times, then sold to a tourist railway.

As for the innovative Chicago Great Western, it did not survive as an independent road but was merged into the Chicago and North Western system.

An example of rail motorcar schedules on the CGW. Reproduced from THE OFFICIAL RAILWAY GUIDE® © 1940, NRPCo.

		42	24	•44	Mls.	*March 1, 1940.*	41	•43		
						LVE.] *(Cent. time.)* [ARR.				
			P M	A M		+.. **Minneapolis** ..ᶁ		P M		
.....	.....	.....	*300	†7 45	0	+.. **Minneapolis** ..ᶁ	....	7 00	.....	
		.....	3 30	8 20	10.5	lve.. +**St. Paul** ᶁ..arr.	....	6 30		
		.....	4 20	9 15	43.2	lve.+ **Randolph** ᶁ..arr.	....	5 38		
				9 26	49.5	+...Cannon Falls....ᶁ	....	5 26		
		.....		f9 43	59.3	+........ Welch	....	f5 07		
		.....		10 05	70.4	+.... **Red Wing** ....ᶁ	....	4 42		
		.....		– –	73.2	..... Trout Brook	....	– –		
		.....		– –	77.4	.....Hay Creek.....	....	– –		
		.....		f10 38	83.5	+.......Clay-ank.......	....	f4 10		
		.....		10 44	86.6	+......Goodhue......ᶁ	....	4 05		
		.....			90.2	Δ.....White Willow.....	....			
		.....		11 05	96.5	+.....**Zumbrota**....ᶁ	....	3 47		
		.....		– –	100.2	.... Lena	....			
		.....		11 22	105.4	+.....Pine Island....ᶁ	....	3 30		
		.....		fr13 38	113.6	.... Douglas	....	f3 15		
			P M	11 59	122.2	arr.+ **Rochester** ..lve.	A M	†3 00		
		.....	*1000	6 00	122.2	lve..**Rochester** ᶁ arr.	7 15	P M		
		.....	10 17	y –	129.8	.......**Simpson**......ᶁ	6 53			
		.....	f10 25	y –	133.4	........Judge........	f6 45			
		.....	10 35	y –	137.1	+....Stewartville ....ᶁ	6 37			
		.....	10 49	y –	142.5	.... Racine ......ᶁ	6 26			
		.....	11 07	r y	150.2	+.. **Spring Valley** ..ᶁ	6 11			
		.....	11 21	y –	155.8	......Ostrander......ᶁ	6 00			
		.....	11 35	n7 18	163.9	+......Le Roy......ᶁ	5 45			
		.....	11 50	7 30	171.0	+......**McIntire**......ᶁ	*5 30			
			P M	P M		ARRIVE]	[LEAVE	A M		
		.....	8 45	.....	.....	+. **Chicago** (*C. T.*) ..	*8 15	.....	.....	
			A M			ARRIVE]	[LEAVE	P M		

MINNEAPOLIS, ST. PAUL, ROCHESTER AND McINTIRE.

Via Dodge Center and C. & N. W. Ry.

For number of table upon which each station is located, see General Index of Stations in back part of Guide.

47

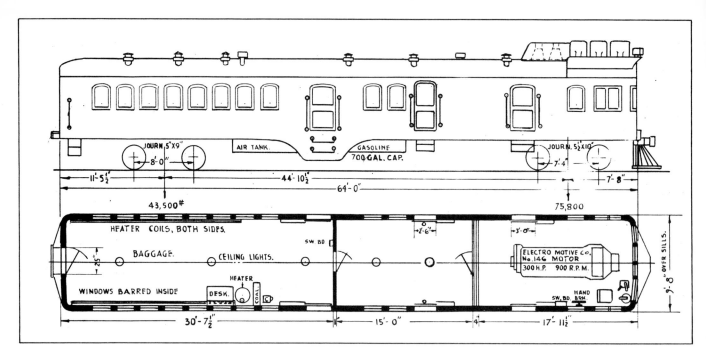

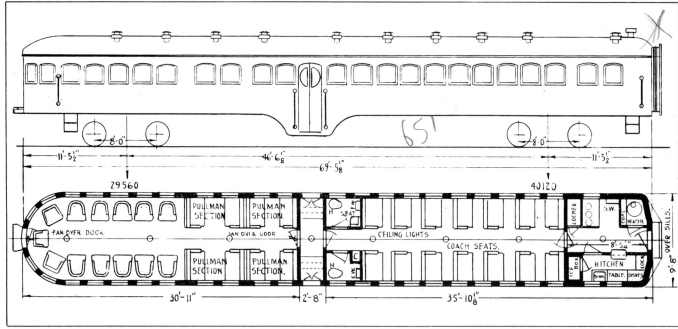

Drawings (above) are of the McKeen **BLUEBIRD** train, a Chicago Great Western feature of the 1920s. At right is McKeen car 1003 after its acquisition second-hand in 1928 and rebuilding to gas-electric drive.

All: James H. Harrison Collection.

Chicago Great Western

ROAD NO.	BUILDER	DATE	BLDR. NO.	ENGINE & DRIVE	BODY TYPE	LGTH.	WT.	DISPOSITION	REMARKS
M 200	Russell	1922	—	Wis. 120hp GM	4win OP Bag. 16p	38'	14t	To Hyman. Mich. 12/29	Front hood, 12 fold. seats in bag. sect.
M 205	Russell Sykes	1923	—	Sterl. 180hp GM	8win Bag. 30p	53'	22½t	Scr. 1933	Front hood
M 207	St. Louis Sykes	1924	1329	Sterl. 180hp GM	8win Bag. 22p	53'	25t	Scr. 1931	Front hood
M 209	St. Louis Sykes	1924	1329	Sterl. 180hp GM	8win 30p	48'	26t	Scr. 1938	Front hood, conv. to bag. only, 7/28
M 300	St. Louis EMC	1924	1323 100	Wint. 106 175hp GE	12win Bag. 54p	59'	38t	Burned 1930	First EMC-designed car
M 400	Brill Service	1922	21585	Midwest 68hp GM	10win Bag. 38p	42'	15½t	Scr. 1930	—
1000[1]	McKeen	1910	—	McKeen "A" 200hp GM	14win CE Bag. 83p	70'	35t	Rblt. 1929, re-no. 1004	Re-eng. 1914, McKeen, Type "C"
1000[2]	McKeen EMC	1910 1929	22	Wint. 146 300hp GE	9win RPO Bag.	64'	60t	Rblt. to switch eng. 10/58	Ex-1002, rblt. as "Bluebird" power car, sold 1964 to Kettle Moraine Ry. (tourist)
1001	McKeen	1910	—	McKeen 200hp GM	14win CE Bag. 83p	70'	34t	Rblt. to tlr., 1928	Square windows (To MT. 1001)
1002	McKeen	1910	—	McKeen 200hp GM	14win CE Bag. 76p	70'	34t	Rblt. to 1000[2], 1929	Square windows, Climax steam engine installed 1923
1003	McKeen EMC	— 1928	18	McKeen 200hp GM	14win CE Bag. 42p	70'	35t	Scr. 8/50	Acq. 2nd hand 1928, rblt. to GE, 1928, re-eng. Wint. 275hp GE, 48t
1004	McKeen EMC	1910 1928	19	Wint. 120 275hp GE	14win CE Bag. 43p	70'	48t	Scr. 10/50	Ex-1000[1], rblt. GE, 1928
1005	Std. Steel	1930	—	Sterl. 400hp GE	6win RPO Bag. 22p	74'	78t	Scr. 6/56	Acq. 1932, may have been demo. Double-end
1006	Pullman EMC	1932	6415 503	Wint. 191 600hp GE	RPO-Bag.	80'	89½t	Scr. 1951	Rblt. to heater car, 1948
1007	Pullman EMC	1932	6415 504	Wint. 191 600hp GE	RPO-Bag.	80'	89½t	Scr. 9/56	Rblt. to heater car, 1948, re-eng. Vik. D, 1951
1008	Pullman EMC	1932	6415 505	Wint. 191 600hp GE	RPO-Bag.	80'	89½t	Scr. 3/51	Damaged in Kansas City flood, 1951
1009	Pullman EMC	1932	6415 506	Wint. 191 600hp GE	RPO-Bag.	80'	89½t	Scr. 10/53	Re-eng. Sterl. D, 1947
1050	Federal	1912	—	4-20hp Elec.-Btry.	10win Bag. 36p	50'	29½t	Ret. to bldr., 1913	Wooden car; had 220-cell Edison btry.

Trailers

ROAD NO.	BUILDER	DATE	BLDR. NO.	ENGINE & DRIVE	BODY TYPE	LGTH.	WT.	DISPOSITION	REMARKS
MT 201	Russell-Sykes	1922	—	—	10win 36p	31'	10t	To Hyman, Mich., 12/29	—
MT 206	Russell-Sykes	1923	—	—	12win 44p	39½'	14t	Scr. 1931	—
MT 208	St.L.-Sykes	1924	1330	—	12win 52p	44½'	18t	Scr. 1935	—
MT 210	St.L.-Sykes	1924	1330	—	12win 52p	44½'	21½t	Scr. 1950	Rblt. 1928 with RPO, 8win 28p
MT 1001	Co. Shops	1928	—	—	23win 74p	66½'	33t	Scr. 5/41	Ex-McKeen mtr. 1001, "Bluebird" coach
MT 1002	Co. Shops	1928	—	—	21win 57p	69½'	35t	Scr. 8/48	Ex-McKeen mtr. acq. 2nd hand; "Bluebird" obs. diner
1025	McKeen	1910	—	—	Bag.-RPO	31'	12½t	Scr. 1937	Wrecked 11/36

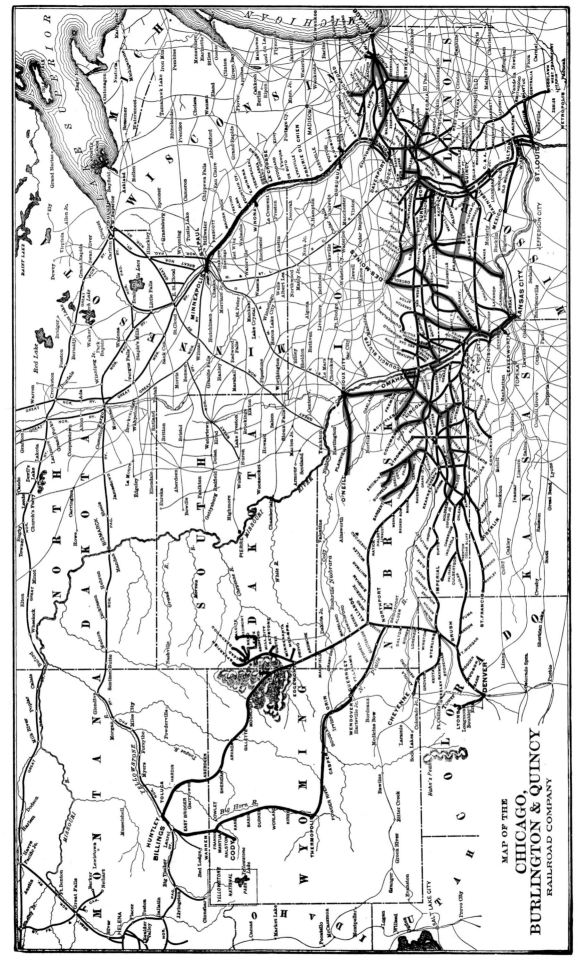

MAP OF THE
CHICAGO,
BURLINGTON & QUINCY
RAILROAD COMPANY

Heavy gray lines indicate doodlebug runs on the Burlington. *Author's Collection*

Burlington

The doodlebug was on its way to becoming an extinct species when this photo of Burlington unit 9772 and coach 6000 was taken in Lincoln, NB, on May 5, 1961. *J. Seacrest; G. Lloyd Collection*

T HE BURLINGTON RAILROAD made headlines with its fleet of "Zephyr" streamliners in the 1930s as a daring idea utilizing lightweight, streamlined trains powered by internal combustion to lure the passenger back to the rails. But the way had already been paved for the motor train by the Burlington's extensive use of the self-propelled railcar in the 1920s.

The CB&Q was an early convert to the self-propelled railcar, and used them equally for secondary main line runs and for branch-line locals. And the Burlington had a lot of branches. By the early 1930s the road had accumulated the biggest fleet of cars of any American railroad up to that time.

On the Burlington as no other railroad the distinction between the railcar and the early streamlined train was not easy to make. The very first streamliner—the Pioneer Zephyr—was an articulated unit incorporating not only engine compartment but baggage and RPO section and could well be called a streamlined doodlebug, except that such a name would hardly be in keeping with the new train's dynamic image. From this beginning, in 1934, sprang a whole generation of streamlined trains which left the "railcar" concept far behind.

Although the early Zephyrs might look like a close relative of the doodlebug, their performance was something else. For the streamliner was meant for speed, while the doodlebug was destined to dwadle along the branches.

The traditional railcar operated on the Burlington from 1922 until 1966. Unlike many contemporary roads, the Burlington never operated any Budd RDC cars, but a few of the sturdy Electro-Motive units of the 1920s stuck it out to the end.

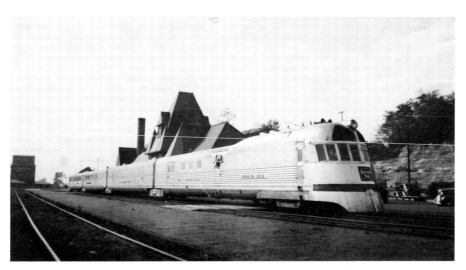

The INJUN JOE motor, shown here on the MARK TWAIN ZEPHYR, is now at the Kansas City Railway Museum. *Author's Collection*

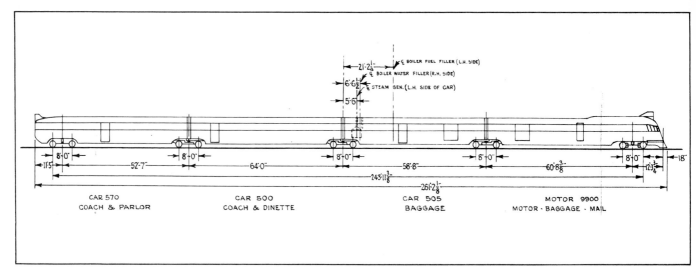

CAR 570 COACH & PARLOR	CAR 500 COACH & DINETTE	CAR 505 BAGGAGE	MOTOR 9900 MOTOR - BAGGAGE - MAIL

999

Burlington Lines

Everywhere West | **Burlington Route**

The General Pershing and Mark Twain Zephyrs—
Between St. Louis and Kansas City
CHICAGO, BURLINGTON & QUINCY RAILROAD CO.

Table 37—ALBIA AND DES MOINES.

□No. 179	□No. 27	Mls.	*March,* 1940.	□No. 178	□No. 28	
*1015 A M	‡*1130 P M	....	lve..**Chicago** (C.T.)..arr.	*755 P M	*600 A M	....
*905 A M	1145 P M	....	lve..**St. Louis** (C.T.)..arr.	*925 P M	*1245 P M	....
b1000 A M		....	lve...**Peoria**.....arr.	*635 P M	†640 A M	....
*545 P M	*820 A M	....	lve..**Ottumwa**..arr.	f1205 P M	*915 A M	....
*630 P M	*920 A M	0	lve..+**Albia**↕..arr.	1120 A M	835 P M	....
644 "	935 "	10	....Lovilia..↕	1102 "	818 "	
649 "	940 "	12	....Hamilton..↕	1057 "	f814 "	
654 "	945 "	14	+....Bussey....↕	1052 "	810 "	
705 "	954 "	19	....**Tracy**....↕	1042 "	758 "	
711 "	1001 "	23	....**Harvey**....↕	1035 "	750 "	
f720 "	f1009 "	29	....Flagler....↕	f1027 "	f741 "	
733 "	1020 "	33	+..Knoxville..↕	1020 "	733 "	
f740 "	f1027 "	37	....Donnelley..↕	f1008 "	f723 "	
751 "	1040 "	43	+..Pleasantville..↕	959 "	715 "	
800 "	1051 "	49	....Swan....↕	946 "	703 "	
f807 "	f1058 "	54	....Ford....↕	f939 "	f656 "	
f814 "	f1105 "	57	....Clarkson..↕	f934 "	f651 "	
835 "	1130 "	68	..**East Des Moines**..	915 "	635 "	
840 P M	1135 A M	68	+..**Des Moines**..↕	*910 A M	*630 P M	
			ARRIVE] (C.T.) [LEAVE			

Table 44.
FORT MADISON AND BIRMINGHAM.

....	⚲No. 97 Mixed.	Mls	*December 4,* 1939.	⚲No. 98 Mixed.	....
			LEAVE] [ARRIVE		
....	†745 A M	0	+..**Fort Madison**..↕	315 P M	....
....	810 "	6	....Sawyer....↕	250 "	....
....	830 "	11	..West Point..↕	235 "	....
....	850 A M	17	..Pilot Grove..↕	218 P M	....
	-- --	23	....**Hamill**....↕	-- --	
....	920 A M	25	....Houghton....↕	145 P M	....
....	940 "	30	arr....**Salem**....lve.	125 "	....
....	950 "	30	lve....**Salem**....arr.	120 "	....
....	1010 A M	35	....Houghton....↕	100 "	....
....	1022 A M	39	....Cottonwood....	1250 P M	....
....	1040 "	44	....Hillsboro....↕	1235 "	....
....	1105 "	51	....Stockport....↕	1210 P M	....
....	1130 A M	57	..**Birmingham**..↕	†1145 A M	....
			ARRIVE] [LEAVE		

Table 38—DES MOINES-OSCEOLA-WELDON.

....Bus	Bus	●37	Bus.	●35	Mls	*February,* 1940.	●36	Bus	●38	Bus.	Bus
	P M	A M	P M	P M	A M		P M	P M	A M	P M	P M
....	§545	§915	†510	√110	†840	0	+..**Des Moines**..↕	145	455	1145	118	1115
						4	....Burch....					
....			536	907	11	....Norwalk....↕	116	1118		
....			547	915	17	....Prole....↕	105	f1108		
....			552	925	20	..Martensdale..↕	1259	f1104		
....			558	931	22	....Wick....↕	1254	f1100		
....			606	941	26	..St. Marys..↕	1249	f1055		
....			614	950	29	..St. Charles..↕	1241	1048		
....			628		36	....Truro....↕	1229	1036		
....			644		46	..New Virginia..↕	1211	1018		
....			652		52	....Jamison....↕	1202	f1010		
710	1045	705	245	1045	57	arr.+**Osceola**↕lve.	f150	335	†958	§158	§957
P M	A M	P M	245	A M	57	lve..**Osceola**..arr.	A M	335	P M	A M	P M
			f--		64	....Leslie....↕	f--			
			x310		70	....**Weldon**....↕	*315			
			P M			ARRIVE] [LEAVE	P M			

Table 46—RED OAK AND NEBRASKA CITY.

91	No. 11	Mls	*September 24,* 1939.	92	No. 2	....
P M	Motor.		LEAVE] [ARRIVE	P M	Motor.	
†140	*707 A M	0	+....**Red Oak**....↕	1220	725 P M	....
152	719 "	7	+....Coburg....↕	1202	713 "	
202	730 "	13	+....Essex....↕	1150	701 "	
219	744 "	19	+..**Shenandoah**..↕	1130	647 "	
235	757 "	25	....Farragut....↕	1115	632 "	
250	807 "	30	....Riverton....↕	1100	622 "	
315	823 "	39	....Hamburg....↕	†1045	605 "	
P M	836 "	46	....Payne....↕	‡AM	521 "	
	855 A M	52	+..**Nebraska City**..↕		*500 P M	
			ARRIVE]		[LEAVE	

Table 4

Bus.	Bus.	Bus
P M	P M	P M

First of the new streamliners on the CB&Q was the PIONEER ZEPHYR. Drawing (above) shows motor unit in detail.

Author's Collection

Albia-Des Moines and Des Moines-Osceola runs were held down by doodlebugs. Reproduced from THE OFFICIAL RAILWAY GUIDE® 1940, NRPCo. ©

Burlington trailer 3664 is shown at Cheyenne, WY, in May of 1955. It was rebuilt from EMC motor 9817. *A. C. Phelps*

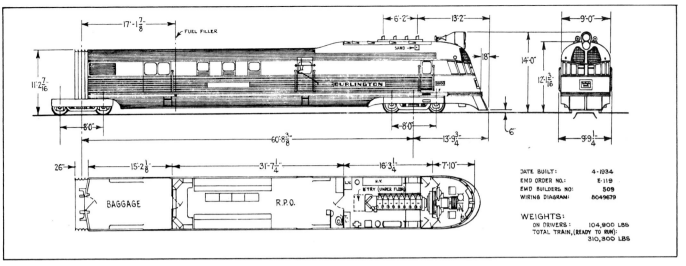

DATE BUILT:	4-1934
EMD ORDER NO.:	E-119
EMD BUILDERS NO.:	509
WIRING DIAGRAM:	8049679

WEIGHTS:
ON DRIVERS: 104,900 LBS
TOTAL TRAIN, (READY TO RUN):
310,300 LBS

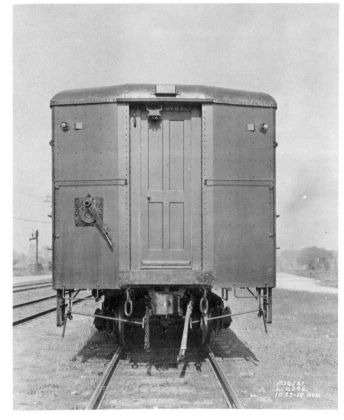

EMC - Pullman units 9768-9767 (above) display clean lines in front and rear photos. Unit at right is the 9099 at Monmouth, IL, in July of 1942.
Two: Author's Collection; W. C. Whittaker Collection

Chicago, Burlington & Quincy

ROAD NO.	BUILDER	DATE	BLDR. NO.	ENGINE & DRIVE	BODY TYPE	LGTH.	WT.	DISPOSITION	REMARKS
9450 (450)	EMD Pullman	1928	288 6145	Wint. 120 275hp GE	17win 77p	65'	52t	Rblt. tlr. 3650, 11/48	—
9500 (500)	Edwards Kel. Sprngfd.	1922	—	K-S 60hp GM	8win CE Bag. 41p	35'	9½t	Scr. 9/34	Re-eng. 103hp Cont.
501	Mack Cummins	1922	60009	Mack AC 45hp GM	7win Bag. 29p	35'	10t	Scr. 6/34	To Rapid City Black Hills & West., 3/28, 8, ret. 9/33
9502 (502)	Edwards Buda	1924	—	2-Buda 60hp GM	9win Bag. 41p	43'	21½t	Scr. 9/34	—
9503 (503)	Edwards Buda	1925	—	2-Buda 60hp GM	9win Bag. 41p	43'	21½t	Scr. 12/34	—
504	Edwards Buda	1925	—	2-Buda 60hp GM	9win Bag. 41p	43'	21½t	To Colo. & Sou., 3/26	C&S 500
9505 (505)	Edwards Buda	1926	—	2-Buda 60hp GM	9win Bag. 37p	43'	21½t	Scr. 6/38	—
9506 (506)	Edwards Buda	1926	—	2-Buda 60hp GM	9win Bag. 27p	43'	21½t	To Laramie No. Park & West. 3/31	LNP&W 9506
9507 (507)	Edwards Buda	1926	—	2-Buda 60hp GM	9win Bag. 22p	43'	21½t	Scr. 9/38	—
9508 (508)	Edwards Buda	1926	—	2-Buda 60hp GM	9win Bag. 22p	43'	21½t	To LNP&W, 3/31	LNP&W 9508
9525 (526)	EMC Pullman	1928	286 6145	Wint. 120 275hp GE	7win Bag. 39p	65'	55t	Rblt. tlr. 3651, 11/41	—
9526 (526)	EMC Pullman	1928	289 6145	Wint. 120 275hp GE	5win Bag. 22p	65'	52t	Scr. 4/57	Re-no. 9097, 8/39
9527 (527)	EMC Pullman	1928	295 6145	Wint. 120 275hp GE	7win Bag. 32p	65'	52t	Rblt. tlr. 3652, 10/41	Re-no. 9098, 8/39
9528 (528)	EMC Pullman	1928	287 6145	Wint. 120 275hp GE	7win Bag. 39p	65'	52t	Scr. 10/38	—
9529 (529)	EMC Pullman	1928	334 6203	Wint. 120 275hp GE	7win Bag. 29p	65'	53t	Rblt. tlr. 3654, 2/49	Re-no. 9099, 8/39
9509 (550)	Brill	1925	22504	Brill-WH 250hp GE	11win DE Bag. 42p	60'	46½t	Scr. 9/38	Re-no. 509, 8/28
9530 (552)	Edwards Porter	1925	—	2-Buda 100hp GM	9win RPO Bag. 42p	66'	35½t	Scr. 3/31	Re-eng. by EMC 220hp Wint. 106A, 1929. Re-no. 810, 7/25, then 530, 8/28
9725 (555)	EMC St. Louis	1927	207 1424	Wint. 120 275hp GE	RPO-Bag.	65'	53½t	Rblt. tlr. 1075, 6/43	Re-no. 725, 1/28
9726 (556)	EMC St. Louis	1927	208 1424	Wint. 120 275hp GE	RPO-Bag.	65'	53½t	Scr. 2/55	Re-no. 726, 1/28
9724 (557)	EMC St. Louis	1927	232 1443	Wint. 120 275hp GE	3win RPO Bag. 12p	65'	54t	Rblt. tlr. 2716, 7/43	Re-no. 811, 1/28, then 9811
9727 (558)	EMC St. Louis	1927	234 1442	Wint. 120 275hp GE	RPO-Bag.	65'	53½t	Rblt. tlr. 1076, 4/43	Re-no. 727, 1/28
9728 (559)	EMC St. Louis	1927	230 1442	Wint. 120 275hp GE	RPO-Bag.	65'	53t	Rblt. tlr. 1077, 8/43	Re-no. 728, 1/28
9812 (560)	EMC St. Louis	1927	236 1444	Wint. 120 275hp GE	?-win RPO Bag. 17p	65'	53t	Rblt. tlr. 3653, 6/43	Re-no. 812
9850 (569)	Mack Pullman	1928	161102 6172	2-Mack AR 120hp GE	7win RPO Bag. 32p	75'	57½t	Wrecked 4/43	Re-no. 9569. Rblt. 1934 w/eng. from 9567
9835 (570)[1]	EMC St. Louis	1927	209 1425	Wint. 120 275hp GE	8win RPO Bag. 37p	75'	54t	To. Ala. Tenn. & Nor. 51, 10/36	Re-no. 835, 1/28
9570 (570)[2]	EMC Pullman	1928	299 6145	Wint. 148 400hp GE	3win RPO Bag. 39p	75'	67½t	Scr. 8/66	Re-no. 9772, 12/33. Re-eng. 400hp Hamltn. 685A Dist., rblt. RPO-Bag. 1933
9836 (571)[1]	EMC St. Louis	1927	210 1425	Wint. 120 275hp GE	8win RPO Bag. 37p	77'	54t	To AT&N 52, 10/36	Re-no. 836, 1/28

ROAD NO.	BUILDER	DATE	BLDR. NO.	ENGINE & DRIVE	BODY TYPE	LGTH.	WT.	DISPOSITION	REMARKS
9571 (571)[2]	EMC Pullman	1928	335 6203	Wint. 120 275hp GE	7win DE Bag. 29p	75'	56t	Rblt. tlr. 3660, 6/40	Re-eng. 400hp Ham. 685A Dist.
9837 (572)	EMC St. Louis	1927	231 1448	Wint. 120 275Hp GE	7win RPO Bag. 32p	75'	57½t	Rblt. tlr. 3662, 11/43	Re-no. 837, 1/28
9838 (573)	EMC St. Louis	1927	237 1447	Wint. 120 275hp GE	6win RPO Bag. 24p	75'	58t	Rblt. tlr. 3657, 7/51	Re-no. 838, 1/28
9839 (574)	EMC St. Louis	1927	240 1447	Wint. 120 275hp GE	6win RPO Bag. 24p	75'	58t	Rblt. tlr. 2752, 12/41	Re-no. 839, 8/28
9840 (575)	EMC St. Louis	1927	239 1447	Wint. 120 275hp GE	6win RPO Bag. 24p	75'	58t	Rblt. tlr. 3666, 7/53	Re-no. 840, 8/28
9565 (585)	EMC St. Louis	1927	211 1426	Wint. 120 275hp GE	?-win Bag. 55p	75'	57½t	Rblt. tlr. 3661, 12/41	Re-no. 565, 8/28; then 9851, 1/37
9566 (586)	EMC St. Louis	1927	233 1446	Wint. 120 275hp GE	?-win Bag. 57p	75'	57½t	Rblt. tlr. 3665, 8/51	Re-no. 566, 8/28; then 9852, 1/37
9567 (587)	EMC St. Louis	1927	235 1446	Wint. 120 275hp GE	12win Bag. 57p	75'	57½t	Wrecked 1/33	Engine went to 9850; re-no. 567, 8/28
9568 (588)	EMC St. Louis	1927	238 1445	Wint. 120 275hp GE	?-win Bag. 49p	75'	57½t	Rblt. tlr. 9568, 7/51	Re-no. 568, 8/28; then 9853, 1/37
9625 (625)	EMC Pullman	1928	290 6145	Wint. 120 275hp GE	6win RPO Bag. 53p	65'	56t	Rblt. tlr. 3656, 4/51	Re-no. 9815, 1/33
9626 (626)	EMC Pullman	1928	291 6145	Wint. 120 275hp GE	7win RPO Bag.-Pass.	65'	56t	Scr. 10/59	Re-no. 9816, 2/33; Re-eng. DE
9627 (627)	EMC Pullman	1929	292 6145	Wint. 120 275hp GE	7win RPO Bag.-Pass.	65'	56t	Rblt. tlr. 3655, 3/50	Re-no. 9814, 7/32
9628 (628)	EMC Pullman	1928	293 6145	Wint. 120 275hp GE	7win RPO Bag.-Pass.	65'	56t	Rblt. tlr. 3668, 9/54	Re-no. 9818, 8/36
9629 (629)	EMC Pullman	1928	294 6145	Wint. 120 275hp GE	7win RPO Bag.-Pass.	65'	56t	Rblt. tlr. 3664, 11/51	Re-no. 9817, 4/34
9665 (665)	EMC Pullman	1928	300 6145	Wint. 148 400hp GE	?-win RPO Bag. 60p	75'	76t	Wrecked 1/33	—
9666 (666)	EMC Pullman	1928	301 6145	Wint. 148 400hp GE	?-win RPO Bag. 60p	75'	76t	To GM&N, 11/37	Re-no. 9771, 11/32; rblt. to RPO-Bag. with Ham. 400hp Dist. eng.
9729 (729)	EMC Pullman	1928	296 6145	Wint. 120 275hp GE	RPO-Bag.	65'	54t	Wrecked 9/41	—
9730 (730)	EMC Pullman	1928	297 6145	Wint. 120 275hp GE	RPO-Bag.	65'	54t	Scr. 2/55	—
9731 (731)	EMC Pullman	1928	298 6145	Wint. 120 275hp GE	RPO-Bag.	65'	54t	Scr. 2/55	—
9732 (732)	EMC Pullman	1928	338 6203	Wint. 120 275hp GE	RPO-Bag.	65'	54t	Scr. 2/55	—
9733 (733)	EMC Pullman	1928	339 6203	Wint. 120 275Hp GE	RPO-Bag.	65'	54t	Rblt. tlr. 1078, 7/49	—
9734 (734)	EMC Pullman	1929	342 6230	Wint. 148 400hp DE	RPO-Bag.	65'	66½t	Scr. 3/51	Re-eng. 400hp Ham. 685A Dist.
9735 (735)	EMC Pullman	1929	343 6203	Wint. 148 400hp DE	RPO-Bag.	65'	66½t	To. Sou. Industrial 9735, 6/69	—
9765 (765)	EMC Pullman	1929	340 6203	Wint. 148 400hp DE	RPO-Bag.	75'	70t	Scr. 1/39	—
9766 (766)	EMC Pullman	1930	341 6203	Wint. 148 400hp DE	RPO-Bag.	75'	70t	Scr. 4/57	—
9767	EMC Pullman	1930	458 6390	Wint. 148 400hp DE	RPO-Bag.	75'	71t	Scr. 12/61	Re-eng. 400hp Ham. 685A Dist.
9768	EMC Pullman	1930	459 6390	Wint. 148 400hp DE	RPO-Bag.	75'	71t	Scr. 9/66	Re-eng. 400hp Ham. 685A Dist.
9769	EMC Pullman	1930	460 6390	Wint. 148 400hp DE	RPO-Bag.	75'	71t	To. Sou. Industrial, 2/66	Re-eng. 400hp Ham. 685A Dist.

ROAD NO.	BUILDER	DATE	BLDR. NO.	ENGINE & DRIVE	BODY TYPE	LGTH.	WT.	DISPOSITION	REMARKS
9770	EMC Pullman	1930	461 6390	Wint. 148 400hp DE	RPO-Bag.	75'	71t	Scr. 8/66	Re-eng. 400hp Ham. 685A Dist.
9841 (841)	EMC Pullman	1928	281 6145	Wint. 120 275hp DE	7win RPO Bag. 32p	75'	57½t	Scr. 10/66	Re-eng. 275hp Cat. 375 DE
9842 (842)	EMC Pullman	1928	285 6145	Wint. 120 275hp DE	6win RPO Bag. 24p	75'	58t	Rblt. tlr. 3658, 8/51	Dbl. end
9843 (843)	EMC Pullman	1928	278 6145	Wint. 120 275hp DE	6win RPO Bag. 37p	75'	58t	Rblt. tlr. 3659, 8/51	Dbl. end
9844 (844)	EMC Pullman	1928	280 6145	Wint. 120 275hp DE	6win RPO Bag. 27p	75'	58t	Scr. 8/60	Re-eng. 275hp Cat. 375 DE
9845 (845)	EMC Pullman	1928	279 6145	Wint. 120 275hp DE	8win RPO Bag. 27p	75'	57½t	Scr. 8/61	Re-eng. 275hp Cat. 375 DE
9846 (846)	EMC Pullman	1928	282 6145	Wint. 120 275hp DE	6win RPO Bag. 24p	75'	57½t	Rblt. tlr. 3667, 9/53	—
9847 (847)	EMC Pullman	1928	283 6145	Wint. 120 275hp DE	6win RPO Bag. 24p	75'	57½t	Rblt. tlr. 2726, 12/42	—
9848 (848)	EMC Pullman	1928	284 6145	Wint. 120 275hp DE	6win RPO Bag. 24p	75'	57½t	Scr. 1/55	Re-no. 9773, 12/41
9849 (849)	EMC Pullman	1928	336 6203	Wint. 120 275hp DE	6win RPO Bag. 24p	65'	52t	Scr. 8/60	Re-eng. 275hp Cat. 375 DE
9813 (850)	EMC Pullman	1928	337 6203	Wint. 120 275hp GE	6win RPO Bag. 24p	65'	52t	Rblt. tlr. 2715, 4/43	Re-no. 813, 8/29; then 9096
9900	EMC Budd	1934	509	Win. 8201A 600hp DE	RPO- Bag. Artic.	74'	52½t	Donated to Museum Sci. & Industry, Chicago, 5/60	''Pioneer Zephyr''
9901	EMC Budd	1935	530	Win. 8201A 600hp DE	Bag. Kitch. Artic.	67'	50t	Burned 12/44	''Twin Zephyr,'' leased to Burl.-Rock Isl. as ''Sam Houston Zephyr,'' 1938
9902	EMC Budd	1935	531	Win. 8201A 600hp DE	Bag. Kitch. Artic.	67'	50t	Scr. 5/56	To B-RI 1938, returned 9/48 to repl. 9901
9903	EMC Budd	1935	521	Win. 8201A 600hp DE	RPO- Bag. Artic.	77'	51t	Sold 6/60	''Injun Joe,'' now at K.C. Ry. Museum
9908	EMC Budd	1939	—	12-567A 1000hp DE	Power-Bag.	80'	101t	To Nat. Museum of Transp.	''Silver Charger''

''Zephyr'' Trailers

ROAD NO.	BUILDER	DATE	BLDR. NO.	ENGINE & DRIVE	BODY TYPE	LGTH.	WT.	DISPOSITION	REMARKS
100	Budd	1939	96106	—	5win 60p	64'	—	Scr. 5/56	Added to 9902, 6/39 in use on B-RI
101 102	Budd	1935	96055- 99	—	5win 40p 7win 24p	58½' 68½'	—	—	5-stool diner-coach, used with 9902 24p coach, 24-seat obs., used with 9902
500	Budd	1938	—	—	5win 40p	64'	—	To. Kan. City RR Mus.	Added to 9900, 6/38
505	Budd	1934	94600-50	—	5win 20p	57½'	—	To. Chi. Mus. Sci. & Ind.	Buffet, bag. sect. For 9900. Rblt. to full bag., 6/38, had boiler & steam gen.
506	Budd	1935	96200	—	Bag.	64'	—	To. Kan. City RR Mus.	''Becky Thatcher,'' for 9903 (Mark Twain)
525	Budd	1935	96055-99	—	5win 40p	58½'	—	Scr. 3/52	Used on 9900 (6/35-6/36), 9902 (6/36-12/36), 9900 (12/36-6/38), 9901 (6/38-12/44). 5-stool diner
550	Budd	1935	96100	—	5win 40p	58½'	—	Scr. 3/52	Used on 9901. 5-stool diner
551	Budd	1935	96200	—	6win 20p	64'	—	To Kan. City RR Mus.	''Huckleberry Finn'' for 9903. 12-seat diner
570	Budd	1935	94600-50	—	8win 40p	63½'	—	To Chi. Mus. Sci. & Ind.	For 9900, 40p + 12 seat obs.
571	Budd	1935	96055-99	—	7win 24p	69½'	—	Scr. 3/53	For 9901, 24p + 24 seat obs.
572	Budd	1935	96200	—	9win 40p	75½''	—	To Kan. City RR Mus.	''Tom Sawyer'' for 9903. 40p + 16 seat obs.

Rock Island

Porthole windows are a dead giveaway of this McKeen motor converted and remotored by EMC in 1925. Knife-nose gave way to a flat front, but otherwise the carbody was little changed.   *Richard Reynolds.*

IN ITS LAST YEARS, the Chicago, Rock Island & Pacific became somewhat remarked for its rather amazing variety of Diesel locomotives. Eight different builders were represented on the roster, and six "one-of-a-kind" types were acquired. Taken together with numerous rebuildings, the Rock did indeed have a rich variety to offer the diesel watcher.

It should not be a surprise to learn that this penchant for the unusual in motive power goes all the way back to the very beginnings of internal combustion on the railroad.

While this policy of non-standardization may have been a financial folly, it certainly led to an interesting railcar roster, starting in 1907 with a little Fairbanks-Morse four-wheel type 19 open car.

Shortly thereafter along came a weird-looking Stover four-wheeler, a couple of steam-driven cars, then the larger McKeen and General Electric cars. After a short pause for World War I, a Mack ACX-type railbus appeared, then the only Mack ACP type ever sold — a completely unsuccessful gas-mechanical unit which was soon sent back to the factory.

The Rock Island was the only road to purchase more than one of the Mack type AQ gas-electric cars, buying five out of the total production run of nine. At this same period the Rock also was receiving the so-called baggage car locomotives, which were baggage cars converted to power units, plus the similar box cab type locomotives — all built by St. Louis-EMC.

A group of four other St. Louis conventional railcars, plus a Standard Steel-built car, completed the list until after World War II, when five Budd

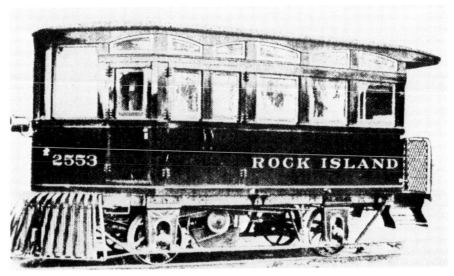

This tiny Stover car originally bore number 2553 on the CRI&P; it later was first 9005.   *R. H. Carlson Collection*

57

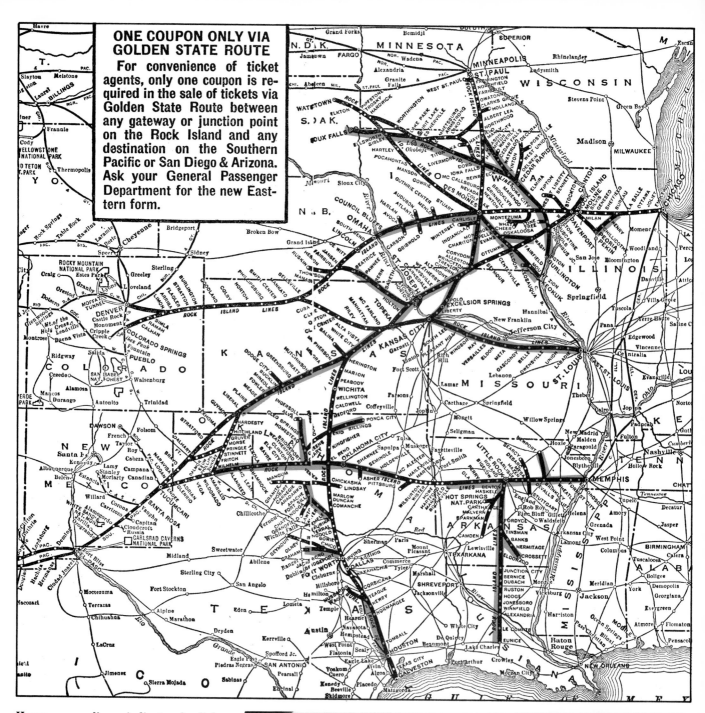

Heavy gray lines indicate doodlebug runs on the Rock Island (above). Reproduced from THE OFFICIAL RAILWAY GUIDE® © 1939 NRPCo. Budd RDC car 9003 (right) was used on Memphis-Amarillo run in the 1950s.

Author's Collection; R. H. Carlson

Power-baggage unit 9008 was built in 1929 by St. Louis-EMC. Just as in diesel locomotives, the Rock Island had a bewildering variety of doodlebugs.

Railway Negative Exchange

RDC cars were purchased. Only the Brill salesman struck out with the CRI&P, it appears.

Most of the Rock Island's railcars were converted to work equipment or scrapped in the late 1940s or 1950s, but some of the box-cab locomotives were used until the middle 1960s.

It is interesting to note that the Rock's first streamlined trains, the 1930s *Rockets*, marked the transition from the Union Pacific and Burlington's concept of the streamlined motor train in which the power unit was also a baggage car, to the present-day concept of the locomotive as a completely separate unit.

The early EMC-built Rock Island TA type locomotives had certain features, however, such as the trucks, which were more closely patterned after railcar practice than the locomotives that followed them.

On the Burlington-Rock Island, the jointly (with the Burlington) owned line from Dallas to Houston, an example of each concept, the *Sam Houston Zephyr* and the *Texas Rocket* were for a short time used at the same time in double daily service.

Mack railcar (above) shows the years at Cedar Rapids, IA. McKeen car 9023 (below) is in its original condition at an unidentified roundhouse.

R. H. Carlson; Author's Collection

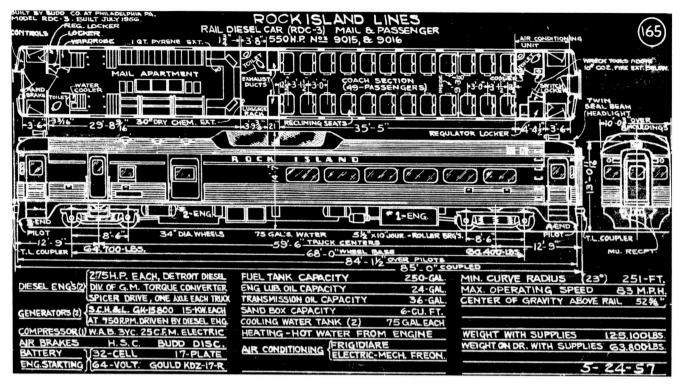

ROCK ISLAND LINES
RAIL DIESEL CAR (RDC-3) MAIL & PASSENGER
550 H.P. Nos 9015, & 9016

BUILT BY BUDD CO. AT PHILADELPHIA PA.
MODEL RDC-3. BUILT JULY 1956.

(165)

DIESEL ENG'S (2)	275 H.P. EACH, DETROIT DIESEL DIV. OF G.M. TORQUE CONVERTER SPICER DRIVE, ONE AXLE EACH TRUCK	FUEL TANK CAPACITY	250-GAL.	MIN. CURVE RADIUS (23°)	251-FT.
		ENG. LUB. OIL CAPACITY	24-GAL.	MAX. OPERATING SPEED	83 M.P.H.
		TRANSMISSION OIL CAPACITY	36-GAL.	CENTER OF GRAVITY ABOVE RAIL	52⅝"
GENERATORS (2)	S.C.H. & L. GK-15800 15-KW. EACH AT 750 R.P.M. DRIVEN BY DIESEL ENG.	SAND BOX CAPACITY	6-CU. FT.		
		COOLING WATER TANK (2)	75 GAL. EACH		
COMPRESSOR (1)	W.A.B. 3YC. 25 C.F.M. ELECTRIC	HEATING - HOT WATER FROM ENGINE		WEIGHT WITH SUPPLIES	125,100-LBS.
AIR BRAKES	H.S.C. BUDD DISC.	AIR CONDITIONING	FRIGIDAIRE ELECTRIC-MECH. FREON.	WEIGHT ON DR. WITH SUPPLIES	63,800-LBS.
BATTERY	32-CELL 17-PLATE				
ENG. STARTING	64-VOLT. GOULD KDZ-17-R			5-24-57	

The 9015 and 9016 were the Rock Island's last-purchased RDC units. This diagram shows the coach and RPO sections in detail.   *James H. Harrison Collection*

Among the more elegant doodlebug designs was that of Rock Island's 9049 (left) in vest-pocket ROCKET service between Des Moines and Washington, IA. Steam motor 2551 (below) helped introduce railcar service on the CRI&P and had a Baldwin prime mover.
James H. Harrison Collection; Author's Collection

Chicago, Rock Island & Pacific

ROAD NO.	BUILDER	DATE	BLDR. NO.	ENGINE & DRIVE	BODY TYPE	LGTH.	WT.	DISPOSITION	REMARKS
9000[1] (2552)	ACF Alco	1908	44444	Alco 250hp steam	11win Bag. 40p	56'	50t	Rblt. combo 1076, 1917	Scr. 3/48
9000[2]	Co. Shops EMC	1927	— RIC-6	2-Wint. 120 275hp Dis.E	Power-Bag.	45'	86½t	Scr. 4/49	Ex-mail car 5996, conv. GE, 2/39. Orig. blt. by Pullman, 1911
9001	Co. Shops EMC	1927	— RIC-7	2-Wint. 120 275hp Dis.E	Power-Bag.	45'	85t	Scr. 11/58	Ex-mail car 5997, conv. GE, 4/39 Orig. blt. by Pullman, 1911
9002	Budd	1953	5906	2-GM6-280 275hp DH	RDC-3 RPO Bag. 48p	85'	60t	Engine removed 12/64	Conv. to coach 902, bag. sect. removed 1955, RPO section enlarged
9003	Budd	1953	5907	2-GM6-280 275hp DH	RDC-3 RPO Bag. 48p	85'	60t	Engine removed 1/65	Conv. to coach 903, bag. sect. removed 1955. Sold to CNJ 1965 (for parts)
9004	Budd	1955	6020	2-GM6-280 275hp DH	RDC-3 RPO Bag. 48p	85'	60t	Engine removed 2/65	Conv. to coach 904, bag. sect. removed 1955
9005[1] (2553)	Stover	1909	—	Stover 60hp GM	6win 20p	—	6t	To Searcy, Kensett, AR	Used on Mo. & Nor. Ark. RR
9005[2]	Co. Shops EMC	1929	— RIC-15	2-Wint. 148 400hp Dis.E	Power-Bag.	45'	108½t	Scr. 12/57	Ex-mail car 5992, conv. GE, 3/37; re-eng. 2-Ham. 400hp D, 1947. Orig. blt. by Pullman, 1911
9006	Co. Shops EMC	1929	— RIC-16	2-Wint. 148 400hp Dis.E	Power-Bag.	45'	98½t	Scr. 10/58	Ex-mail car 5993, conv. GE, 4/37; re-eng. 2-Cat. 400hp D, 1951. Orig. blt. by Pullman, 1911
9007	Co. Shops EMC	1929	— RIC-17	2-Wint. 148 400hp Dis.E	Power-Bag.	45'	106½t	Sold for scrap 11/58	Ex-mail car 5995, conv. GE, 7/37; re-eng. 2-Ham. 400hp D, 1/40. Orig. blt. by Pullman, 1911
9008	St. Louis EMC	1929	1503 393	2-Wint. 148 400hp Dis.E	Power-Bag.	51'	98½t	Burned 1949	Conv. to GE, 3/37
9009	St. Louis EMC	1929	1503 394	2-Wint. 148 400hp Dis.E	Power-Bag.	51'	104t	Scr. 2/58	Re-eng. 2-Ham. 400hp D, 3/42
9010[1] (2550)	Sheffield Fair-Morse	1907	—	FM 30hp GM	Open 4wh 20p	22'	4½t	Scr. 8/13	Model 19
9010[2]	St. Louis EMC	1929	1503 395	2-Wint. 148 400hp Dis.E	Power-Bag.	51'	104t	Sold for scrap 11/58	Conv. to GE, 6/37; re-eng. 2-Ham. 400hp D, 11/41
9011	St. Louis EMC	1929	1503 396	2-Wint. 148 400hp Dis.E	Power-Bag.	51'	106t	Scr. 5/59	Conv. to GE, 8/37; re-eng. 2-Ham. 400hp D, 8/46
9012	St. Louis EMC	1929	1503 397	2-Wint. 148 400hp Dis.E	Power-Bag.	51'	100½t	Scr. 7/59	Conv. to GE, 7/37; re-eng 2-Cat. 400hp D, 9/50
9013	St. Louis EMC	1929	1503 398	2-Wint. 148 400hp Dis.E	Power-Bag.	51'	104t	Scr. 3/64	Conv. to GE, 3/37; re-eng. 2-Ham. 400hp D, 12/40
9014	St. Louis EMC	1929	1503 399	2-Wint. 148 400hp Dis.E	Power-Bag.	51'	101t	Scr. 12/64	Conv. to GE, 8/37; re-eng. 2-Cat. 400hp D, 2/51
9015[1] (2551)	Ry. Auto Car Baldwin	1909	— 33417	Ganz 80hp steam	6win Bag. 48p	58'	38t	Rblt. to combo 1017, 3/17	Rblt. with 250hp engine
9015[2]	Budd	1956	6303	2-GM6-280 275hp DH	RDC-3 RPO 49p	85'	61t	Traded to Gen. Elec., 1966	Blt. with enlarged RPO section, no bag. Scr. 1969
9016	Budd	1956	6304	2-GM6-280 275hp DH	RDC-3 RPO 49p	85'	61t	Eng. removed 1965	Conv. to RPO-Bag. 1966, blt. same as 9015
9020	McKeen	1909	—	McKeen 200hp GM	9win CE Bag. 48p	58'	37t	Scr. 2/37	Re-eng. 275hp Wint. by EMC, 5/25. Flat front
9021	McKeen	1910	—	McKeen 200hp GM	14win CE Bag. 48p	70'	40t	Burned 12/11	—
9022	McKeen	1910	—	McKeen 200hp GM	14win CE Bag. 48p	70'	40t	Ret. 2/37	Re-eng. 275hp Wint. by EMC, 5/25. Flat front
9023-24	McKeen	1910	—	McKeen 200hp GM	14win CE Bag. 48p	70'	40t	Ret. 1937	Re-eng. 275hp Wint. by EMC, 5/25. Flat front

ROAD NO.	BUILDER	DATE	BLDR. NO.	ENGINE & DRIVE	BODY TYPE	LGTH.	WT.	DISPOSITION	REMARKS
9040	Gen. Elec. Wason	1912	3749 12920	GE-GM16C1 175hp GE	14win Bag. 79p	70'	51t	Scr. 8/37	—
9041	Gen. Elec. Wason	1912	3750 12920	GE-GM16C1 175hp GE	14win Bag. 79p	70'	51t	Sold ED&W, 4/33	El Dorado & Wesson 5
9045	St. Louis EMC	1927	1416 195	Wint. 120 275hp GE	16win Bag. 62p	75'	55t	Conv. work car 6/52	Body sold 9/54
9046	St. Louis EMC	1927	1416 196	Wint. 120 275hp GE	16win Bag. 72p	75'	55t	Scr. 11/48	—
9047	St. Louis EMC	1927	1416 197	Wint. 120 275hp GE	16win Bag. 45p	75'	55t	Scr. 11/51	—
9048	St. Louis EMC	1927	1416 198	Wint. 120 275hp GE	16win Bag. 44p	75'	55t	Scr. 11/48	—
9049	St. Louis EMC	1927	1416 199	Wint. 120 275hp GE	16win Bag. 38p	75'	68t	Burned 1950 on B-RI	Re-eng. 275hp Ster. "Viking" for "Rocket" service. A-C 1937
9050[1]	Mack Pullman	1925	FIB1004	2 Mack AC 120hp GM	10win CE Bag. 36p	54'	24t	Ret. to Mack, 1926	Eng. mounted on trucks
9050[2]	St. Louis EMC	1928	1475 326	Wint. 120 275hp GE	13win RPO Bag. 27p	75'	60t	To Sperry Rail Svc. 141	Power removed 12/44
9051	St. Louis EMC	1928	1475 327	Wint. 120 275hp GE	13win RPO Bag. 42p	75'	60t	Conv. work car 3/52	—
9052	St. Louis EMC	1928	1475 328	Wint. 120 275Hp GE	13win RPO Bag. 32p	75'	60t	Conv. RPO-Bag. 56, 4/48	Scr. 8/54
9053	St. Louis EMC	1928	1475 329	Wint. 120 275hp GE	13win RPO Bag. 32p	75'	60t	Conv. RPO-Bag. 63, 5/45	Scr. 5/55
9054	St. Louis EMC	1928	1475 330	Wint. 120 275hp GE	13win RPO Bag. 32p	75'	57½t	Conv. caboose, 3/45	Scr. 6/57
9055	St. Louis EMC	1928	1475 331	Wint. 120 275hp GE	13win RPO Bag. 40p	75'	59½t	Conv. pas-bag-mail 55, 9/45	Scr. 6/58
9056	St. Louis EMC	1928	1475 332	Wint. 120 275hp GE	13win RPO Bag. 22p	75'	57½t	Scr. 12/51	—
9057	St. Louis EMC	1928	1475 333	Wint. 120 275hp GE	12win RPO Bag. 32p	75'	59½t	Conv. to bunk car, 9/52	—
9070	St. Louis EMC	1929	1502 400	Wint. 148D 400hp GE	9win RPO Bag. 24p	74'	78½t	To weed spray car, then Sperry Rail Svc. 138, 1971	Re-eng. Cat.; pass. sect. removed 1948. Was "Junior Rocket"
9071	St. Louis EMC	1929	1502 401	Wint. 148D 400hp GE	9win RPO Bag. 24p	74'	79t	Scr. 10/59	Re-eng. 400hp Ham. D, 1948
9090	Std. Steel	1928	356	Ster. 400hp GE	10win RPO Bag.-Pas.	75'	81t	Conv. weed spray car, 1965	Re-eng. 400hp Ham. D, 1941, then 400hp Cat. D, 1954
9095	Mack Cummings	1922	60011	Mack AC 60hp GM	7win Bag. 22p	38'	14½t	Ret. 1934	Model ACX, hood front
9100	Mack Cummings	1929	161004	2-Mack AP 120hp GE	12win RPO Bag. 46p	75'	55t	Scr. 5/47	—
9101	Mack Cummings	1929	161005	2-Mack AP 120hp GE	12win RPO Bag. 46p	75'	55t	Conv. caboose 9/43	Scr. 9/53
9102	Mack Cummings	1929	161006	2-Mack AP 120hp GE	12win RPO Bag. 42p	75'	55t	Conv. caboose 6/43	Conv. work car, 11/52
9103	Mack Cummings	1929	161007	2-Mack AP 120hp GE	12win RPO Bag. 39p	75'	55t	Conv. caboose 10/42	Scr. 3/57
9104	Mack Cummings	1929	161008	2-Mack AP 120hp GE	12win RPO Bag. 39p	75'	55t	Conv. caboose 4/43	Scr. 7/54

Trailers

ROAD NO.	BUILDER	DATE	BLDR. NO.	ENGINE & DRIVE	BODY TYPE	LGTH.	WT.	DISPOSITION	REMARKS
454	Budd	1937	—	—	10win 36p	79'	46½t	—	Parlor obs., used with RDCs. Ex-Kansas City Rocket.

Colorado & Southern
(C.B. & Q. Subsidiary)

ROAD NO.	BUILDER	DATE	BLDR. NO.	ENGINE & DRIVE	BODY TYPE	LGTH.	WT.	DISPOSITION	REMARKS
401	Pullman EMC	1928	6145 302	Wint. 148 400hp GE	6win Mail Bag. 24p	75'	67½t	To FW&DC for parts, 2/43	Conv. to Mail-Bag. 1930
402	Pullman EMC	1929	6239 368	Wint. 148 400hp GE	Bag.-2 doors	75'	68½t	Ret. 9/45	—
500	Edwards	1925	—	2-Cont. 144 103hp GM	9win Bag. 39p	43'	22t	Sold 9/29	Ex-CB&Q 504, acq. 3/26

The C&S 402 was a Pullman-Electro Motive car purchased in 1929. It is shown at Denver on July 21, 1936.
Author's Collection

Wichita Valley
(C.B. & Q. Subsidiary)

ROAD NO.	BUILDER	DATE	BLDR. NO.	ENGINE & DRIVE	BODY TYPE	LGTH.	WT.	DISPOSITION	REMARKS
20	Pullman EMC	1930	6390 462	Wint. 148 400hp GE	Mail-Bag.	75'	70½t	To FW&DC M-20, 6/33	—

Fort Worth & Denver City
(C.B. & Q. Subsidiary)

ROAD NO.	BUILDER	DATE	BLDR. NO.	ENGINE & DRIVE	BODY TYPE	LGTH.	WT.	DISPOSITION	REMARKS
M-20	Pullman EMC	1930	6390 462	Wint. 148 400hp GE	Mail-Bag.	75'	70½t	Sold for scrap, 8/50	Wrecked 11/42, parts from C&S 401 used to rebuild. Mail section removed

Chicago & North Western

Electro-Motive unit 9905 was rigged up for snow fighting in this April 3, 1939 view taken in Milwaukee.

James Buckley Collection

CNW Rail Motorcar Runs—1940

Route	Train No.	Mileage
Carroll-Sioux City IA	17-18	131
Tama-Wall Lake IA	25-6	146
Milwaukee-Adams WI	407-408	114
Janesville-Fond du Lac WI	15-28	86
Rapid City-Deadwood SD	715-712	44
Whitewood-Newell SD	812-815	42
Huron-Pierre SD	503-504	119
Sioux City IA-Huron SD	23-24	187.5
Ames-Hawdren IA	52-57	197
Hudson-Ashland WI	361-364	163
Omaha-Winner NB	11-22	298
Belle Plaine-Sanborn IA	16-21	242
Eagle Grove-Fox Lake IA	14-15	99
Madison-Lancaster WI	617-620	86
Green Bay-Long Lake WI	504-517	109
Powers-Iron River MI	201-202	67
Fond du Lac-Marshfield WI	9-10	122
Eland-Green Bay WI	216-317	70
Antigo MI-Ashland WI	116-117	171
Powers-Escanaba MI	10-11	22
Tracy-Pierre SD	106-107	309
Lander WY-Chadron NB	612-621	341

ONE WOULD EXPECT the Chicacgo & North Western, with its many granger branches, to have used the rail motorcar in large numbers, and it did. Including three Budd RDC cars and a Baldwin diesel locomotive that had a baggage section, 47 cars were owned at various times.

But the C&NW and its subsidiary, the Omaha, did not go in for railcar variety. Other than the RDCs, about all the North Western could offer in the way of oddballs was a lone McKeen and three rebuilt steam coaches. The bulk of the fleet consisted of standard Pullman or St. Louis-built units.

But wait: there was certainly something out-of-the-ordinary about some of those Pullman railcars, wherein the proliferation of appendages on the roof for all manner of vents, bells, radiators, pipes, lights and horns made for a marvellously grotesque piece of rolling machinery. On some cars these protuberances were hidden behind metal shrouding which gave the vehicles a top-heavy streamlined look.

As passenger service was progressively withdrawn from the branches, many of the railcars were rebuilt as trailers and several wound up in maintenance-of-way service. When the C&NW acquired the Minneapolis & St. Louis, it took over a few of that road's cars, but as far as can be determined they were not used in common carrier traffic but only in MW service.

The Northwestern bought three Budd RDC cars in 1950, but never really found a home for them. For awhile they operated in Chicago commuter service, but were traded in 1957 to the Chesapeake & Ohio for passenger coaches. Ironically, in 1979 a used RDC was purchased from Conrail—for use as a rail-detector car.

Streamlined unit 9915 rests (above) at Madison, WI, in 1951. Compare the lines with 9914 at Council Bluffs, IA, in 1949 and its many roof decorations.
Ray W. Buhrmaster; W. C. Whittaker Collection

Chicago & North Western

ROAD NO.	BUILDER	DATE	BLDR. NO.	ENGINE & DRIVE	BODY TYPE	LGTH.	WT.	DISPOSITION	REMARKS
1	McKeen	1980	—	McKeen 200hp GM	13win CE 75p	57'	30t	Scr. 12/27	Square rear windows
5000A	Baldwin	1948	73464	Bal. 606 1000hp DE	Power-Bag.	80½'	160t	Scr. 1958	6-wheel AIA trucks
9500	Jones Oneida	1883 1935	—	2-Cont. 104hp GM	— Bag. 38p	—	—	Wrecked 12/27	Orig. combo 872, then coach 2773, then 9915[1]
9501	Barn. & Smith Oneida	1884 1925	—	2-Cont. 70hp GM	17win 60p	—	31t	Rblt. to work car	Orig. coach 2680, then 9916[1]. 6-wheel trucks
9502	Barn. & Smith Oneida	1886 1925	—	2-Cont. 104hp GM	11win Bag. 36p	—	38½t	Rblt. to work car	Orig. coach ?, then 9917[1]
9900	St. Louis EMC	1926	1352 141	Wint. 106 175hp GE	12win Bag. 39p	60'	39t	To Sperry Rail Svc. 126, 3/37	Blt. as EMC demo. 108, 5/25, then rblt.
9901-03	St. Louis EMC	1926	1394 148-50	Wint. 106A 220hp GE	9 win RPO Bag. 42p	73'	47t	Rblt. tlrs. 9950, 1942; and and 9951-42, 1945	9901 seated 27p
9904-08	St. Louis EMC	1927	1422 201-05	Wint. 106A 220hp GE	9win RPO Bag. 35p	74'	53½t	Rblt. tlrs. 9953, 4, 6, 7, 1945; 9955, 1944	—

ROAD NO.	BUILDER	DATE	BLDR. NO.	ENGINE & DRIVE	BODY TYPE	LGTH.	WT.	DISPOSITION	REMARKS
9909	Pullman EMC	1928	6141 270	Wint. 106A 220hp GE	9win RPO Bag. 40p	75'	56t	Wrecked 7/53	—
9910-11	Pullman EMC	1928	6141 267-68	Wint. 106A 220hp GE	9win RPO Bag. 40p	75'	56t	9910 scr. 4/52; 9911 destroyed 7/53	9911 weighed 58½t
9912	Pullman EMC	1928	6141 269	Wint. 120 275hp GE	9win RPO Bag. 40p	75'	58½t	Destroyed 12/50	Rblt. as Bag.-pas.
9913-14	Pullman EMC	1928	6143 272-73	2-Wint. 120 275hp GE	RPO-Bag	67'	67t	Sold M.S. Kaplan, 1/54	9914 rblt. to all-Bag.
9915-17[1]	(See 9500-02)								
9915-17[2]	Pullman EMC	1928	6143 274-76	2-Wint. 120 275Hp GE	RPO-Bag.	67'	66t	Sold for scrap in 1957, 54, 52	9915 rblt. '48. (2) Sterl. 275hp D., streamlined front
9918-19	Pullman EMC	1928	6195 317-18	Wint. 120 275hp GE	RPO-Bag.	75'	54t	Rblt. work cars 12/51	—
9920	Pullman EMC	1928	6195 319	Wint. 120 275hp GE	9win RPO Bag. 40p	75'	55½t	Rblt. work car 12/51,	—
9921	Pullman EMC	1928	6195 320	Wint. 120 275Hp GE	8win Bag. 35p	75'	53½t	Sold for scrap 12/53	—
9922	Pullman EMC	1928	6195 321	Wint. 120 275hp GE	11win RPO 53p	68'	53½t	Rblt. work car 12/51	—
9923-24	Pullman EMC	1929	6233 361-62	Wint. 148D 400hp GE	14win 68p	67'	61½t	Sold for scrap 1/52, 2/44	9924 wrecked 10/43 Dakota City, Iowa
9925	Pullman EMC	1929	6233 353	Wint. 146 300hp GE	9win RPO Bag. 40p	77'	58½t	Rblt. work car 12/51	—
9926	Pullman EMC	1929	6233 354	Wint. 146 300hp GE	8win RPO Bag.-Pas.	77'	58½t	Sold for scrap 6/57	Re-eng. 300hp Sterl. D., "streamlined" front installed 1948
9927	Pullman EMC	1929	6233 357	2-Wint. 146D 300hp GE	7win RPO Bag. 30p	77'	80t	Sold for scrap 1/54	—
9928-29	Pullman EMC	1928	6233 355-56	Wint. 146D 300hp GE	RPO-Bag.	67'	56t	9928 rblt. work car 12/51; 9929 sold for scrap 4/52	—
9930-32	Pullman EMC	1929	6233 358-360	2-Wint. 146D 300hp GE	RPO-Bag.	77'	77½t	9930, 32 sold for scrap 2/54; 9931 burned 7/35	—
9933-34	Budd	1950	5003-04	2-GM6-280 275hp DH	RDC-1 80p; 88p	85'	63½t	To C&O 9061-62, 9/57	Traded for passenger coaches
9935	Budd	1950	5009	2-GM6-280 275hp DH	RDC-2 Bag. 66p	85'	59t	To C&O 9060, 9/57	Traded for passenger coaches

Chicago, St. Paul, Minneapolis & Omaha
(Subsidiary of Chicago & Northwestern)

ROAD NO.	BUILDER	DATE	BLDR. NO.	ENGINE & DRIVE	BODY TYPE	LGTH.	WT.	DISPOSITION	REMARKS
2000	Pullman EMC	1928	6144 277	2-Wint. 120 275hp GE	RPO-Bag.	67'	66t	—	—
2001	Pullman EMC	1928	6141 271	Wint. 120 275hp GE	?-win Bag. 80p	74'	50t	—	—
2002	Pullman EMC	1929	6231 364	2-Wint. 146D 300hp GE	6win Bag. 20p	67'	73½t	Burned	Rblt. to Baggage car
2003-04	Pullman EMC	1929	6231 365-66	2-Wint. 146D 300hp GE	7win Bag. 30p	67'	73t	—	—
2005	Pullman EMC	1929	6231 367	2-Wint. 146D 300hp GE	RPO-Bag.	74'	77½t	—	"Namakagon"

NOTE: A number of motors were rebuilt to trailers. See remarks.

Chicago & Eastern Illinois

ROAD NO.	BUILDER	DATE	BLDR. NO.	ENGINE & DRIVE	BODY TYPE	LGTH.	WT.	DISPOSITION	REMARKS
245	ACF	1937	1590	H-S 190 200hp GM	15win mail 61p	76'	31t	To KCM&O (Mex) 103, 1943	''Salem''
342	ACF	1937	1590	H-S 190	15win mail	75'	31t	To Louisiana NW 400, 1943	''Mt. Vernon''
RDC 1	Budd	1955	6222	2-GM2-803 275hp GH	RDC-1 89p	85'	60t	To CN D-109, 8/64	—

Trailers

467	Pullman Std.	1946	6720	—	54p	—	—	To L&N 6/69	Ex-Pere Marquette 30, acq. 1950. Used with RDC

We see the MT. VERNON, built by ACF in 1937, at Danville, IL, on August 3, 1939. The ACF cars, and later the Budd car, were typically used on the run to Southern Illinois via Salem, IL.   *C. A. Brown*

The Milwaukee Road

IN BETTER DAYS, the Milwaukee Road was noted for the variety of equipment built by the craftsmen of its own shops. The passenger cars built for the streamlined Hiawatha trains come immediately to mind, but there also were many types of freight cars and even two railcar locomotives.

These self-propelled units, numbered 5900 and 5901, looked like diesel locomotives, down to a shortened EMC-style nose, but they contained 41-foot baggage compartments. They were built in 1948 and were the last railcars built for the CMSP&P.

Extensive rebuildings were done on many of the Milwaukee's railcars. For

This "locomotive" with its F-style nose and baggage compartment was built in the Milwaukee Road's own shops.
C. A. Brown

67

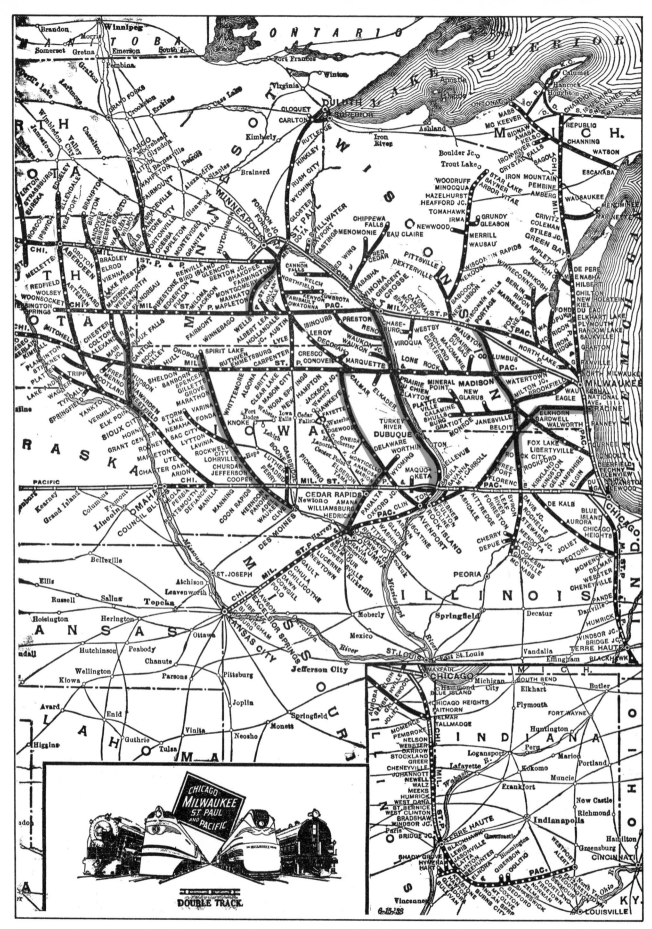

Heavy gray lines indicate doodlebug runs on the eastern part of the Milwaukee Road. Reproduced from THE OFFICIAL GUIDE® © 1938 NRPCo.

68

Standard Steel EMC-built 5925 has its portrait made at Marquette, IA, on September 23, 1939.
C. T. Felstead; Ray W. Burhmaster Collection

(Right) The X671 was a boomer doodlebug, purchased from the Northwestern Pacific in 1941 and later converted to a line car for the Milwaukee's electrification. *Tom Gray*
(Below) A two-car consist at the Kansas City Union Station circa 1940. Motor car is the 5927. *Gordon Lloyd*

instance, Standard Steel cars 5925 to 5934 were constructed in 1927 as combines, and in 1929 were rebuilt to baggage-RPO configuration, with extensive changes in the cooling system.

The two cars that the Milwaukee purchased from the Southern Pacific in 1941 were also changed to RPO-baggage cars. One of these cars, ex-Northwestern Pacific 902, was rebuilt to a line car for the electrified zone, and was used as such up until 1965, making it the last railcar on the system, even outliving the 5900 and 5901 which were scrapped in 1961 after only 12 years of service.

As might be expected, most of the doodlebug runs were on the eastern end of the system; in fact, by 1940, there were no railcar runs west of the Dakotas. In the early days when the General Electric cars held sway, there were runs from Seattle to Enumclaw and another from Everett to Monroe, both in the state of Washington.

In 1918 the Bellingham Bay & British Columbia Railroad was acquired, along with the short line's two cars, a small Fairbanks-Morse and a 70-foot McKeen car. These two units were the only non-electric drive cars the Milwaukee ever had, and were soon retired.

Chicago, Milwaukee, St. Paul & Pacific

ROAD NO.	BUILDER	DATE	BLDR. NO.	ENGINE & DRIVE	BODY TYPE	LGTH.	WT.	DISPOSITION	REMARKS
5900[1] (1)	Gen. Elec. Wason	1912	3754 12900	GE 16C1 175hp GE	15win Bag. 80p	72'	56t	Rblt. to line car	—
5900[2]	Co. Shops	1948	—	GM 567A 1000hp DE	Loco.-Bag.	85'	111t	Scr. 1/61	6-wheel trucks, F-style nose
5901[1] (2)	Gen. Elec. Wason	1912	3755 12900	GE 16C1 175hp GE	15win Bag. 80p	72'	56t	Ret. 1932	—
5901[2]	Co. Shops	1948	—	GM 567A 1000hp DE	Loco.-Bag.	85'	111t	Scr. 1/61	Same as 5900[2]
5902 (3)	Gen. Elec. Wason	1913	3756 12900	GE 16C1 175hp GE	15win Bag. 80p	72'	56t	Ret. 1932	Re-eng. 200hp Wint. 120, 1940; pass. sect. rblt. 10 win.
5903 (4)	Gen. Elec Wason	1913	3757 12900	GE 16C1 175hp GE	15win Bag. 80p	72'	56t	Ret. 1947	Re-eng. 200hp Wint. 120, 1940; pass. sect. rblt. 6 win.
5904	Gen. Elec. Wason	1912	3759 12920	GE 16C1 175hp GE	13win Bag. 77p	70½'	51t	Rblt. to line car, 10/20	Ex-Chi. Milw. & Puget Sound 300
5905	Gen. Elec. Wason	1912	3760 12920	GE 16C1 175hp GE	13win Bag. 77p	70½'	51t	Rblt. to line car, 10/20	Ex-Chi. Milw. & Puget Sound 301
5906 (5)	Gen. Elec. Wason	1913	3758 12900	GE 16C1 175hp GE	12win Bag. 46p	72'	56t	—	Rblt. flat-front, re-eng. Foos D., 9/27. Wt. 66t
5907	Fair-Morse	—	—	FM GM	—	—	—	Ret. by 1921	Ex-Bel. Bay & Brit. Col. 1, acq. 1918
5908	McKeen	1909	—	McKeen 200hp GM	14win CE Bag.-Pas.	70'	34t	Ret. by 1921	Ex-Bel. Bay & Brit. Col. 2. "Kulshan" acq. 1918
5925-29	Std. Steel EMC	1928	307 219-23	Wint. 120 275hp GE	12win Bag.-Pas.	76'	70t	Ret. by 1954	Rblt. to RPO-Bag. 1929
5930-34	Std. Steel EMC	1928	307 251-55	Wint. 120 275hp GE	12win Bag.-Pas.	76'	70t	Ret. by 1954	Rblt. to RPO-Bag. 1929. Fair-Morse D. installed in 5932, 1935
5935-36	Pullman EMC	1928	6120 256-57	Wint. 120 275hp GE	12win Bag.-Pas.	76'	69t	5935 ret. 1951; 5936 rblt. to tlr.	Rblt. to 6 win RPO-Bag. 22p
5937	Pullman EMC	1928	6120 258	Wint. 120 275hp GE	12win Bag. 42p	76'	60t	Ret. 1954	—
5938	Pullman EMC	1928	6120 259	Wint. 120 275Hp GE	6win RPO Bag.-Pas.	76'	69t	Ret. 1951	—
5939	Pullman EMC	1928	6120 260	Wint. 120 275hp GE	12win Bag. 42p	76'	69t	Ret. 1952	—
5940[1]	Pullman Ryan	1928	6228	Ryan steam 450hp V8	—	—	—	—	Steam car
5940[2]	Pullman EMC	1930	6297 436	Wint. 148D 400hpGE	RPO-Bag.	76½'	79t	Ret. 1947	Ex-SP 6, acq. 1941; pas. sect. rblt. to RPO
5941[1]	Pullman Ryan	1928	6287	Ryan steam 450hp V8	RPO-Bag.	65'	70t	To Amer. Cyan. 1939	"Locomotor" steam car
5941[2]	Pullman EMC	1930	6297 437	Wint. 148D 400hp GE	RPO Bag. 34p	76½'	85t	Conv. to line car	Ex-NWP 902, acq. 1941; pass. sect. rblt. to RPO
5942	Pullman Ryan	1931	6287	Ryan steam 450hp V8	RPO-Bag.	65'	70t	Rblt. to tlr. 1875, 4/40	—

Columbus & Greenville

ROAD NO.	BUILDER	DATE	BLDR. NO.	ENGINE & DRIVE	BODY TYPE	LGTH.	WT.	DISPOSITION	REMARKS
M 75	Brill	1925	2					u. & NW, 4/31	Ex-demo, pur. 11/30
M 76-77	Brill	1928	2					demotorized 1948; 7 conv. storage room,	—
T-75	Brill	1926	22					ntanamo & West.)	Sold to G&W, 1937
T-86-7	Brill	1928	22					)/40	Conv. to boarding cars B-50, 51; scr. 1972

Note swastika emblem on Columbus & Greenville motor M-76, photographed at the Brill plant when the car was brand-new in 1928.
Author's Collection

This is the car that started General Electric on the road to the gas-electric doodlebug era: No. 1000. It was never actually owned by the Delaware & Hudson but it ran extensive tests on that road, and led to the GE's line of distinctive rail motorcars.

C. P. Munck Collection

Delaware & Hudson

ROAD NO.	BUILDER	DATE	BLDR. NO.	ENGINE & DRIVE	BODY TYPE	LGTH.	WT.	DISPOSITION	REMARKS
1000	Barn. & Smith Gen. Elec.	1906	—	Wolseley 140hp GE	12win Bag. 40p	65'	48t	Owned by GE	GE demo.; sold to Elec. Short Line MN
2000	Gen. Elec. Wason	1911	3721	GE 16A5 175hp GE	13win CE Bag. 91p	68'	46t	To Clinchfield 75, 6/17, then Apalachicola Nor., 1919	—

The **BRIGHAM YOUNG** heads a two-car PROS-PECTOR motor train, shown at Denver in 1941. Unfortunately the two D&RGW motor trains had a very short life.

Harold K. Vollrath Collection

Denver & Rio Grande Western

ROAD NO.	BUILDER	DATE	BLDR. NO.	ENGINE & DRIVE	BODY TYPE	LGTH.	WT.	DISPOSITION	REMARKS
M 1	Budd	1941	—	2-Her. 192hp GE	8win Bag. 44p	75'	—	Returned to bldr., 7/42	"John Evans." Prospector train, with tlr.
M 2	Budd	1941	—	2-Her. 192hp GE	8win Bag. 44p	75'	—	Returned to bldr., 7/42	"Brigham Young." Prospector train, with tlr.
592	Pullman Ry. Motors	1898 1927	—	2-Cont. 100hp GM	11win 40p	57'	38t	Rblt. to combo. 1938, ret. 1/51	Orig. passenger coach

NOTE: M-1 and M-2 each had 78' tlr., 10 win., buffet lounge, sleeper.

Detroit, Toledo & Ironton

ROAD NO.	BUILDER	DATE	BLDR. NO.	ENGINE & DRIVE	BODY TYPE	LGTH.	WT.	DISPOSITION	REMARKS
35-36	Pullman	1925	4926	2 Hall-Sc. 150hp GE	12win RPO Bag. 48p	72½'	66t	35 rblt. to tlr; 36 to Minn. West. 39	Engine under body

Duluth, Missabe & Iron Range

ROAD NO.	BUILDER	DATE	BLDR. NO.	ENGINE & DRIVE	BODY TYPE	LGTH.	WT.	DISPOSITION	REMARKS
W 56	Co. Shops TCRT	1939	—	GM 160hp DM	5win wood streetcar	—	—	—	Ex-Duluth streetcar, blt. by Twin City Rapid Transit, Mpls.
1	Budd	1952	5701	2 GM 275hp DH	RDC-3	85'	—	To NP B42, 3/63	To Amtrak, then Brit. Col. Ry.

This former Duluth streetcar, built at the Twin City Rapid Transit shops in St. Paul, shuttled employes around the DM&IR yards near Superior, WI.   *Author's Collection*

Rather homely was the DM&N's M-55 but it served long and well. It is pictured here at Proctor, MN, on August 29, 1939. That exhaust pipe apparently was carefully bent to follow closely the contours of the side of the car.
C. T. Felstead; Ray W. Buhrmaster Collection

Duluth, Missabe & Northern
(Merged into Duluth, Missabe & Iron Range)

ROAD NO.	BUILDER	DATE	BLDR. NO.	ENGINE & DRIVE	BODY TYPE	LGTH.	WT.	DISPOSITION	REMARKS
M 55	Ohio Falls Ry. Mot. Co.	1901 1927	—	2-Cont. 70hp GM	17win 64p	—	—	—	Orig. coach 55
M 108	ACF Ry. Mot. Co.	1908	—	2-Cont. 104hp GM	5win Bag. 30p	74'	50t	—	Orig. combo. 108

Duluth & Iron Range
(Merged into Duluth, Missabe & Iron Range)

ROAD NO.	BUILDER	DATE	BLDR. NO.	ENGINE & DRIVE	BODY TYPE	LGTH.	WT.	DISPOSITION	REMARKS
MC 1	Bar. & Smith Ry. Mot. Co.	1907 1926	—	2-Cont. 104hp GM	8win Bag. 36p	62'	46t	—	Orig. combo. 19

Duluth, South Shore & Atlantic

ROAD NO.	BUILDER	DATE	BLDR. NO.	ENGINE & DRIVE	BODY TYPE	LGTH.	WT.	DISPOSITION	REMARKS
500	Budd	1955	6220	2-GM 275hp DH	RDC-1	85'	—	To CP 9049, 5/58	—

Duluth, Winnipeg & Pacific

ROAD NO.	BUILDER	DATE	BLDR. NO.	ENGINE & DRIVE	BODY TYPE	LGTH.	WT.	DISPOSITION	REMARKS
D301	Budd	1956	6602	2-GM 275hp DH	RDC-3 Bag.-Pas.	85'	—	To CN D355, 10/61	No RPO section

Erie

Erie's 5003 pulls a pair of Stilwell coaches in this 1948 view at Little Falls, NJ. The motor was one of the few doodlebugs built entirely by Standard Steel Car Co.   *C. A. Brown*

WHILE THE ERIE probably is best remembered for its fleet of "Stilwell" roofed gas-electric cars, it did have several other distinctions in the history of the self-propelled railcar. The Erie was, in fact, a railcar pioneer.

A steam storage car, built by the Kinetic Power Co., was tried out in 1897, but apparently not purchased.

However in the same year, an old emigrant coach was equipped with a Schenectady Locomotive Co. vertical-boilered 0-4-0 type steam mechanism, and in 1898 another of these units was purchased.

These two units were soon retired, mostly because of poor power and poor steaming qualities. Despite this failure, another steam car, this time with a Ganz-designed two-cylinder compound, was tried in 1907. The result was the same and the Erie soon turned to internal combustion.

To start with, the Erie borrowed the Union Pacific's McKeen car, number 7 — the first to be built with McKeen's

Built before the turn of the century was this Schenectady steam motor, lettered for the New Jersey and New York before road was merged into the Erie.

Harold K. Vollrath Collection

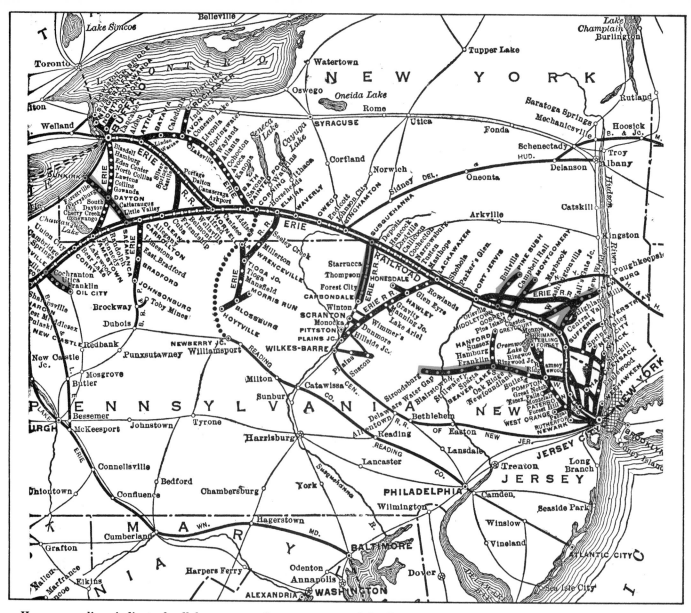

Heavy gray lines indicate doodlebug runs on the eastern part of the Erie. Reproduced from THE OFFICIAL RAILWAY GUIDE® © 1941, NRPCo.

These passengers doubtless look forward to the warm and cozy interior of Erie motorcar 5006 at the Newark, NJ, stop on a snowy day in February, 1947.
P. Kutta Collection

The 5004 and train make the station stop at Athenia, NJ (right) on June 28, 1939. Newburgh, NY (below) was the end of one Erie branch line which offered this Brill-built lightweight as an accommodation. Photo dates to about 1929.

P. Kutta Collection; Robert G. Foley Collection

In later years the Erie used its doodlebugs in commuter-type service in the greater New York area. Here, on July 23, 1949, unit 5005 and train pauses at Paterson, NJ.

P. Kutta Collection

trademarked round windows—and kept it for tests long enough to receive Erie lettering. This led to an order for two McKeen cars, which lasted until 1922.

In the years from 1923 to 1925 the Erie acquired the largest fleet of Brill gas-mechanical cars of any American railroad. Ten model 55, four model 75 and a matching trailer made up the fleet. From 1926 to 1930, seven gas-electric cars were bought, plus car 5000—a pioneering oil-electric that was probably more locomotive than railcar.

Then in 1931 the road purchased the aforementioned Stilwell cars, used mostly in New York City commuter service. In 1951 the entire railcar fleet was retired.

Erie

ROAD NO.	BUILDER	DATE	BLDR. NO.	ENGINE & DRIVE	BODY TYPE	LGTH.	WT.	DISPOSITION	REMARKS
?	Schenectady	1897	—	0-4-0 steam	16win 50p	—	—	—	Ex-immigrant car; vertical boiler
680	Schenectady	1898	—	0-4-0 steam	10win Bag. 40p	—	—	Ret. 1902	Ex-combo; vertical boiler
3000	Ry. Auto Car	1907	—	2-Ganz 60hp steam	13win Bag. 50p	58'	45t	—	—
4000[1]	McKeen	1906	7	McKeen 200hp GM	13win CE Pass.	55'	30t	To UP 7, 1907	Probably on loan; first round-window car
4000[2]	Brill Service	1923	21870	Midwest 68hp GM	10win Bag. 38p	43'	15t	Sold 1935 to Cuba (?)	Model 55
4001[1]	McKeen	1908	—	McKeen 200hp GM	?-win CE Bag.-Pass.	55'	30t	Ret. 1922	—
4001[2]	Brill Service	1923	21870	Midwest 68hp GM	10win Bag. 38p	43'	15t	Rblt. to tlr. 4011, 1/35	Model 55
4002[1]	McKeen	1909	—	McKeen 200hp GM	13win CE Bag.-Pass.	70'	35t	Ret. 1922	—
4002[2]-03[1]	Brill Service	1924	22086	Midwest 68hp GM	10win Bag. 38p	43'	15½t	Sold 1935 to Cuba (?); 4003 wrecked, 1924	Model 55
4003[2]	Brill Service	1925	22243	Midwest 68hp GM	10win Bag. 38p	43'	16t	Sold 1935 to Cuba (?)	Model 55
4004-08	Brill	1924	See note	Midwest 68hp GM	10win Bag. 38p	43'	16t	Sold 1935 to Cuba (?)	Model 55; 4004 Bldr. No. 22086; 4005-6, no. 22087; 4007, no. 22088; 4008, no. 22112
4050-51	Brill	1924	22089	Brill-WH 190hp GM	13win Bag. 59p	55'	28t	4050 rblt. to coach, 1/33	Model 75
4052-53	Brill	1925	22306	Brill-WH 190hp GM	13win Bag. 59p	55'	28t	4053 rblt. to tlr. 4013, 3/36	Model 75
4070	Brill	1926	22305	Brill-WH 250hp GE	13win Bag. 53p	60'	48t	—	Model 250
4071	Brill	1926	22309	Brill-WH 250hp GE	13win Bag. 44p	60'	48t	—	Model 250
4072	Brill	1926	22322	Brill-WH 250hp GE	13win Bag. 48p	60'	48t	Conv. to loco. 18, 6/41	Model 250
5000	St. Louis WH	1930	1523	2-WH B 300hp OE	RPO-Bag.	78'	103½t	—	RPO section reduced, 12/35
5001	Std. Steel	1930	371	Ster. GE 300hp GE	RPO-Bag.	75½'	89t	Ret. 1951	RPO section reduced, 11/34
5002-04	Std. Steel	1930	See note	Ster. GE 300hp GE	14win RPO 42p	75½'	89t	Ret. 1951	5002-3 Bldr. no. 370; 5004, no. 372
5005-13	Bethlehem EMC	1931	466-74	2-Win. 146D 300hp GE	11win Bag. 44p	73'	88t	All ret. 1951; 5012 donated to Ohio Ry. Mus.	5012 used for a time on NYS&W, same number
5014-15	Bethlehem EMC	1931	475-76	2-Win. 146D 300hp GE	11win Bag. 44p	73'	88t	To Amer. Agg., 1951	—

Trailers

ROAD NO.	BUILDER	DATE	BLDR. NO.	ENGINE & DRIVE	BODY TYPE	LGTH.	WT.	DISPOSITION	REMARKS
4010	Brill	1923	21871	—	10win 38p	35'	—	Rblt. to m/w, 12/35	—
4011	Brill	1923	21870	—	10win 38p	43½'	—	—	Ex-motor 4001[2], conv. 1/35. Bag. sect.
4012	Brill	1924	22112	—	10win 38p	43½'	—	—	Ex-motor 4008, conv. 1/35. Bag. sect.
4013	Brill	1924	22306	—	13win 59p	55'	—	—	Ex-motor 4053, conv. 3/36. Bag. sect.

Florida East Coast

ROAD NO.	BUILDER	DATE	BLDR. NO.	ENGINE & DRIVE	BODY TYPE	LGTH.	WT.	DISPOSITION	REMARKS
200	Gen. Elec. Wason	1916	3791 17275	GE 16C9 175hp GE	17win Bag.-Pass.	70'	51½t	To Minn., Northfl. & Sou. 12, 1919	—

Georgia & Florida
(Merged into Southern Railway System)

ROAD NO.	BUILDER	DATE	BLDR. NO.	ENGINE & DRIVE	BODY TYPE	LGTH.	WT.	DISPOSITION	REMARKS
81	St. Louis Fair.-Morse	1939	1598	F.M. PC 750hp DE	Mail-Bag.	81'	114t	Sold for scrap, 5/64	Ex-Sou. 41, acq. 9/54

Trailers

ROAD NO.	BUILDER	DATE	BLDR. NO.	ENGINE & DRIVE	BODY TYPE	LGTH.	WT.	DISPOSITION	REMARKS
(2 cars)	St. Louis	1939	1599	—	21win 76p	73'	57t	Sold for scrap, 5/64	Ex-Sou. MT-40, 41. Probably not used with 81

The Gulf, Mobile & Northern was a pioneer in the use of streamlined trains. Here is REBEL power unit 353, with baggage and RPO section, at Jackson, TN, on May 11, 1936.
Harold K. Vollrath Collection

Gulf, Mobile & Ohio

One of the relatively small railroads which ultimately made up the GM&O system was the New Orleans Great Northern, which in 1925 purchased this Brill Model 75 car. It is shown at the Brill plant before delivery.

GM&O Rail Motorcar Runs—1941

Route	Train No.	Mileage
Bloomington IL-Kansas City MO	20-21	351
Bloomington-Roodhouse IL	27-28	106
Roodhouse-Godfrey IL	34-35	20
St Louis MO-Jackson TN	3-4	261.6
Jackson TN-Meridian MS	11-12	251.1
Artesia MS-Montgomery AL	111-115	181
Artesia MS-Tuscoola AL	112-116	74
Tuscoola Al-Montgomery AL	109-110	107
Jackson TN-Jackson MS	5-6	302
Union-Meridian MS	15-16	33
New Orleans LA-Jackson TN	1-2	487
Mobile AL-Union MS	21-22	181

Latter two were "Rebel" trains.

HOW ISAAC B. "IKE" TIGRETT built a small, struggling railroad into a system that extended from the Gulf of Mexico to the Great Lakes has been well documented as one of the Cinderella stories of railroading. By coincidence, each of the railroads that made up this system was a user of rail motorcars and in general had similar histories in their operation.

Starting with the Gulf, Mobile & Northern, Tigrett acquired the New Orleans-Great Northern. This road had a General Electric gas-electric car built in 1913. The Mobile & Ohio, the second road acquired, operated three Fairbanks-Morse Type 24 four-wheelers that were built at the same time.

The Alton, which formed the northern part of the combined system, had an experimental home-built unit built in

The ST. TAMMANY SPECIAL was a very short run which extended north out of New Orleans. Motor 350 headed up this brightly-painted GM&N train in 1930, giving a sort of streamlined effect a few years in advance of the real thing.
Author's Collection

1906. The roads all acquired standard cars in the 1920s and in 1934 Tigrett's GM&N put into service a streamlined railcar unit dubbed the *Rebel* which set a fast and stylish note in the Bayou country.

Generally, however, the railcars took over the branch line and secondary mainline trains leaving the overnight Pullman consists to be hauled by steam locomotives. The Alton, in addition, had some fast daylight flyers between Chicago and St. Louis which remained locomotive-powered.

By the time the Alton railroad was acquired in the World War II period, the Rebel motor trains had assumed even the long-distance, overnight runs except for one St. Louis-Mobile train. After the Alton came into the system, the "Rebel" image was toned down; the Alton main line through the heart of Illinois was hardly Rebel country and an "Abraham Lincoln Rebel" would have been incongruous indeed!

Alton tracks did carry many of the original *Zephyr* trains, but only because the Burlington Route used Alton rails for half of their trip between Kansas City and St. Louis.

The last GM&O railcar schedule was on the Alton section between Bloomington, Ill., and Kansas City. By the time this run was taken off in April of 1960, it had become somewhat celebrated as one of the last such doodlebug runs in the United States.

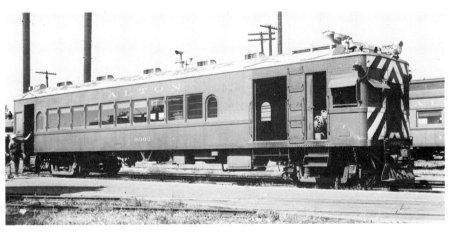

Alton's 6002 (above) was much renumbered in its career on the Chicago & Alton, the reorganized Alton, then the Gulf, Mobile & Ohio. GM&O trailer 2551 (below) sported an unusual open platform. It is shown at Higginsville, MO, in May of 1955.
W. C. Whittaker Collection; A. C. Phelps

Gulf, Mobile & Northern
(Merged into Gulf, Mobile & Ohio)

ROAD NO.	BUILDER	DATE	BLDR. NO.	ENGINE & DRIVE	BODY TYPE	LGTH.	WT.	DISPOSITION	REMARKS
2	Brill Service	1922	21605	Midwest 68hp GM	10win CE Bag. 29p	43'	14½t	Ret. 1929	Ex-NO–GN 2
3	Brill	1925	22197	Brill 75 175hp GM	13win CE Bag.-Pass.	55'	25t	To Consol. RR of Cuba	Ex-NO–GN 3
300	Brill	1923	21898	Midwest 68hp GM	10win Bag. 38p	43'	14½t	To Angelina & Neches Riv. 300, 4/28	—
350-51	Brill	1930	22857	Brill 860 550hp GE	12win Bag. 40p	75'	20t	350 to GM&O 350; 351 wrecked 1937	Assigned to NO–GN
352-53	ACF	1934	1383	Alco 660hp DE	Power RPO Bag.	73'	89½t	To GM&O 352-353	"Rebel" power units
354	ACF	1936	1600	Alco 660hp DE	Power RPO Bag.	73'	89½t	To GM&O 354	"Rebel" power units
9771	Pullman EMC	1928	6145 301	Ham. 685A 400hp GE	RPO-Bag.	75'	76t	To GM&O 1835	Ex CB&Q 9771, acq. 11/37

NOTE: CB&Q cars 9725, 9731, 9849 and 9525 were leased from time to time.

Trailers

ROAD NO.	BUILDER	DATE	BLDR. NO.	ENGINE & DRIVE	BODY TYPE	LGTH.	WT.	DISPOSITION	REMARKS
310	Brill	1924	21982	—	11win 42p	34'	12t	—	—
360	Brill	1930	22860	—	15win 52p	75½'	—	To GM&O 360	Assigned to NO–GN. Bag. sect.
370-1	Brill	1930	22858	—	21win 78p	75½'	—	To GM&O 370, 371	Assigned to NO–GN. Bag. sect.
372-4	ACF	1934	1348	—	19win 54p	76'	—	To GM&O 372-374	"Rebel" buffet-coaches
380-1	ACF	1936	1601	—	20win 40p	81'	—	To GM&NO 380-381	"Rebel" coach-sleepers
390	Brill	1930	22859	—	22win 76p	75½'	—	To GM&O 390	Assigned to NO-GN
395-6	ACF	1934	1385	—	46p	77'	—	To GM&O 395, 396	"Rebel" obs.-sleepers

Mobile & Ohio
(Merged into Gulf, Mobile & Ohio)

ROAD NO.	BUILDER	DATE	BLDR. NO.	ENGINE & DRIVE	BODY TYPE	LGTH.	WT.	DISPOSITION	REMARKS
600 (1)	Fair.-Morse	1913	—	Sheffield 50hp GM	8win 4wh 35p	34'	12½t	Ret. by 1933	Model 24, wooden body
601-2 (2-3)	Fair.-Morse	1915	—	Sheffield 50hp GM	8win 4wh 35p	34'	12½t	601 ret. by 1924; 602 by 1922	Model 24, woden body
1800-01	St. Louis EMC	1926	1403 154-55	Wint. 106A 220hp GE	9win RPO Bag. 40p	72'	47t	To GM&O 1800-1801	"Tennessee" and "Mississippi"
1802	St. Louis EMC	1927	1432 214	Wint. 106A 220hp GE	9win RPO Bag. 40p	72'	49t	To GM&O 1802	—
1820-21	St. Louis EMC	1927	1431 212-13	Wint. 106A 220hp GE	9win RPO Bag. 40p	72'	49t	To GM&O 1820-21	—
1830-32	St. Louis EMC	1928	1471 303-05	Wint. 106A 220hp GE	RPO-Bag.	72'	49t	To GM&O 1830-1832	—

ROAD NO.	BUILDER	DATE	BLDR. NO.	ENGINE & DRIVE	BODY TYPE	LGTH.	WT.	DISPOSITION	REMARKS
					Trailers				
1900-01	Brill	1927	22521	—	17win 72p	59½'	30t	To GM&O 1900, 1901	—
1930-32	St. Louis	1928	1470	—	23win 96p	72½'	30t	To GM&O 1930-32	Open obs. plat.

New Orleans - Great Northern
(Merged into Gulf, Mobile & Northern)

ROAD NO.	BUILDER	DATE	BLDR. NO.	ENGINE & DRIVE	BODY TYPE	LGTH.	WT.	DISPOSITION	REMARKS
1	Gen. Elec Wason	1913	3738	GE 16C1 175hp GE	?-win CE Bag.-Pass.	70'	50t	Ret. 1922, sold 1927	—
2	Brill Service	1922	21605	Midwest 68hp GM	10win CE Bag. 36p	43'	14½t	To GM&N 2	—
3	Brill	1925	22197	Brill 75 175hp GM	13win CE Bag. 48p	55'	25t	To GM&N 3	—

Chicago & Alton
(Reorganized as Alton RR)

ROAD NO.	BUILDER	DATE	BLDR. NO.	ENGINE & DRIVE	BODY TYPE	LGTH.	WT.	DISPOSITION	REMARKS
M 1	Gas-Elec. Motor Car Co.	1905	—	Bty. Assist. 120hp GE	13win 84p	78'	57½t	Rblt. to bag. car, 1909	Ex-coach rblt. to motor, wooden body. 6-wh. trucks
M 4	EMC St. Louis	1925	104 1348C	Wint. 106 185hp GE	12win DE Bag. 44p	59½'	36t	To Alton 6002	—
M 5-6	EMC St. Louis	1925	119-20 1363	Wint. 106 185hp GE	5win Bag. 19p	57'	35t	M5 to Alton 6003; M6 to M-1 work car	—
M 10	Ry. Motors Co. Shops	1925	—	2-Cont. 104hp GM	11win Bag. 32p	58'	42t	Ret. by 1932	Ex-combo 738, blt. Co. Shops, 1892. Wooden body
M 11	Ry. Motors Co.Shops	1926	—	2-Cont. 104hp GM	6win Bag. 16p	58'	43t	Ret. by 1935	Ex-combo 741, blt. Co. Shops, 1892. Wooden body
M 15-16	EMC St. Louis	1928	247-48 1461	Wint. 120 275hp GE	4win RPO Bag. 12p	75'	51t	To Alton 6010, 6021	Pass. seats removed
M 17-18	EMC St. Louis	1928	249-50 1462	Wint. 120 275hp GE	6win RPO Bag. 24p	75'	52t	To Alton 6011, 6012	Pass. seats removed; open platform
					Trailers				
T 2	Brill	1924	22099	—	13win 60p	53'	—	To Alton 6111	Ex-MKT motor M-1, acq. 1934
T 3	Brill	1924	22100	—	15win 60p	57½'	—	To Alton 6112	Ex-MKT tlr. T-1, acq. 1934

NOTE: Alton RR, as reorganized, had on its motor car roster the following ex-C&A cars: 6002, 6003, 6010, 6011, 6012, 6021 (ex-C&A M4, M5, M15, M17, M18, M16). Also trailers 6110, 6111, 6112 (ex T1, T2, T3). Also on roster was motor car M1, ex-C&A M6, used as shop employees car, Chicago.

Gulf, Mobile & Ohio

ROAD NO.	BUILDER	DATE	BLDR. NO.	ENGINE & DRIVE	BODY TYPE	LGTH.	WT.	DISPOSITION	REMARKS
M 1	EMC St. Louis	1925	120 1363	Wint. 106 185hp GE	5win 12p	57'	35t	To maint.-of-way car	Ex-Alton M1, orig. C&A M6 shop car
350	Brill	1930	22857	Brill 860 550hp GE	12win Bag. 40p	75'	70t	—	Ex-GM&N 350, re-eng. 5/50 Superior D. RPO sect. installed c. 1943
352-53	ACF	1934	1383	Alco 660hp DE	Power RPO	73'	89½t	—	"Rebel" power car, ex-GM&N 352-353
354	ACF	1936	1600	Alco DE	Power RPO	73'	89½t	—	"Rebel" power car, ex-GM&N 354
1800-01	EMC St. Louis	1926	154-55 1403	Wint. 106A 220hp GE	9win RPO Bag. 40p	73'	47t	1800 rblt. tlr. 1945; 1801 to W&OD 46, 1946	Ex-M&O 1800-1801. Seats removed 1941
1802	EMC St. Louis	1927	214 1432	Wint. 106A 220hp GE	9win RPO Bag. 40p	73'	47t	Ret. by 1943	Ex-M&O 1802. Seats removed 1941
1820-21	EMC St. Louis	1927	212-13 1431	2-Wint. 106A 220hp GE	6win RPO Bag. 27p	73'	64½t	1821 Re-no. 2500, 1946; ret. by 1957, 1820 ret. by 1943	Ex-M&O 1820 & 1821, 1821 re-eng. 4-Det. D 110hp, 3/50
1830-32	EMC St. Louis	1928	303-05 1471	2-Wint. 106A 220hp GE	RPO-Bag.	72'	64t	Re-no. 2501-2503, 1946; ret. by 1957	Ex-M&O 1830-1832; re-eng. 4-Det. D 110hp, c. 1950
1835	EMC Pullman	1928	301 6145	Ham. 685A 400hp GE	RPO-Bag.	75'	76t	Scrapped 1940's	Ex-GM&N 9771
2500-03	(See above)	—	—	—	—	—	—	—	Ex. 1821, 1830-32
2504	EMC St. Louis	1925	104 1348C	Wint. 106 185hp GE	12win DE Bag. 44p	57½'	36t	Ret. by 1957	Ex-Alton 6002
2505	EMC St. Louis	1925	120 1363	Wint. 106 185hp GE	5win Bag. 16p	57'	35t	Ret. by 1957	Ex-Alton 6003
2506-08	EMC St. Louis	1928	247-49 1461	Wint. 106 185hp GE	4win Bag. 24p	74'	51t	Ret. 1962, 1957, 1962. 2508 weighed 52½t, had 7 win.	Ex-Alton 6010-6012. Re-eng. 250hp GM D, 1940s. RPO & pass. sect. elim. on 2506, 2508
2509	EMC St. Louis	1928	250 1462	Wint. 106 185hp GE	4win Bag. 24p	74'	52½t	Ret. 1962	Ex-Alton 6021. Re-eng. 250hp GM D, 11/49. RPO & pass. sect. eliminated

NOTE: The following trailers were on the GM&O roster: 360, 370-374, 380, 381, 390, 395, 396 (ex-GM&N, same numbers); 1900, 1091, 1930-1932 (ex-M&O, same numbers); plus the following:

Trailers

ROAD NO.	BUILDER	DATE	BLDR. NO.	ENGINE & DRIVE	BODY TYPE	LGTH.	WT.	DISPOSITION	REMARKS
1940	Co. Shops	1943	—	—	9win 40p	73'	—	Re-no. 2554	Conv. from motor 1800. RPO, Bag. sect.
2550	Brill	1927	22521	—	17win 72p	59½'	—	Ret. 1957	Ex-1900
2551-3	St. Louis	1928	1470	—	23win 80p	75'	—	Ret. 1962	Ex. 1930-32. Open plat. obs. 2552-3 seated 40
2554	Co. Shops	1943	—	—	9 win 32p	73'	—	Ret. 1952	Ex-1940. RPO, Bag. sect.
2556-7	Brill	1924	—	—	—	—	—	—	See C&A T2, T3

Grand Trunk Western

ROAD NO.	BUILDER	DATE	BLDR. NO.	ENGINE & DRIVE	BODY TYPE	LGTH.	WT.	DISPOSITION	REMARKS
15805	St. Louis EMC	1925	1376 121	Wint. 106 175hp GE	4win RPO Bag. 17p	60'	46t	Scr. 12/57	Re-eng. Cat. D, 1941
112	Gr. Trunk (Canada)	1910	—	2 cyl. steam horiz. boiler	17win 58p	68½'	85t	Ret. to Canada, CN 15900	Acq. 1914. Open platform

The 15805 (above) was the Grand Trunk Western's sole standard era rail motorcar. It is shown with an ancient wooden combine at the Detroit terminal in August 1946. "The car that wasn't there" (below) was Great Northern 2304 shown at the Brill plant in 1925. The unit, along with trailer 2352, was lettered for the GN but was probably sent instead to the Chicago, Springfield & St. Louis.

Harold K. Vollrath Collection; Robert G. Foley Collection

Great Northern

A sprightly color scheme adorned Great Northern doodlebugs. Here is the 2339 at Grand Forks, ND, in 1949.
W. C. Whittaker Collection

MOST RAILROADS showed little imagination in the paint jobs they applied to their doodlebugs. Dark colors predominated, black, olive drab, dark green or perhaps a dark red, relieved only by zebra stripes on the end, favored by some roads to increase visibility and reduce grade-crossing accidents.

The Great Northern was an exception. In later years, the GN painted its rail motorcars in the orange, green and brown Empire Builder livery—a dedication to color approached only by the Milwaukee Road with its orange and maroon cars.

With some 50 units on the roster at one time or another, the GN could be considered a sizable user of the self-propelled vehicle. As was typical of roads in its area, the GN had only two of the first generation type of car, both General Electric gas-electrics; both wound up on the Pacific Great Eastern in British Columbia.

Four lightweight mechanical-drive cars were purchased in the early 1920s, but the road standaridized on Brill and EMC-St. Louis units until 1930 when a couple of Westinghouse-equipped oil-electrics were added to the roster—one of them the Westinghouse demonstrator which was later resold to the Bangor & Aroostook.

Another exception to the pattern was acquisition of a Mack type AR gas-electric, which was rebuilt to a line car for the Cascade Tunnel electrification. Most of the gas-electrics were in time rebuilt to diesel-electric drive and many survived into the 1950s.

Only one RDC car was acquired; it was used on the Havre-Butte line in Montana. This unit survived until the advent of Amtrak in 1971, and then the car was sold to the new passenger service agency.

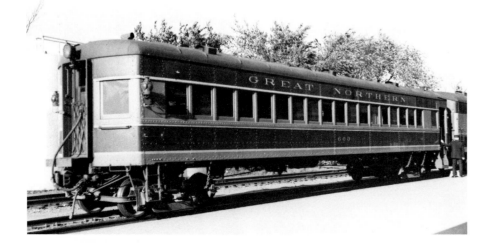

Motor 2314 was rebuilt into trailer 600, shown at Sioux City, IA, in June 1956.
W. C. Whittaker Collection

This "baby" EMPIRE BUILDER (above) was designed to operate between Great Falls and Havre, MT, to connect with the real EMPIRE BUILDER, but was replaced by a diesel locomotive when motor 2322 proved incapable of maintaining the schedule. Drawing (below) is of motor 2323.

James H. Harrison Collection; Author's Collection

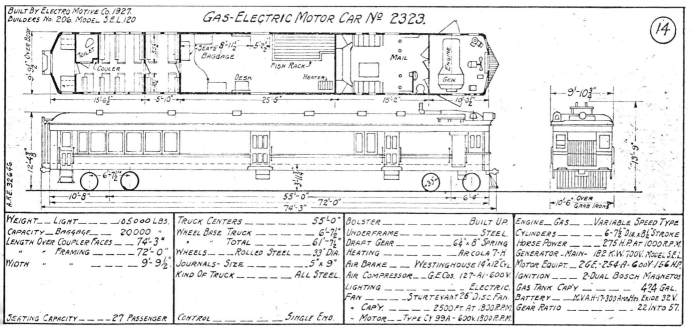

BUILT BY ELECTRO MOTIVE CO. 1927.
BUILDERS No. 206. MODEL S.E.L. 120

GAS-ELECTRIC MOTOR CAR No. 2323.

(14)

WEIGHT __ LIGHT __ __ __ 105000 LBS.	TRUCK CENTERS __ __ __ __ 55'-0"	BOLSTER __ __ __ __ __ __ BUILT UP.
CAPACITY __ BAGGAGE __ __ 20000 "	WHEEL BASE TRUCK __ __ __ __ 6'-7½"	UNDERFRAME __ __ __ __ __ __ STEEL.
LENGTH OVER COUPLER FACES __ 74'-3"	" " TOTAL __ __ __ __ 61'-7½"	DRAFT GEAR __ __ __ __ 64" X 8" SPRING
" " FRAMING __ __ 72'-0"	WHEELS __ __ ROLLED STEEL __ 33" DIA.	HEATING __ __ __ __ __ __ ARCOLA T-H
WIDTH " __ __ 9'-9½"	JOURNALS- SIZE __ __ __ __ 5" X 9"	AIR BRAKE __ __ WESTINGHOUSE 14"X12" CYL.
	KIND OF TRUCK __ __ __ __ ALL STEEL.	AIR COMPRESSOR __ G.E.Cos. 127-A1-600V.
		LIGHTING __ __ __ __ __ __ ELECTRIC.
		FAN __ __ __ STURTEVANT 26" DISC. FAN.
		" CAP'Y. __ __ __ 2500 FT. AT 1800 R.P.M.
SEATING CAPACITY __ __ __ 27 PASSENGER	CONTROL __ __ __ __ SINGLE END.	" MOTOR __ TYPE CY 99A - 600 V. 1800 R.P.M.

ENGINE __ GAS __ __ VARIABLE SPEED TYPE
CYLINDERS __ __ __ __ 6-7½" DIA. X 8½" STROKE
HORSE POWER __ __ __ __ 275 H.P. AT 1000 R.P.M.
GENERATOR -MAIN- __ 182 K.W. 700V. MODEL S.E.L.
MOTOR EQUIP'T. __ 2 G.E.-254-A- 600V. 156 H.P.
IGNITION __ __ __ 2-DUAL BOSCH MAGNETOS
GAS TANK CAP'Y __ __ __ __ 424 GAL.
BATTERY __ M.V.A.H-17-300 Amp.Hrs. EXIDE 32 V.
GEAR RATIO __ __ __ __ __ 22 INTO 57.

Unit 2328 was a 1928 Brill product.
Robert Gray

87

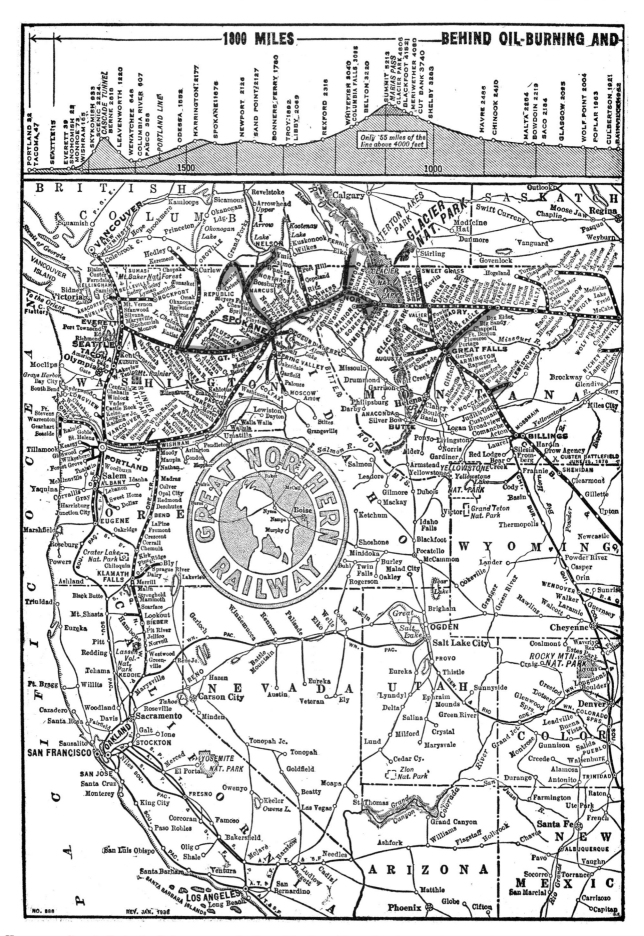

Heavy gray lines indicate doodlebug runs on the Great Northern. Reproduced from THE OFFICIAL RAILWAY GUIDE ® ©
1941 NRPCo.

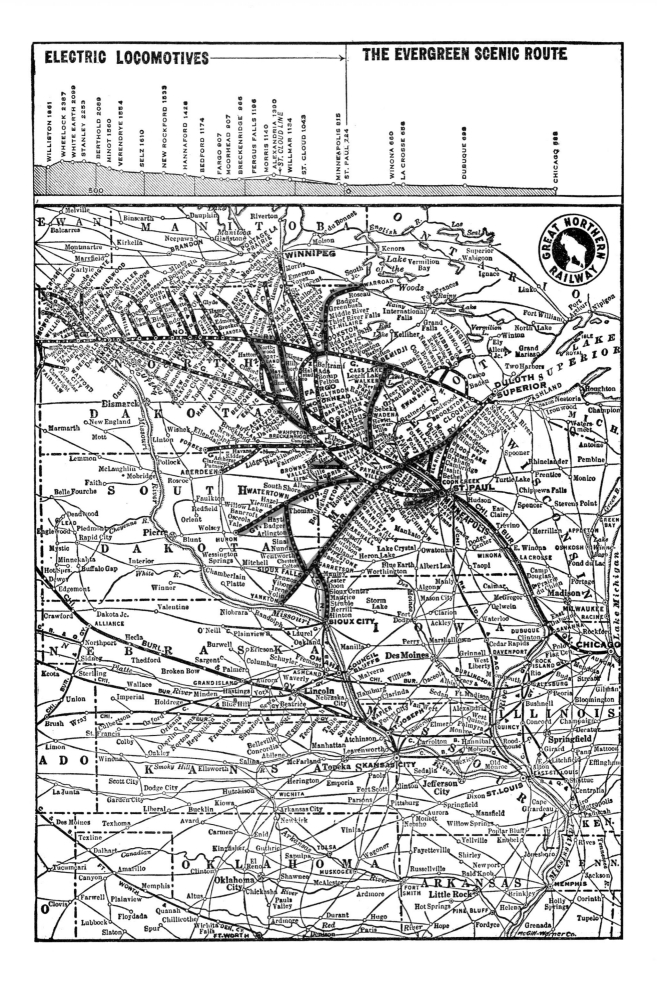

ELECTRIC LOCOMOTIVES

THE EVERGREEN SCENIC ROUTE

GREAT NORTHERN RAILWAY

ROAD NO.	BUILDER	DATE	BLDR. NO.	ENGINE & DRIVE	BODY TYPE	LGTH.	WT.	DISPOSITION	REMARKS
2300[1]	Gen. Elec. Wason	1913	3741 12051	GE 16C1 175hp GE	16win Bag. 86p	70'	52t	To Crowsnest Pass. Coal, 6/19	Became Pac. Gt. East. 106, 5/20
2300[2]	St. Louis EMC	19267	1395 142	Wint. 106A 220hp GE	Bag.	60'	40½t	Scr. 3/52	—
2301[1]	Gen. Elec. Wason	1913	3742 12051	GE 16C1 175hp GE	16win Bag. 86p	70'	52t	To PG&E 104, 2/19	Scr. 1952
2301[2]	St. Louis EMC	1926	1395 143	Wint. 106A 220hp GE	RPO-Bag.	60'	40½t	Scr. 3/52	—
2302	St. Louis EMC	1926	1395 144	Wint. 106A 220hp GE	DE-RPO	60'	40½t	Scr. 5/56	2nd eng. added 1940 from car 2312. Had pass. sect. 1933-40
2303	St. Louis EMC	1926	1395 145	Wint. 106A 220hp GE	Bag.	60'	41t	Scr. 11/57	2nd eng. added 1944 from car 2309.
2304	Brill	1925	22214	Brill 175hp GM	13win Bag.-Pas.	55'	25t	Unk.	Model 75. Never delivered to GN
2305	Mack Cummings	1922	60006	Mack AC 40hp GM	7win Bag. 36p	35'	10t	Scr. 3/29	Model AC
2306	St. Louis FWD	1922	1277 19027	Wau. 65KR 51hp	4win Bag. 15p	25½'	8½t	Rblt. combo 546, 4/37	Scr. 4/57
2307	White Brill	1923	— 21544	White 39hp GM	?-win Bag. 36p	32'	11½t	To Mont. West. 20, 3/29	—
2308	Brill Service	1922	21514	Midwest 68hp GM	10win Bag. 38p	43½'	14t	Body sold 4/37	—
2309	St. Louis EMC	1925	1352 113	Wint. 106 175hp GE	12win Bag. 52p	59'	35t	Rblt. tlr. 572, 11/43	—
2310-12	St. Louis EMC	1925	1360 114-16	Wint. 106A 220hp GE	12win Bag. 42p	59'	35t	2311 rblt. detector car, 1941 2312 rblt. tlr. 568, 6/41	—
2313	St. Louis EMC	1925	1368C 130	Wint. 106 175hp GE	12win DE Bag. 52p	59'	36t	To Mont. West. 31, 1/40	Traded back to GN; donated to Mid. Cont. Ry. Mus., 8/66
2314	Brill	1925	22216	Brill-WH 250hp GE	13win Bag. 52p	62'	48t	Rblt. tlr. 600, 2/47	—
2315-16	St. Louis EMC	1926	1395A 147	Wint. 120 275hp GE	RPO-Bag.	65'	43½t	Scr. 6/58	Re-eng. 275hp Sterl. D, 1948. Orig. 60'
2317	St. Louis EMC	1926	1411 176	Wint. 120 275hp GE	RPO-Bag.	74'	49t	Scr. 7/57	Re-eng. 275hp Sterl. D, 1948
2318-19	St. Louis EMC	1927	1411 177-78	Wint. 120 275hp GE	RPO-Bag.	77'	49t	Scr. 7/59, 3/58	2318 rblt. to 6 win RPO Bag. 22p. Both re-eng. 275hp Sterl. D, 1948. Orig. 74'
2320-21	St. Louis EMC	1926 179-80	1410	Wint. 106A 220hp GE	12win Bag. 42p	60' 62'	47t 50t	Scr. 10/57	2321 rblt. to seat 16
2322	Brill	1927	24481	2-Brill-WH 250hp GE	DE Bag.	68'	47t	Scr. 3/58	Rblt. streamlined body, 1946; re-eng. 500hp Cum. D
2323	St. Louis EMC	1927	1423 206	Wint. 120 275hp GE	6win RPO Bag. 15p	77'	50t	Scr. 12/59	Re-eng. 275hp Sterl. D, 9/47. Orig. 74'
2324	St. Louis EMC	1928	1458 246	Wint. 120 275hp GE	7win RPO Bag. 14p	77'	55t	Scr. 7/59	Re-eng. 275hp Sterl. D, 9/46. Orig. 74'
2325	Brill	1928	22627	Brill-WH 300hp GE	?-win RPO Bag. 34p	77'	60t	Scr. 7/59	Re-eng. 275hp Sterl. D, 3/48. Orig. 73'
2326-30	Brill	1928	22657	Brill-WH 300hp GE	RPO-Bag.	77'	56½t	Scr. 1959	2329 length 79'. All re-eng. 300hp Sterl. D, c. 1948. Orig. 73'
2331	Brill	1929	22764	Brill-WH 300hp GE	RPO-Bag.	77'	64t	Scr. 7/59	Re-eng. 300hp Sterl. D, 1/47
2332-36	St. Louis EMC	1929	1504 405-09	Wint. 148 400hp GE	RPO-Bag.	74'	71t	Scr. 1959	Re-eng. 400hp Sterl. D, c. 1947. 2336 wt. 64t
2337	St. Louis Mack	1929	1506 162006	3-Mack AR 135hp GE	Bag.	77'	70t	Rblt. tower car, 12/36	Re-eng. 400hp Cum. D, 1945

ROAD NO.	BUILDER	DATE	BLDR. NO.	ENGINE & DRIVE	BODY TYPE	LGTH.	WT.	DISPOSITION	REMARKS
2338	St. Louis EMC	1930	1531 443	Wint. 148 400hp GE	RPO-Bag.	74'	72t	Scr. 7/59	Re-eng. 400hp Sterl. D, 7/46
2339	Brill	1930	22850	Brill-WH	RPO-Bag.	78'	71t	Scr. 8/57	Re-eng. 400hp Sterl. D, 12/45. Orig. 75'
2340	St. Louis WH	1930	1532	WH-Beard 400hp OE	RPO-Bag.	74½'	74t	Scr. 5/49	—
2341	Std. Steel WH	1930	369 30	WH-Beard 400hp OE	6win RPO Bag. 22p	76'	81t	To Bang. & Aroost. 5, 11/52	Ex-WH demo. 20
2350	Budd	1956	6302	2-GM6-280 275hp DH	RDC-3 RPO Bag. 48p	85'	59t	To Amtrak 8/72, not used	Resold Brit. Col. Ry. B-31, 12/75

Trailers

ROAD NO.	BUILDER	DATE	BLDR. NO.	ENGINE & DRIVE	BODY TYPE	LGTH.	WT.	DISPOSITION	REMARKS
2351	Brill	1925	21929	—	Bag.	34'	7t	Scr. 2/37	Tlr. for motor 2308
2352	Brill	1925	22215	—	RPO-Bag.	45'	—	—	Tlr. for motor 2304, not delivered

In addition, motors 2306, 2312, 2309, 2314 were rblt. into tlrs. 546, 568, 572, 600 (2306 in 1937, others 1925).

This is the RDC car that ultimtely provided the EMPIRE BUILDER connection for the city of Great Falls. It is shown at Butte, MT, in May of 1957. *Harold K. Vollrath Collection*

Kansas City, Mexico & Orient
(Absorbed into Atchison, Topeka & Santa Fe)

ROAD NO.	BUILDER	DATE	BLDR. NO.	ENGINE & DRIVE	BODY TYPE	LGTH.	WT.	DISPOSITION	REMARKS
M1-M3	Brill	1925	22241	Brill 75 175hp GM	13win Bag. 59p	57'	25t	Became ATSF M102-M104[2]	—
100, 200, 300	White	1925	—	White 40hp GM	3win OP 7p	—	—	Became ATSF Insp. Cars 153-155	Hood front business cars

Trailers

ROAD NO.	BUILDER	DATE	BLDR. NO.	ENGINE & DRIVE	BODY TYPE	LGTH.	WT.	DISPOSITION	REMARKS
T-1, 2	Brill	1925	22242	—	RPO-Bag.	53'	—	Became ATSF T100, 101	—
T-3	—	—	—	—	Bag.	—	—	Ret. 1928	Ex-Ark. Valley Interurban

Illinois Central

The streamlined LAND O'CORN ran for a very short time, but was captured on film on November 20, 1941, crossing the Chicago & West Towns traction line at Riverside, IL.

C. A. Brown

THE ILLINOIS CENTRAL was more famous for the railcars it got rid of than the cars that it kept.

In 1940 and 1941 the IC bought four Motorailers from American Car & Foundry. These streamlined doodle-bugs were launched amid an unprecedented publicity campaign. Full-color, double-page spreads in magazines proclaimed that these were the railcars of the future.

On November 17, 1940, *Miss Lou* made its inaugural run between Jackson, Miss., and New Orleans. The *Illini* was soon put on between Chicago and Champaign, Ill. The two-car *Land O'Corn* began covering the 274-mile run between Chicago and Waterloo, Iowa, in 1941. These were no mere branchline trains, but mainline junior streamliners, and they did attract passengers.

Sadly, the railcars of the future found it not on IC rails but as commuter cars on the New York, Susquehanna and

Western, a New Jersey line. All four cars were sold to the Susquehanna in 1943 after a truncated career on the IC. The *Land O'Corn*, in fact, was in a wreck shortly after going into service and afterwards saw very little use.

In one way, it was success which killed the ACF units on the IC. With World War II coming on, passenger loads were increasing fast and it soon became necessary for the small units to be replaced by regular, high-capacity steam trains.

Prior to this misadventure, the Illinois Central had not become highly involved in doodlebugs, but the road did

try several leading brands. In the early years the IC operated a pair of McKeens and four General Electric gas-electrics. It is mildly surprising that the GE cars outnumbered the McKeens, considering that the IC was at the time considered a Harriman road, and it was Harriman money which backed the McKeen car.

In the mid 1920s four Brill Model 75 gas mechanical cars were added for branch line services, and in 1936 Pullman and EMC completed a locomotive which was considered to be a railcar. It powered the Green Diamond streamliner.

Early IC General Electric motor 115 is coupled to center- entrance car 2092 at an unknown location in 1941. The trailer may have been an ex. motor (117-120 series)

M. D. McCarter Collection

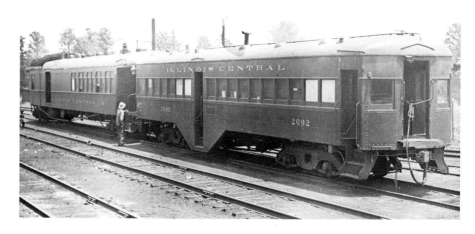

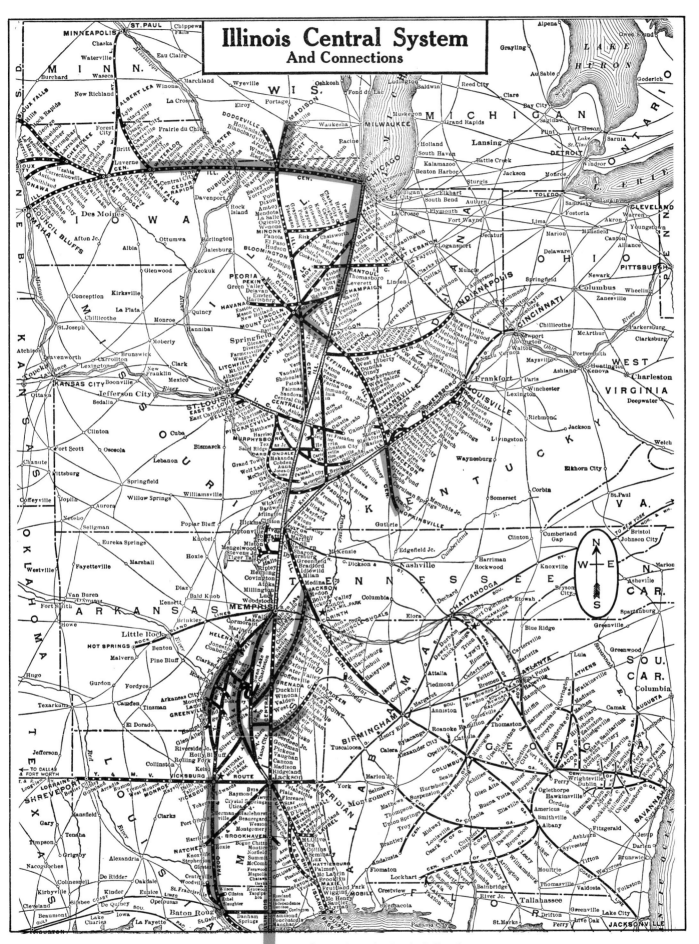

Illinois Central System
And Connections

Heavy gray lines indicate doodlebug runs on the Illinois Central.   *Author's Collection*

Illinois Central

ROAD NO.	BUILDER	DATE	BLDR. NO.	ENGINE & DRIVE	BODY TYPE	LGTH.	WT.	DISPOSITION	REMARKS
111	McKeen	1907	14	McKeen 200hp GM	12win CE Bag.-Pass.	55'	35t	Ret. 1925	Ex-UP 14
112[1]	Gen. Elec. Wason	1914	3781 1550	GE 16C8 175hp GE	17win Bag. 84p	70'	54t	Re-no. 116	—
112[2]	McKeen	—	—	McKeen 200hp GM	82p	70'	34t	Scr. 1925	Ex-PRR 4701(?)
113-15	Gen. Elec. Wason	1914	3782-4 1550	GE 16C8 175hp GE	17win Bag. 84p	70'	53t	Sold 1942	114 weighed 52t
117-19	Brill	1925	22303	Brill 75 175hp GM	13win Bag. 30p	55'	26½t	Conv. to M/W	May have been rebuilt to trailer
120	Brill	1925	22304	Brill 75 175hp GM	13win Bag. 30p	55'	26½t	Conv. to M/W	(see above)
121	Pullman EMC	1936	— 534	EMD 567 1200hp DE	Loco.	—	—	Scr. 8/50	Loco for ''Green Diamond''
130	ACF	1940	2023	Wauk. Hess 225hp DM	17win 72p	75'	45t	To NYS&W 1004, 1943	''Illini'' Dual Engine
131	ACF	1940	2023	Wauk. Hess 225hp DM	16win 64p	75'	45t	To NYS&W 1003, 1943	''Miss Lou'' Dual Engine
140	ACF	1941	2109	Wauk. Hess 225hp DM	19win 72p	75'	48½t	To NYS&W 1005, 1943	''Land O'Corn'' Dual Engine
141	ACF	1941	2110	Wauk. Hess 225hp DM	12win 39p	75'	45t	To NYS&W 1006, 1943	''Land O'Corn;'' one engine powered tlr.

Lehigh & Hudson River

ROAD NO.	BUILDER	DATE	BLDR. NO.	ENGINE & DRIVE	BODY TYPE	LGTH.	WT.	DISPOSITION	REMARKS
M 1	Brill	1928	22687	2-Brill 250hp GE	14win DE Bag. 52p	73'	76t	Wrecked 5/31	—

The Lehigh & Hudson River's sole motorcar, M1, is readied for departure from the Brill plant under its own power for home rails at Warwick, NY, 1928.

Historical Society of Pennsylvania

Lehigh & New England

ROAD NO.	BUILDER	DATE	BLDR. NO.	ENGINE & DRIVE	BODY TYPE	LGTH.	WT.	DISPOSITION	REMARKS
91[1]	Brill	1923	21802	White 43 40hp GM	10win CE 36p	31½'	9t	—	—
90	Brill	1926	22275	Brill 225hp GE	16win CE DE, 86p	—	43t	To Ark. Vy., 1940	—
91[2]	Brill	1928	22590	Brill 250hp GE	15win CE DE, 81p	—	47½t	To Ark. Vy., 1940	—

Lehigh Valley

With icicles hanging down from the roof, Lehigh Valley motor car 25 awaits midwinter assignment circa 1926.

Robert G. Foley Collection

ALTHOUGH the Lehigh Valley did not buy a rail motorcar until 1923, it soon jumped in with both feet and became an enthusiastic doodlebug operator. The first car, a Brill type 55 gas-mechanical unit, and the second, a model 75 Brill, were the only mechanical drive cars on the system. The Model 55 was used until 1934 when it was sold for use elsewhere, after putting in some 200,000 miles of hard use.

From then on until the arrival of the two Budd RDC cars in 1951, all motorcars were gas-electric driven.

By 1930 the Lehigh Valley had given the doodlebug a major role in its passenger network. The road owned 26 motors along with 25 lightweight trailers which matched the power units. It was a fleet specifically tailored for providing all local passenger traffic—

main line or branch line—on the system.

If the rise of the railcar on the LV had been swift, so was its decline. By 1940 all that was left was the Rochester-Rochester Jct. shuttle, Ithaca to Auburn, Maunch Chunk to Hazelton, and the commuter operations in the New York City area.

Hazelton seems to have been a good source of passenger revenue to the

95

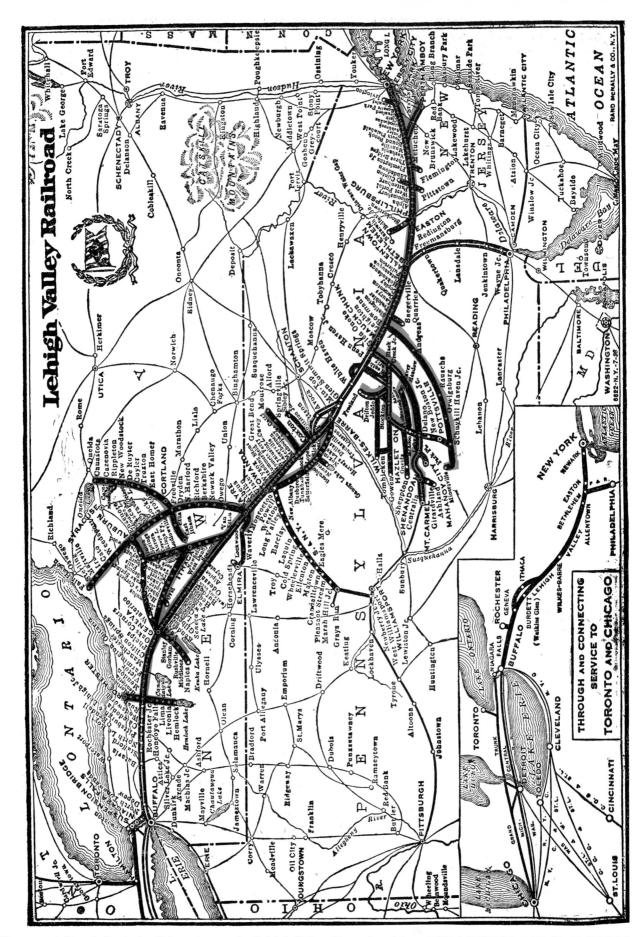

Heavy gray lines indicate doodlebug runs on the Lehigh Valley. Reproduced from THE OFFICIAL RAILWAY GUIDE® ©
1941 NRPCo.

Lehigh Valley down through the years, a city of 40,000 not on any main railroad line. The LV provided numerous railcar trips to connect Hazelton with the main line. This operation led to the road's final purchase of railcars—two Budd RDCs.

The steady erosion of passenger traffic on the mainline sealed the fate of the RDCs, and they were sold in 1958 and 1962. Ironically, because the Pennsylvania Public Utilities Commission would not allow its removal even after there were no mainline passenger train for it to connect to, the last RDC was the last passenger train on the entire railroad! This vestigal service finally ended in February of 1961.

The mail is loaded (above) onto Lehigh Valley motor at Geneva, NY, in 1952. Car 17 (below) was streamlined for service on the original Asa Packer train, shown here at Jersey City NJ on March 18, 1939.

P. Kutta Collection; Author's Collection

Baggage trailer T-75 was built by Brill for service behind doodlebugs.
Historical Society of Pennsylvania

Lehigh Valley

ROAD NO.	BUILDER	DATE	BLDR. NO.	ENGINE & DRIVE	BODY TYPE	LGTH.	WT.	DISPOSITION	REMARKS
3	Brill Service	1923	21877	Serv. 68hp GM	10win Bag. 43p	42'	15t	To West Riv., 1934	Then Tenn. RR M-2
4	Brill	1925	22218	Brill-WH 175hp GM	13win Bag.-Pas.	55'	25t	Rblt. to tlr. T-54	Model 75
5	Brill	1927	22563	Brill-WH 250hp GE	13win Bag. 53p	60'	45t	To Alaska RR 115, 2/38	—
10	Osgd Bdly EMC	1930	10990 456	2-Wint. 146 300hp GE	10win Bag. 42p	74'	77t	Scr. 11/52	—
11	Osgd Bdly EMC	1930	10995 457	2-Wint. 146 300hp GE	5win Bag. 18p	74'	76½t	Scr. 12/50	—
14	St. Louis EMC	1926	1386A 369	Wint. 106A 220hp GE	14win 66p	59'	40½t	To Sperry Rail Svc. 123, 2/36	Blt. for B&O but rejected. Rblt., acq. 1/29
15	St. Louis EMC	1926	1386A 363	Wint. 106A 220hp GE	14win Bag. 49p	59'	40t	To Sperry Rail Svc. 128, 3/39	'Blt. for B&O but rejected. Rblt., acq. 2/28
16	Osgd Bdly EMC	1929	10285 370	2-Wint. 146D 300hp GE	5win Bag. 21p	74'	76½t	Scr. 9/51	—
17	Osgd Bdly EMC	1929	10280 371	2-Wint. 146D 300hp GE	10win Bag. 30p	74'	77t	Scr. 1/51	Streamlined for ''Asa Packer'' train
18	Osgd Bdly EMC	1928	9580 266	2-Wint. 106A 220hp GE	5win RPO Bag. 21p	73½'	67t	Scr. 11/52	—
19	Bethlehem EMC	1928	— 265	2-Wint. 106A 220hp GE	5win Bag. 21p	74'	66½t	Scr. 11/51	—
20	St. Louis EMC	1927	1452 241	2-Wint. 106A 220hp GE	12win Bag. 53p	57'	40½t	To Sperry Rail Svc., 11/37	—
21	Osgd Bdly EMC	1927	8971 191	2-Wint. 106A 220hp GE	4win RPO Bag. 16p	73'	66t	Scr. 11/51	—
22	Osgd Bdly EMC	1927	8972 192	2-Wint. 106A 220hp GE	12win Bag. 36p	73'	63t	Scr. 11/51	—
23	Osgd Bdly EMC	1927	8974 193	2-Wint. 106A 220hp GE	13win Bag. 60p	73'	62½t	Scr. 7/48	—
24	Osgd Bdly EMC	1927	8973 194	2-Wint. 106A 220hp GE	13win Bag. 54p	73'	63t	To Apal. Nor. 24, 1/38	—
25	St. Louis EMC	1925	1375 132	2-Wint. 106A 220hp GE	RPO-Bag.	60'	40t	Scr. 1/37	—
26-28	St. Louis EMC	1925	1376 135,4,6	2-Wint. 106A 220hp GE	12win Bag. 52p	59'	38½t	To Sperry Rail Svc. 125, 131, 130, 1/37, 11/40, 12/40	27 orig. seated 40, rblt. with RPO Sect., Seating reduced to 22
29	St. Louis EMC	1925	1376-A 133	2-Wint. 106A 220hp GE	13win Bag. 42P	59'	38½t	To Sperry Rai Svc. 129, 4/38	
30-31	Brill	1926	22423-24	2-Brill-WH 250hp GE	5win Bag. 19p	73'	64t 66t	Scr. 6/45, 4/45	Re-eng D
32-33	Brill	1926	22426-25	2-Brill-WH 250hp GE	RPO-Bag.	73'	66t	Scr. 5/45, 1/40	Re-eng. D
34	Brill	1927	22427	2-Hall Sc. 275hp GE	5win RPO Bag. 19p	73'	69t	Scr. 10/50	Re-eng. D
35	Brill	1927	22428	2-Hall Sc. 275hp GE	6win Bag. 24p	73'	68½t	Scr. 5/45	Re-eng D
36	Brill	1928	22619	275hp GE 275Hp GE	6win Bag. 19p	73'	72t	Scr. 10/48	Re-eng. D
40	Budd	1951	5410	2-GM 275hp DH	RDC-1	85'	—	To Reading 9163, 1/62	—
41	Budd	1951	5416	2-GM 275hp DH	RDC-2	85'	—	To CPR 9116, 9/58	—

ROAD NO.	BUILDER	DATE	BLDR. NO.	ENGINE & DRIVE	BODY TYPE	LGTH.	WT.	DISPOSITION	REMARKS
					Trailers				
T 50	St. Louis EMC	1925	1377 101	—	17win 80p	59'	22t	Sold 1938	—
T 51-2	Brill	1926	22431	—	76p	—	27t	T 51 rblt. M/W, 7/34	—
T 53	Osgd Bdly	1928	9585	—	78p	—	29½t	Sold 5/42	—
T 54	Brill	1925	22218	—	75p	57½'	—	Ret. 4/47	Rbld. of motor 4
T 59	Osgd Bdly	1930	10985	—	15win 78p	75½'	—	Ret. 1951	—
T 60-1	Osgd Bdly	1927	8976	—	15win 64p	60½'	32t	—	—
T 62	Brill	1926	22428	—	—	—	—	Sold 1937	—
T 63-4	Osgd Bdly	1927	8976	—	78p	60½'	32t	Sold 10/49	—
T 65-7	Brill	1926	22429	—	17win	57½'	29½t	Sold 1/37	T 67 blt. 1927
T 68	Bethlehem	1928	—	—	78p	60½'	—	Ret. 1949	—
T 69	Brill	1928	22620	—	64p	60'	—	Ret. 1951	—
T 70-2	Osgd Bdly	1929	10290	—	103o	—	38½t	—	—
T 73-4	Osgd Bdly	1929	10295	—	64p	60½'	33t	T 73 sold 5/42; T 74 ret 1951	—
T 75	Brill	1927	22430	—	Bag.	—	31t	Ret. 1946	—
T 76	Osgd Bdly	1927	8977	—	Bag.	—	27t	To Apal. Nor. T 76, 1/38	—
T 77	Bethlehem	1928	—	—	—	60½'	—	Ret. 1949	—
T 85	Osgd Bdly	1927	8978	—	RPO-Bag.	60½'	—	Ret. 1948	—

Long Island Rail Road

ROAD NO.	BUILDER	DATE	BLDR. NO.	ENGINE & DRIVE	BODY TYPE	LGTH.	WT.	DISPOSITION	REMARKS
1	Federal	1911	—	Edison Btry. Elec.	7win 4 wheel 20p	28'	—	Scr. 12/26	—
2	Federal	1914	—	Edison Btry. Elec.	7win 4 wheel Bag. 32p	32'	11½t	—	Train doors in ends
4	Federal	1914	—	Edison Btry. Elec	9win 4 wheel 40p	32'	11½t	—	Train doors in ends
1134	Brill	1927	22594	Brill 55 68hp GM	10win Bag. 44p	43'	14½t	To Atl. & West., 12/39	—
3101	Budd	1955	6219	2-GM6-280 275hp DH	12win RDC-1 107p	85'	59t	Wrecked 10/67	—
3121	Budd	1955	6015	2-GM6-280 275hp DH	9win RDC-2 84p	85'	59½t	To B&O 1972, 8/68	—
4001-04	Budd Garrett	1975	—	Garett Turbo-Elec.	20win 120p	85'	90t	—	M-1 ''Metropolitan'' body, withdrawn 11/77
4005-08	Gen. Elec. United Air	1974	—	U-A Turbo-Elec.	20win 120p	85'	90t	Rblt. to elec. 1980-81	M-1 ''Metropolitan'' body, withdrawn 11/77

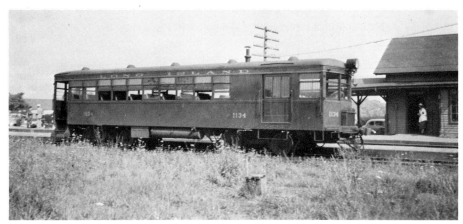

Brill's sole contribution to the Long Island Rail Road's gas-electric doodlebug roster was car 1134.   *Author's Collection*

Long Island was an early operator of battery cars (below). Car 2 was assigned to the West Hempstead branch. A train composed of gas-turbine electrics 4001-4002-4005-4006 glides into Mineola, NY (Bottom) on June 3, 1977.

Both: George E. Votava

Long Island Railroad

UNLIKE all of the nation's railroads, the golden age of the doodlebug arrived on the Long Island Rail Road in the 1970s.

Between June of 1976 until November of 1977 the Long Island, now a part of New York's Metropolitan Transit Authority, operated eight turbine-electric railcars.

The units, evenly split between Garrett and United Aircraft turbine power plants, were actually owned by the U. S. Department of Transportation

and were operated on the non-electrified Port Washington branch.

These cars used the standard "Metropolitan" body and trucks employed in hundreds of electric MU cars already in service on the LIRR. As is often the case with experimental units, the results did not justify the high cost and the cars were scheduled for rebuilding into regular electric MU sets.

The first self-propelled units on the LIRR were a trio of four-wheel battery

cars purchased between 1911 and 1914. The size of small streetcars, they were employed for a time on short shuttle runs. There was a single Brill Model 55, acquired in 1927, which was sold in 1939.

The Long Island also operated a pair of RDC cars starting in 1955. One was wrecked, the other sold. During the 1920s and 1930s the Long Island leased a number of rail motors from parent Pennsylvania Railroad.

Louisville & Nashville

LITTLE IS KNOWN about the operation of the Louisville & Nashville's two early rail motor cars, one of them a steam car built in the company shops in 1907. But the "Old Reliable" had little truck with the doodlebug in the standard era, owning only one car.

This one car, however, Brill-built No. 3600, did carve out a modest legend for itself on the L&N system. So far as anyone can remember, the car spent its entire career of more than two decades on a single run, trains 11-12 on the Columbia, Tenn., to Florence, Ala. route.

It was given the nickname "Huckety Buck," again, no one is certain why. Unless laid up for repairs, car 3600 (sometimes with a trailer) made its daily run for some 27 years without variation. The L&N never found another run suitable for the rail motor-car, and the unit remained an orphan on the system to the end.

A legend in its own time was Brill-built 3600, the Louisville & Nashville's HUCKETY-BUCK. It remained a one-of-a-kind on the L&N.

Author's Collection

Louisville & Nashville

ROAD NO.	BUILDER	DATE	BLDR. NO.	ENGINE & DRIVE	BODY TYPE	LGTH.	WT.	DISPOSITION	REMARKS
3000	Co. Shops	1907	—	Steam	7win Bag. 54p	67'	—	To Grand Trunk 3	Then CN 15902
3001	—	1911	—	Gas-mech.	—	—	—	Ret. by 6/25	—
3600	Brill	1928	22733	Hall-Scott 275hp GE	13win Bag. 61p	72'	46½t	Scr. 1955	"Huckety Buck" train

Louisiana & Arkansas
(Absorbed into Kansas City Southern)

ROAD NO.	BUILDER	DATE	BLDR. NO.	ENGINE & DRIVE	BODY TYPE	LGTH.	WT.	DISPOSITION	REMARKS
125	Brill	1928	22713	Brill 55 68hp GM	10win Bag. 38p	43'	14½t	—	—
126	Brill	1929	22828	Brill 275 250hp GE	12win DE Bag.-Pas.	73'	60t	To Fonda Johns. & Glov., 1938	Acq. 1935, Chas. Beach 300

Maine Central

ROAD NO.	BUILDER	DATE	BLDR. NO.	ENGINE & DRIVE	BODY TYPE	LGTH.	WT.	DISPOSITION	REMARKS
700	Brill	1922	21503	Brill 55 68hp GM	10win Bag.-Pass.	42'	14½t	—	—
901	Ing. Rand St. Louis	1933	— 1559	2-IR 300hp DE	Mail-Bag.	72'	110t	Ret. 7/49, body rblt. for M/W service	Ex-Demo OE600

Minneapolis & St. Louis

ROAD NO.	BUILDER	DATE	BLDR. NO.	ENGINE & DRIVE	BODY TYPE	LGTH.	WT.	DISPOSITION	REMARKS
GE-1 -2	St. Louis EMC	1929	1519 438-39	Wint. 146D 300hp GE	8win RPO Bag. 32p	75'	64t	May have been rblt. tlr.	"Peoria," "New Ulm"
GE-3	St. Louis EMC	1930	1519 440	Wint. 146D 300hp GE	8win RPO Bag. 32p	75'	64t	May have been rblt. tlr.	"Oskaloosa"
GE-4	St. Louis EMC	1931	1552 494	Wint. 146D 300hp GE	8win RPO Bag. 32p	75'	65t	Burned 1/46	—
GE-25 -26	St. Louis EMC	1930	1545 448-49	Wint. 148 400hp GE	RPO-Bag.	75'	73½t	GE-25 rblt. weed sprayer GE26 to C&NW	"Albert Lea," "Ft. Dodge." Both re-eng. 400hp Cat. D, 1950. GE-26, 22p section added
GE-27	St. Louis EMC	1930	1545 450	Wint. 148 400hp GE	RPO-Bag.	75'	73½t	Sold for scrap, 4/61	"Des Moines." Re-eng. 2-Cum. 200hp D, 1946; then 400hp CAT. D397 D, 1950. 22p section added
GE-28	St. Louis EMC	1930	1545 451	Wint. 148 400hp GE	RPO-Bag.	75'	73½t	Sold for scrap, 4/61	"Watertown." Re-eng. 400hp Cat. D, 1950. 22p section added
GE-29	St. Louis EMC	1931	1550 491	Wint. 148 400hp GE	RPO-Bag.	75'	73½t	To C&NW	"Montgomery." Re-eng. 400hp Cat. D, 8/50
GE-30 -31	St. Louis EMC	1931	1551 492-93	Wint. 148 400hp GE	RPO-Bag.	75'	72t	GE-30 rblt. tlr. 451, 1954 GE31 to C&NW	GE-30 re-eng. 400hp Cat. D397, 2/50; removed and re-inst. in GE-31, 1954
32-33	Budd	1957	6605-06	2-GM6-280 275hp DH	RDC-4 3win 17p	75'	55t	Traded to C&O 9080, 9081, 12/58	"Gopher," "Hawkeye." Bag. Sect. mod. to seat 17

Trailers

ROAD NO.	BUILDER	DATE	BLDR. NO.	ENGINE & DRIVE	BODY TYPE	LGTH.	WT.	DISPOSITION	REMARKS
50-55	Budd	1948	—	—	11win 64 pass.	85'	—	Sold to CRI&P 1957 (no. 361-366)	Had own heating and lighting system
405-407	Co. Shops	1947	—	—	Baggage	44'	21t	—	Ex. frt. cars, alum.

Note: Numerous conventional passenger cars were used as trailers.

Minneapolis & St. Louis

Zebra striping on Minneapolis & St. Louis motorcar GE-29 (above) was for high visibility. Photo (below) shows one of the postwar streamlined lightweight coaches the M&STL used behind the motors. View was taken at Manly, IA, on July 7, 1948.   *Author's Collection; W. F. Armstrong*

IN JULY OF 1923, the Minneapolis & St. Louis Railroad was placed in receivership by the Minneapolis Steel & Machinery Co. for money owed for some locomotive repairs. This sad state was to last for nearly 20 years, and precluded the purchase of major equipment until 1929, when the M&SL started buying rail motorcars to modernize its passenger service.

The doodlebug seems to have suited the M&SL very well. In 1932 the last steam locomotive-hauled passenger train, a joint M&SL-Wabash Minneapolis-St. Louis Pullman run, was taken off and all passenger service (except for a few mixed trains) was given by the 11 doodlebugs that had been acquired up to that time.

In 1948, after the M&SL had emerged from receivership, the company made a series of surprising moves. First, six Budd stainless steel air-conditioned lightweight passenger coaches were purchased to be run as trailers behind the rail cars.

Then, in 1957, two Budd RDC-4 railcars were purchased. Primarily a RPO baggage and express model, these

RDC-4s had been modified with a tiny passenger section for 17 seats. They sometimes were seen pulling a specially modified aluminum boxcar, a combination the Budd Co. reportedly was not very happy about.

In any event, soon after the Budd cars arrived, their reason for being evaporated with cancellation of the railroad's mail contracts. With passenger loads already nearly nonexistent, the M&SL traded the RDC cars to the Chesapeake & Ohio. The Budd pas-

senger coaches went to the Rock Island.

To provide service on the remaining runs until abandonment permission came down, four of the old Baggage-RPO motors were modified to include a small passenger section, and were restored temporarily to service. Then the M&SL was merged into the Chicago & Northwestern, which unceremoniously slammed the "Peoria Gateway" closed by abandoning the M&SL's Peoria Branch, and all passenger service ended.

11 Gas-Electric
Rail Motor Cars
release 25 steam locomotives

MORE than two years ago, the Minneapolis & St. Louis Railroad Company decided to substitute gas-electric for steam power in order to reduce the cost of operation. To-day, this road operates 20 of its 22 passenger schedules with 11 gas-electric rail motor cars—25 steam locomotives have been replaced—and the company is saving at a rate of more than $300,000 a year. Each rail car averages 118,850 miles per year, and the total annual mileage for the 11 cars is more than 1,300,000.

The Minneapolis & St. Louis is one of 41 American railroads using G-E equipped gas-electric rail motor cars. During the last two years, thirteen of these roads have purchased a total of 52 G-E equipped cars—because substantial savings could be made quickly and surely. For further information, address the G-E office nearest you or General Electric Company, Schenectady, New York.

391-48

GENERAL ⊕ ELECTRIC

Minneapolis, St. Paul & Sault St. Marie (Soo Line)

ROAD NO.	BUILDER	DATE	BLDR. NO.	ENGINE & DRIVE	BODY TYPE	LGTH.	WT.	DISPOSITION	REMARKS
1	McKeen	1914	127	McKeen 200hp GM	14win CE Bag. 84p	70'	38½t	To Elec. Short Line, 1920	—
M 1	St. Louis EMC	1925	1360C 117	Wint. 106 175hp GE	12win Bag. 52p	58'	40t	To Sperry Rail Svc. 137, 1947	Conv. to welding c ar, 10/42

Missouri & Arkansas

ROAD NO.	BUILDER	DATE	BLDR. NO.	ENGINE & DRIVE	BODY TYPE	LGTH.	WT.	DISPOSITION	REMARKS
102	Gen. Elec. Wason	1912	3739	GE 16C1 175hp GE	14win CE Bag. 62p	70'	47t	Traded to Mid. Vly. M-7, 1927	—
103[1]	Gen. Elec. Wason	1912	3748	GE 16C1 175hp GE	14win CE Bag. 62p	70'	47t	Wrecked 1914	—
103[2]	Gen. Elec. Wason	1914	3780	GE 16C3 175hp GE	14win CE Bag. 62p	70'	47t	Traded to MV M-8, 1927	—
605	Brill	1937	23618	Brill 92hp GM	10win Bag. 28p	43'	16t	Scr. 1949	Last Model 55 car built
705, 726	ACF	1938	1799	H-S 200hp GM	9win RPO Bag. 33p	76'	33t	705 wrecked 8/46; 726 scr. 1949	705 "Thomas C. McRae;" 726 "John E. Martineau"

Missouri & Arkansas 705 poses in Chicago when brand new on June 23, 1938. *James Buckley*

Not too many more doodlebugs would be sold after this trade ad appeared in 1932. *Railway Age—Author's Collection*

The Katy's only Budd car, the 20, is serviced (right) Waco, TX, in May of 1957. An earlier car, lightweight M-10, suns itself at the depot in Joplin, MO., in May of 1936.
R. H. Carlson; Harold K. Vollrath Collection

Missouri - Kansas - Texas

ROAD NO.	BUILDER	DATE	BLDR. NO.	ENGINE & DRIVE	BODY TYPE	LGTH.	WT.	DISPOSITION	REMARKS
M-1	Brill	1924	22099	Brill 75 175hp GM	13win Bag. 59p	55'	27½t	To Chi. & Alton, tlr. 1101	Rblt. to tlr. by C&A
M-10	St. Louis EMC	1925	1368 131	Wint. 106 175hp GE	12win Bag. 59p	59½'	39t	—	—
M-11	St. Louis EMC	1931	1556 500	Wint. 148 400hp GE	Mail-Bag.	78'	79t	—	—
M-12	St. Louis Brill	1931	1557	Brill-WH 415hp GE	Mail-Bag.	78'	75½t	—	—
162 (20)	Budd	1956	6301	GMC 275hp DH	RDC-3 Bag. 49p	85'	63t	Traded to C&O 9081, 1962	Resold CN D356, 1965. Blt. with RPO comp.

Trailers

ROAD NO.	BUILDER	DATE	BLDR. NO.	ENGINE & DRIVE	BODY TYPE	LGTH.	WT.	DISPOSITION	REMARKS
T100	Brill	1924	22100	—	15win 60p	59½'	—	To C&A, tlr. 1100	—

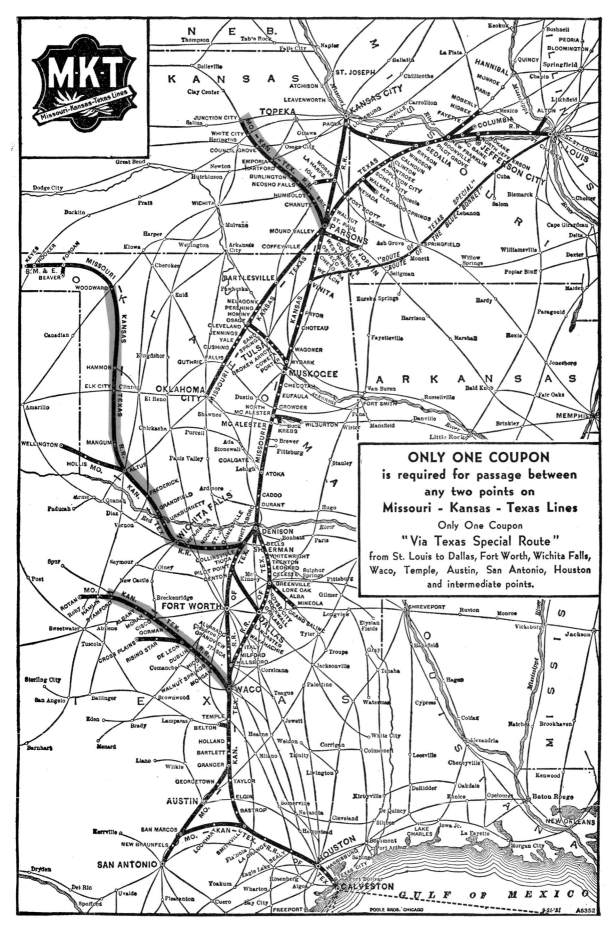

Heavy gray lines indicate the doodlebug runs on the Katy. Reproduced from THE OFFICIAL RAILWAY GUIDE® © 1941 NRPCo.

ONLY ONE COUPON
is required for passage between
any two points on
Missouri - Kansas - Texas Lines
Only One Coupon
"Via Texas Special Route"
from St. Louis to Dallas, Fort Worth, Wichita Falls,
Waco, Temple, Austin, San Antonio, Houston
and intermediate points.

Missouri Pacific

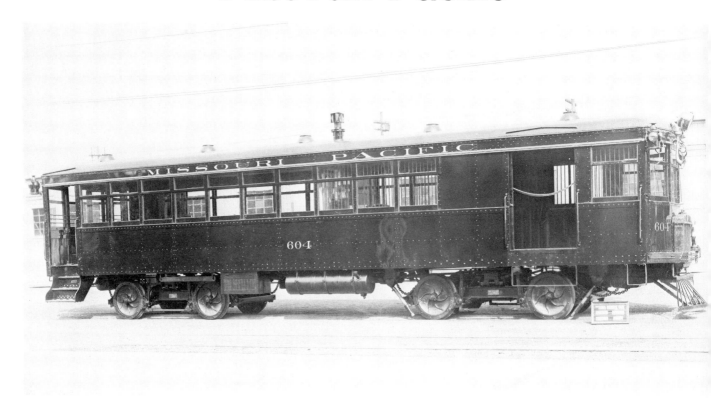

Missouri Pacific was an enthusiastic operator of lightweight Brill Model 55s. Car 604 gets its official photo taken at the Brill plant before delivery, 1925.
Historical Society of Pennsylvania

THE MISSOURI PACIFIC was one of the very first railroads anywhere to look on the self-propelled car as a way to cut costs on lightly-patronized branch line trains. Its efforts in this direction go back to early Civil War days.

Today's Missouri Pacific was formed by the 1917 merger of the Missouri Pacific Railway and the St. Louis, Iron Mountain & Southern; the former running west to Kansas and the latter

south to Arkansas and Texas. In 1861 the Iron Mountain coverted a passenger coach built in 1857 or 1858 into a motorcar by installing a single-drive steam mechanism.

Little is known of this car, except that it was operated as the Carondelet accommodation train to south St. Louis County and that it continued in service until sometime in 1863 when it may have been requisitioned by the Union military railroad system for war use.

From this start in 1861 the MP system progressed through an interesting variety of small and large standard railcars and wound up by purchasing, in 1948, a small fleet of railbuses for use on a converted electric interurban out of Houston, Texas. These operated for only a few short years but the Missouri Pacific's experience with the rail motorcar thus lasted nearly a century—surely a U. S. record.

After its pioneer Civil War car, the Missouri Pacific did not buy another railcar for nearly 60 years. In 1912 the road purchased a single General Electric gas-electric, a type quite popular in its Southwestern area. This car remained an only child until 1924 when the MP began to buy a group of Brill Model 55 gas-mechanical cars. By 1926, eight of these small-but-tough units were on the property.

By the mid-1930s four of the Model 55s were downgraded into "Jim Crow" trailers with freight car trucks and spartan accommodation.

This General Electric car built in 1912 survived long enough to be photographed at San Benito, TX, in 1942. *R. H. Carlson*

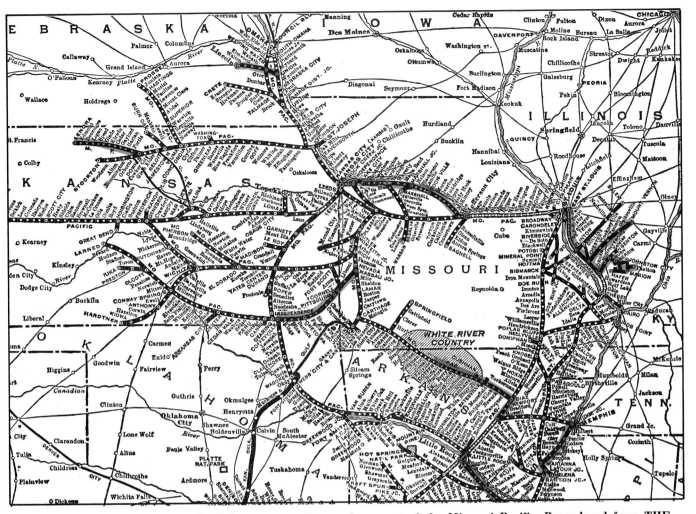

Heavy gray lines indicate the doodlebug runs on the northern part of the Missouri Pacific. Reproduced from THE OFFICIAL RAILWAY GUIDE® © 1941 NRPCo.

Before delivery, Sykes-engined car 609 rests at the St. Louis Car Co. plant in 1925.

Missouri Pacific

After the Brills, the Missouri Pacific added a fleet of five Sykes-St. Louis Car motors which proved to be so mechanically poor that within a year they were re-engined with the Electro-Motive-Winton-General Electric drive. Rebuilt, they proved themselves very reliable and this led to the purchase of seven other EMC-St. Louis cars in the years 1926 through 1939. In 1942, the company purchased one of the American Car & Foundry streamlined *Motorailers*, a double-ended unit for operation as a stub train connecting with the famed Eagle streamliners.

The Missouri Pacific also purchased a modified EMD E6A diesel locomotive which had only one engine instead of two; in the place of the missing power unit was a 35-foot baggage compartment. If this unit, number 7100, is admitted to be a rail motorcar, then it was the last to run on the MP, being retired in 1962. It also was considered by some to be EMD's last-built rail motorcar.

Much of the railroad's railcar history unfolded on the Texas and Louisiana lines, which jumped in and out of the MP corporate family over the years in a complex series of financial maneuvers. A brief bit of history is in order:

The parent Missouri Pacific was originally put together by the rascally 19th century financier, Jay Gould. By the 1880s he had assembled a railroad empire that extended from Buffalo, N. Y. ot the Mexican border at Laredo, Texas. By 1884 the empire began to come apart.

In the resulting crash, the International-Great Northern, the line that carried the MP from Longview, Texas, to Houston and Laredo, tumbled into bankruptcy and was separated from the MP, though it continued operating agreements with the former parent.

Later, the MP again began to expand, this time toward the West Coast via the Rio Grande and the Western Pacific. A parallel empire was being forged in the Southwest by B. F. Yoakum, who planned a railroad—

The hood-front Sykes cars, when rebuilt, looked like this. This is unit 626 (ex 606) at Chester, IL, on July 17, 1948, pulling one of the 1001-class trailers. *C. A. Brown*

Few doodlebugs were double-ended. Here is a rare bi-directional shovelnose ACF streamlined car 670, used by the MP for years on the stub to Lincoln, NB.
Author's Collection

based on the Rock Island and the Frisco—stretching all the way from Chicago to Mexico City.

By 1909 Yoakum had, by building, buying and obtaining trackage rights, a railroad running from New Orleans to Brownsville, Texas, on the Mexican border. This collection of roads included the New Orleans, Texas & Mexico Railroad as its dominant member, and was collectively known as the Gulf Coast Lines.

In 1913 the Rock Island and Frisco were forced into bankruptcy, and the Gulf Coast Lines became completely independent. When the Frisco emerged from bankruptcy by 1923 it decided to expand its operations in Texas, eyeing the Gulf Coast Lines as its key acquisition. There was no physical link between the two networks, and to remedy

this the Frisco applied to the ICC to buy the Gulf Coast Lines plus the International-Great Northern, to form the link.

This move upset the Missouri Pacific, for, although it no longer owned the I-GN, it continued to exchange a great deal of traffic with it and, for all practical purposes, the I-GN was a functional part of the MP system. The MP promptly appealed the Frisco application to the ICC, which not only denied the Frisco's application to buy the I-GN but gave the MP permission to buy not only the I-GN but the Gulf Coast Lines as well.

This the MP quickly proceeded to do, shutting the Frisco out of South Texas for good. A number of small, independent railroads were gobbled up by the MP or the rival Southern Pacific at

about this time, as the two giants sought to consolidate their positions.

One of the small independents purchased by the MP was the Houston North Shore, an unfinished electric interurban running from Houston to Goose Creek, Texas. In its purchase of the various Texas independent roads, the MP acquired in a very short time a fleet of seven General Electric gas-electric cars (five of them ex-Frisco), six Brill type 55 gas-mechanical cars and a matching trailer.

The only new railcar equipment purchased for these lines was two Evans Autorailers and the previously-mentioned Twin Coach railbuses to replace electric cars on the Houston North Shore.

There wasn't much in the way of beauty about her, but Evans railbus 105 plied the Houston North Shore tracks out of Houston for several years after the MP abandoned electric interurban service on the line to Goose Creek. Unit 105 is at North Baytown on December 8, 1946. *M. D. McCarter Collection*

Missouri Pacific

ROAD NO.	BUILDER	DATE	BLDR. NO.	ENGINE & DRIVE	BODY TYPE	LGTH.	WT.	DISPOSITION	REMARKS
500	Gen. Elec. Wason	1911	3716 10400	GE 16A1 175hp GE	16win CRE Bag. 86p	72'	49½t	Destroyed 1928	Ex-SLSF, NOT&M 2105, acq. 4/23
501	Gen. Elec. Wason	1912	3724	GE 16A3 175hp GE	15win CE Bag. 91p	71'	51½t	Scr. 2/36	Ex-SLSF, NOT&M 2107, acq. 4/23
502-03	Gen. Elec. Wason	1912	3725-26	GE 16A3 175hp GE	15win CE Bag. 91p	71	51t	Rblt. tlr. 1943	Ex-SLSF, NOT&M 2108, acq. 4/23. Ex-SLSF, NOT&M 2109, acq. 4/23
504	Gen. Elec. Wason	1912	3733 12200	GE 16C1 175hp GE	15win CE Bag. 91p	71'	51t	Scr. 6/46	Ex-SLSF, NOT&M 2115, acq. 4/23
514-15	Brill	1924	21910	Brill 55 68hp GM	10win CE Bag.-Pas.	43'	17t	514 scr. 1936; 515 to Ga.-Car., 1939	Ex I-GN 1001-1002
516	Brill	1924	21913	Brill 55 68hp GM	RPO-Bag.	43'	17t	Scr. 1936	Ex I-GN 1003
527	Brill	1924	21983	Brill 55 68hp GM	18win Bag. 40p	43'	14t	To Ga. Nor. 5/40	Ex-SAU&G 200, used as Biz. Car. 1929-32
531[1]	Gen. Elec. Wason	1911	3717 9931	GE 6M16 175hp GE	17win CE Bag. 97p	66'	47t	Ret. 3/32	Ex-Houston & Brazos Valley 55.
531[2]	Twin Coach	1947	41 SCR 1	Twin 404 180hp GM	11win bus 43p	33'	11½t	Re-no. 701	Ex-Houston North Shore. (See following roster for others)
532	Gen. Elec.	1912	3722 9931	GE 16A5	14win CE Bag. 41p	68'	48t	—	Ex-H&BV 56
536	Brill	1924	22121	Brill 55 68hp GM	10win Bag. 42p	43'	14t	To Ga.-Car., 1939	Ex-Asherton & Gulf 103, then St. Mary's RR 100
600 (Orig.)	Gen. Elec. Wason	1912	3727	GE 16A3 175hp GE	16win CE Bag. 83p	70'	53t	See below	—
600 (Rblt.)	EMC Co. Shops	1930	GEC8	Wint. 106A 220hp GE	14win CE Bag. 74p	70'	62t	Scr. 9/48	New flat front end, seats put in Bag. sect.
601-02	Brill	1924	21957-58	Brill 55 85hp GM	10win Bag. 22p	43'	16t	Rblt., tlr. 1012-1013, 11/36	602 seated 26
603	Brill	1924	21959	Brill 55 85hp GM	10win Bag. 36p	47'	18t	Wrecked 7/39	—
604-05	Brill	1925	22203	Brill 55 85hp GM	10win Bag. 26p	47'	17½t	604 scr. 6/41, 605 burned 9/28	—
606-10[1]	St. Louis Sykes	1925	1370	Sterl. 175hp GM	13win 48p	52'	29½t	Rblt., re-no. 625-629, 5/28	—
606[2]	Brill	1926	22352	Brill 55 85hp GM	10win Bag. 28p	43'	18t	Scr. 11/40	—
607-08[2]	Brill	1926	22352	Brill 55 85hp GM	10win Bag. 30p	43'	15½t	Rblt. tlrs. 1011, 1014	608[2] seated 42
625-26	EMC Co. Shops	1928	MSCK-11, 9	Wint. 106A 220hp GE	13win 48p	52'	41½t	625 to Mo.-Ill. 625, 9/44; 626 scr. 8/50	Ex 606-607[1]
627-29	EMC Co. Shops	1928	MSCK-12-14	Wint. 106A 220hp GE	13win 46p	52'	41½	627, 628 scr. 1950; 629 rblt. tlr. 4/43	Ex 608-610[1]. 628 seated 48
650	St. Louis EMC	1926	1400 160	Wint. 106A 220hp GE	12win Bag. 38p	57'	42t	Scr. 7/54	—
651	St. Louis EMC	1926	1401 159	Wint. 106A 220hp GE	15win 46p	57'	41½t	Scr. 8/50	—
652	St. Louis EMC	1926	1402 156	Wint. 106A 220hp GE	12win Bag. 40p	70½'	48½t	Rblt. 12/35, Co. Shops, to 10win RPO-Bag. 32p. Scr. 9/50	Wt. incr. to 56t
653	St. Louis EMC	1926	1402 158	Wint. 106A 220hp GE	13win Bag. 40p	70½	48½t	Scr. 9/40	Bag. sect. enlarged 7/30. Wt. incr. to 52t
654	St. Louis EMC	1926	1402 158	Wint. 106A 220hp GE	13win Bag. 40p	70½'	48½t	Rblt. 12/33, Co. Shops, to 10win RPO-Bag. 30p. Scr. 8/50	Wt. incr. to 54½t

ROAD NO.	BUILDER	DATE	BLDR. NO.	ENGINE & DRIVE	BODY TYPE	LGTH.	WT.	DISPOSITION	REMARKS
660-61	St. Louis EMC	1931	1553 495-96	Wint. 148 400hp GE	RPO-Bag.	77'	82t	Scr. 8/50, 4/51	—
670	ACF	1942	2223	2-Wauk. 210hp OM	9win RPO Bag. 47p	75'	57½t	Scr. 2/61	Re-eng. 2-Cum. 300hp DH, 1/55
7100	GM-EMD	1940	1082	EMD-12567 1000hp DE	Loco.-Bag.	70'	123½t	Scr. 2/62	E6-A carbody less 1 eng.

Trailers

ROAD NO.	BUILDER	DATE	BLDR. NO.	ENGINE & DRIVE	BODY TYPE	LGTH.	WT.	DISPOSITION	REMARKS
502-03	Co. Shops	1943	—	—	27win 83p	70½'	25t	To MW Serv., 1940	Re-np. NOT&M 4125, 4126
517	Brill	1924	21911	—	14win 42p	42½'	—	Scr. 1936	Ex-IGN 1004
629	Co. Shops	1943	—	—	13win 46p	52'	32t	Scr. 7/48	Ex Motor 629
1001-05	St. Louis Sykes	1925	1371	—	RPO-Bag.	49½'	27t	1002 to Mo.-Ill. 1002, 9/44	All scr. c. 1948-50, ex. 1002, scr. 4/54

In addition, motor 607[2], 601, 602, 608, rblt. into tlrs. 1011-1013 (1936) and 1014 (1938).

International - Great Northern
(Purchased by New Orleans, Texas & Mexico [MP] in 1924)

ROAD NO.	BUILDER	DATE	BLDR. NO.	ENGINE & DRIVE	BODY TYPE	LGTH.	WT.	DISPOSITION	REMARKS
1001-02	Brill	1924	21910	Midwest 68hp GM	10win CE Bag. 43p	43'	17t	To MP 514-515	—
1003	Brill	1924	21913	Midwest 68hp GM	3win RPO Bag.	43'	17t	To MP 516	—

Trailers

ROAD NO.	BUILDER	DATE	BLDR. NO.	ENGINE & DRIVE	BODY TYPE	LGTH.	WT.	DISPOSITION	REMARKS
1004	Brill	1924	21911	—	14win 52p	42½'	—	To MP 517	—

Houston North Shore
(Purchased by Beaumont, Sour Lake & Western [MP] in 1927)

ROAD NO.	BUILDER	DATE	BLDR. NO.	ENGINE & DRIVE	BODY TYPE	LGTH.	WT.	DISPOSITION	REMARKS
100	Evans	1939	113	Reo 101hp GM	1win bus Bag.	—	10½t	Scr. 12/47	Model D-1 ''Autorailer''
105	Evans	1943	169	Reo 127hp GM	4win bus Bag. 19p	35'	15t	Sold Comm'l Metals,	Model D-20 ''Autorailer''
701 (531)	Twin Coach	1947	41 SCR 1	Twin 404 180hp GM	11win bus 45p	33'	11½t	Scr. 11/55	Model 41 bus body, center exit inst. 6/49
602 (702)	Twin Coach	1948	41 SCR 2	Twin 404 180hp GM	10win bus 43p	33'	11½t	Scr. 1/58	Model 41 bus body
703	Twin Coach	1948	41 SCR 3	Twin 404 180hp GM	10win bus 43p	33'	11½t	Scr. 11/55	Model 41 bus body
604 (704)	Twin Coach	1948	41 SCR 4	Twin 404 180hp GM	10win bus 43p	33'	11½t	Donated Nat. Mus. Transp., 1/62	Model 41 bus body
605 (705)	Twin Coach	1948	41 SCR 5	Twin 404 180hp GM	10win bus 43p	33'	11½t	To Gen. Export & Metal, 2/62	Model 41 bus body
706	Twin Coach	1948	41 SCR 6	Twin 404 180hp GM	10win bus 43p	33'	11½t	Scr. 11/55	Model 41 bus body

A much smarter-appearing railbus was Twin Coach No. 701, also used on the MP-owned Houston North Shore out of Houston in the postwar years. This was a model 41 city bus on flanged wheels.

Missouri Pacific

Houston & Brazos Valley
(Purchased by New Orleans, Texas & Mexico [MP] in 1924)

ROAD NO.	BUILDER	DATE	BLDR. NO.	ENGINE & DRIVE	BODY TYPE	LGTH.	WT.	DISPOSITION	REMARKS
55	Gen. Elec. Wason	1911	3717 9931	GE GM16 175hp GE	18win CE Bag. 97p	66'	47t	To MP 531	Ex-Demo 5, then Bang. & Aroost. 5, then AC&Y 55, acq. 12/22
56	Gen. Elec Wason	1912	3722 9931	GE 16A5 175hp GE	14win CE Bag. 91p	68'	48t	To MP 532	Ex-Bang. & Aroost. 6, then AC&Y 56, acq. 2/23

Gulf Coast Lines
New Orleans, Texas & Mexico; St. Louis, Brownsville & Mexico; Beaumont, Sour Lake & Western
(Purchased by Missouri Pacific in 1924)

ROAD NO.	BUILDER	DATE	BLDR. NO.	ENGINE & DRIVE	BODY TYPE	LGTH.	WT.	DISPOSITION	REMARKS
2104-05	Gen. Elec. Wason	1911	3715-6 10400	GE 16A1 175hp GE	16win CE Bag. 86p	72'	49½t	2104 ret. to SLSF, 1922; 2105 to MP 500	Ex-SLSF 2104-2105, acq. 1916
2107-09	Gen. Elec. Wason	1912	3724-6 —	GE 16A3 175hp GE	15win CE Bag. 91p	71'	51½t	To MP 501-503	Ex-SLSF 2107-2109, acq. 1916
2115-16	Gen. Elec. Wason	1912	3733-4 12200	GE 16C1 175hp GE	15win CE Bag. 91p	71'	51t	2115 to MP 504; 2116 to Mac. & Birm., 1919	Ex-SLSF 2115-2116, acq. 1916

ONE OF THE CLAIMS to fame of Muskogee, Oklahoma, is that it was the headquarters of an important group of regional railroads operated in a rather unusual fashion. The Muskogee group of railroads consisted of the Midland Valley Railroad, which ran from Wichita, Kansas, to Hartford, Ark., 328 miles, and controlled the Muskogee Corp. which owned two other railroads.

These were the Kansas, Oklahoma & Gulf, which extended from Baxter Springs, Kan., to Denison, Tex., and, after 1930, the Oklahoma City-Ada-Atoka Railway.

Most of the track mileage was in Oklahoma and the two biggest lines, the MV and the KO&G, intersected at Muskogee. The OC-A-A had originally been a branch of the Missouri, Kansas & Texas but after that line (known as the Katy Railroad) was reorganized as the Missouri-Kansas-Texas in 1923, the branch, which extended from Oklahoma City to Atoka, Okla., 133 miles, was left out.

The Muskogee Co. purchased this line and thereafter operated the three roads as pretty much one railroad, although they were never consolidated under one name. In fact, most of the locomotives and cars carried the names of all three companies.

The Midland Valley in the years from 1913 to 1927 acquired a group of mostly second-hand General Electric gas-electric cars. The KO&G, which started out as the Missouri, Oklahoma & Gulf, had in 1912 purchased six of the rare Drake gas-electric cars. By the time of its inclusion in the group in 1925, these cars had been converted to maintenance

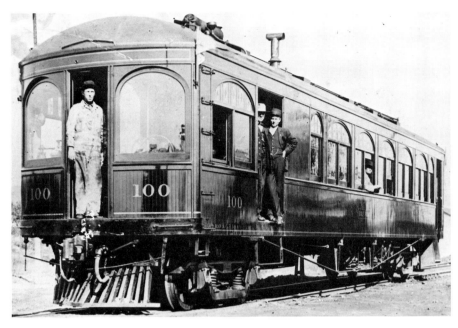

Looking for all the world like an electric interurban car of the period, Missouri, Oklahoma & Gulf Drake car 100 appears at Muskogee in 1911. Crew and passengers alike patiently await the photographer to complete his task.

Harold K. Vollrath Collection

equipment or disposed of. The OC-A-A in the years 1924 to 1928 purchased two Sykes gas-mechanical cars, plus three matching trailers.

As time went on the number of motor car runs was reduced to only a pair of Muskogee to Denison trains. Around 1940, parts from several of the GE cars were combined into three highly rebuilt cars.

This rebuilding enlarged the baggage section greatly, added a RPO compartment, and reduced seating to 30. Most

of the cars, but not all, had had the characteristic General Electric center entrance. This was eliminated, but the open rear platforms were retained, as was the drive mechanism. It seems a bit strange that this cumbersome and antiquated drive wasn't modified at the time, as was done on GE cars on other railroads at the time.

The resulting cars, numbered M-8, M-21 and M-23, still possessed the traditional rounded front end and open rear platforms, but were otherwise much rebuilt. They held down the last run until 1954. A decade later the Muskogee group was broken up; the Midland Valley and the KO&G were sold to the Missouri Pacific while the Santa Fe took the OC-A-A.

Although shuffled around the Muskogee group roads, the General Electric cars were altered very little in appearance over the years. This is KO&G M-23, circa 1939. *Author's Collection*

Muskogee Group

Kansas, Oklahoma & Gulf
(Merged into T&P)

ROAD NO.	BUILDER	DATE	BLDR. NO.	ENGINE & DRIVE	BODY TYPE	LGTH.	WT.	DISPOSITION	REMARKS
100-05	Drake St. Louis	1912	— 932	Drake 90hp GE	12win DE Bag. 54p	56'	32½t	104 to Elec. SL 304, 1913; 100 rblt. to insp. car; others to M/W	100 sold to Garland Coal, 12/27; 101, 103. 105 used as diners
M-21[1]	Gen. Elec. Wason	1916	3792	GE 16C10 175hp GE	14win Bag. 62p	70'	51½t	Scr. 1939	Ex-MV M-3, acq. 1929; orig. Elec. SL 312
M-21[2]	Gen. Elec. Co. Shops	— 1939	—	GE 16C 175hp GE	7win RPO Bag. 30p	70'	51½t	Scr. 1954	Rblt. using parts from other cars
M-22	Gen. Elec. Wason	1912	3736	GE 16A5 175hp GE	14win Bag. 80p	70'	49t	Scr. 1939	Ex-MV M-6, orig. Dan Patch 10
M-23[1]	Gen. Elec. Wason	1912	3780	GE 16C1 175Hp GE	14win Bag. 85p	70'	52t	Scr. 1939	Ex-MV M-8[1]; orig. Mo. & No. Ark. 103[2], acq. 1929
M-23[2]	Gen. Elec. Co. Shops	— 1939	—	GE 16C 175hp GE	7win RPO Bag. 30p	70'	—	Scr. 11/54	Rblt. using parts from other cars

Midland Valley
(Merged into T&P)

ROAD NO.	BUILDER	DATE	BLDR. NO.	ENGINE & DRIVE	BODY TYPE	LGTH.	WT.	DISPOSITION	REMARKS
M-1	Gen. Elec. Wason	1913	3740 12000	GE 16C1 175hp GE	14win Bag. 86p	70'	52t	Ret. 1934	—
M-2	McKeen	1911	103	McKeen 200hp GM	15win CE Bag. 82p	70'	39½t	To UP M-6, 1925	Ex-Sand Springs 2, acq. 1916
M-3	Gen. Elec. Wason	1916	3792	GE 16C10 175hp GE	14win Bag. 62p	70'	51½t	To KO&G 21, 1929	Ex-Elec. SL 312, acq. 1917
M-4	Gen. Elec. Wason	1912	3728	GE 16C1 175hp GE	14win CE Bag. 91p	70'	52t	Ret. 11/43	Ex-Hawk. & Fla. Sou. 26, acq. 1923. Orig. SLSF 2110
M-5	Gen. Elec. Wason	1912	3751	GE 16C1 175hp GE	8win Bag. 42p	42'	39t	Scr. 12/35	Ex-Hawk. & Fla. Sou. 25, acq. 1922. Orig. P&LE 500
M-6	Gen. Elec. Wason	1912	3736	GE 16A5 175hp GE	14win Bag. 80p	70'	49t	To KO&G M-22, 1928	Ex-Okla., N.M. & Pac.; orig. Dan Patch 10
M-7	Gen. Elec. Wason	1912	3739	GE 16C1 175hp GE	14win Bag. 85p	70'	51t	—	Ex-M&NA 102, acq. 1927
M-8[1]	Gen. Elec. Wason	1914	3780	GE 16C1 175hp GE	14win Bag. 85p	70'	53½t	To KO&G M-23, 1929	Ex-M&NA 103[2], acq. 1927
M-8[2]	Gen. Elec. Co. Shops	— 1935	—	GE 16C1 175hp GE	8win RPO Bag.-Pass.	70'	—	Scr. 11/54	Rblt. using parts from other cars

Trailers

ROAD NO.	BUILDER	DATE	BLDR. NO.	ENGINE & DRIVE	BODY TYPE	LGTH.	WT.	DISPOSITION	REMARKS
T 1-2	Brill	1915	19602	—	19win 104p	57½'	—	Scr. 1939, 1924	Acq. 11/17, ex-Dan Patch
T 3	Wason	1912	12630	—	15win 56p	38½'	—	Scr. 1939	Ex-P&LE 700, then Hawk. & Fla. Sou. 100, acq. 1923
T 4	Wason	1913	13500	—	19win 104p	48½'	—	Scr. 2/46	Prob. ex-ONM&P, orig. Dan Patch
T 10	St. L.-Sykes	1928	1489	—	9win 32p	40'	18½t	To M/W	Ex OC–A–A MT 130

Oklahoma City-Ada-Atoka
(Purchased by Atchison, Topeka & Santa Fe)

ROAD NO.	BUILDER	DATE	BLDR. NO.	ENGINE & DRIVE	BODY TYPE	LGTH.	WT.	DISPOSITION	REMARKS
M 126	St. Louis Sykes	1928	1488	Sterl. 225hp GM	Bag.	41'	24½t	—	—
M 300	St. Louis Sykes	1924	1329B	Sterl. 175hp GM	—	53'	20t	—	—

Trailers

ROAD NO.	BUILDER	DATE	BLDR. NO.	ENGINE & DRIVE	BODY TYPE	LGTH.	WT.	DISPOSITION	REMARKS
MT 130	St. L.-Sykes	1928	1489	—	9win 32p	40'	18½t	To MV T10	—
MT 131	St. L.-Sykes	1928	1490	—	50p	40'	18½t	—	—
MT 301	St. L.-Sykes	1924	1330B	—	—	45½'	13½t	—	—

Nashville, Chattanooga & St. Louis
(Merged into Louisville & Nashville)

ROAD NO.	BUILDER	DATE	BLDR. NO.	ENGINE & DRIVE	BODY TYPE	LGTH.	WT.	DISPOSITION	REMARKS
1	Brill	1924	21972	Brill 55 68hp GM	10win Bag.-Pass.	43'	14½t	Gone by 4/27	—
699	Elec. Car & Loco,	1919	—	Beach 150hp DE	12win CE Bag. 51p	59'	56½t	To Roby & Nor. 1923, conv. to elec.	—

Still working for the Big Four, Brill-built M-1208 pauses at some long forgotten location with a venerable wooden coach in tow.
Author's Collection

New York Central

This Barney & Smith baggage-club car was motorized by NYC company forces in 1927.
Bob Lorenz Collection

PRIOR TO 1937 the various railroads that made up the New York Central System were operationally separate. Rolling stock, including rail motorcars, was numbered in a separate system on each road, resulting in some duplication. The general reorganization of properties in 1937 included a master renumbering to eliminate any duplication and resulted in a NYC system-wide roster.

The New York Central was an enthusiastic user of rail motorcars in the 1920s and 1930s and for the most part the system steered clear of unusual and oddball units. However, there was a mysterious wooden baggage car of the Lake Shore & Michigan Southern which was converted into some type of mechanical-drive gas car way back in 1907. The result did not suit the

Big Four Route 123 was a 1922 Brill-Service lightweight—originally the Service company's demonstrator.
Robert G. Foley Collection

Brill built New York Central X-8015 as a rail detector car, using the standard heavyweight doodlebug body. It is shown at Sharonville, OH, on February 3, 1968. *Louis A. Marre Collection*

In the time-honored tradition of the "local," motor M-203 takes its station stop at Clyde, OH. Conductor waits on platform for the mail to be loaded.

Bob Lorenz Collection

LS&MS, for the car was soon reconverted into a baggage car.

The Pittsburgh & Lake Erie purchased a very short General Electric gas-electric car along with a matching trailer with the idea of using the set in commuter service in the Pittsburgh area. It proved to be unable to maintain the schedule, and was sold after about two years.

It is therefore not surprising that no other cars were acquired until the middle 1920s when some Brill gas-mechanical and gas-electric, and Electro-Motive gas electrics were acquired, along with a couple of Mack gas-electrics for good measure.

Slightly out of the ordinary was the conversion of a wooden baggage-club car to one of the first diesel-electric railcars. Using a McIntosh & Seymour engine, the New York Central shops did this job in 1927. The Cleveland, Cincinnati, Chicago & St. Louis (Big Four Route) and a subsidiary (Evansville, Indianapolis & Terre Haute) invested in a fleet of very cranky Sykes cars, and bought some former interurban cars of the Michigan Railways for use as trailers, as did the Cincinnati Northern.

The Michigan Central, which on its own never received or owned any railcars, was assigned some of the NYCRR units plus a couple of the ex-Michigan Railways electric cars for the Buffalo-Detroit local run.

Five Multiple unit cars from the New York City electrified zone were rebuilt as trailers for rail motorcars but were soon converted back to their original use.

Several of the New York Central System's railcars were sold to other operators, but most were around until the 1950s, when the NYC placed in service a fleet of Budd RDC cars. These, in turn, were passed on to the Penn Central.

One, the M-497, an RDC-3 RPO-Baggage-coach, made headlines during the reign of NYC President Alfred Perlman when it was fitted with a jet engine. Thus equipped, it streaked along the Toledo-Chicago main line at 183.8 miles per hour. As flashbulbs popped, there were cheers and murmurings of a fleet of ultra high-speed railcars. A few days later, the whole idea was forgotten.

Running on the Boston & Albany, NYC Budd RDC car M-464 stops at Worcester, MA, on April 12, 1953.
M. D. McCarter Collection

New York Central System

ROAD NO.	BUILDER	DATE	BLDR. NO.	ENGINE & DRIVE	BODY TYPE	LGTH.	WT.	DISPOSITION	REMARKS
M-1	Brill	1925	22127	Brill 75 190hp GM	13win Bag. 52p	55'	30½t	—	Model 75, nee NYCRR M-1
M-2	Brill	1925	22259	Brill 75 190hp GM	13win Bag. 50p	58'	28t	—	Model 75, nee NYCRR M-2
M-3 -5	Brill	1925	22259	Brill 75 190hp GM	13win Bag. 50p	58t	28½t	—	Model 75 nee NYCRR M-3-5; M-4 weighed 30½t, M-5 29t
M-6 -7	Brill	1925	22260	Brill 75 190hp GM	13win Bag. 47p	58'	30t 28½t	—	Model 75, nee NYCRR M-6, 7
M-8	Co. Shops Barney & Sm	1927 1906	— —	Mac. & Sym. 200hp DE	10win DE Bag. 48p	74'	93½t	—	Nee NYCRR M-8, was bag.-club 107 wooden
M-9	Brill	1928	22543	Brill-WH 250hp GE	15win DE Bag. 71p	76'	59½t	—	Nee NYCRR M-9
M-10	Brill	1928	22545	2-Brill-WH 250hp GE	15win DE Bag. 65p	76'	79½t	Rblt. Clearance Car, 6/55	Nee NYCRR M-10
M-11	Brill	1928	22547	2-HS 275hp GE	15win DE Bag. 52p	75½'	80t	To Sperry Rail Svc. 136, 4/48	Nee NYCRR M-11. Orig. had RPO
M-12 -13	Std. Steel	1928	309	Sterl. TT6 300hp GE	13win DE Bag. 58p	75½'	64t	—	Nee NYCRR M-12, 13. M-13 seated 65
M-14	Osgd Bdly Mack	1928	9115 161001	2-Mack AP 120hp GE	16win DE Bag. 65p	76½'	58t	To Wash. & Old Dom. 45	Nee NYCRR M-14. Ex-Mack demo M-200, Model AQ
M-15	Std. Steel	1928	309	Sterl. TT6 300hp GE	13win DE Bag. 57p	75½'	65t	—	Nee NYCRR M-15
M-70	Mack Pullman	1928	162001	3-Mack AP 120hp GE	15win DE Bag. 70p	76½'	57½t	To Mon. Ry., 1/40	Ex-P&LE M-70, Mack demo, Model AR
M-200	Brill	1925	22128	Brill 75 190hp GM	RPO-Bag.	55'	33t	To Sou. Ga. Ry.	Nee NYCRR M-101, Model 75; 58' long
M-201 -203	St. Louis EMC	1925	1364 216-18	Wint. 120 275hp GE	RPO-Bag.	60½'	47t	—	Nee Cincinnati Nor. M-101-103
M-204	Brill	1926	22370	Brill-WH 250hp GE	RPO-Bag.	6&'	46t	—	Nee CCC&St.L M-1208, Model 250
M-205	Brill	1930	22861	Brill-WH 535hp GE	RPO-Bag.	77½'	74½t	—	Nee CCC&St.L M-1210, Model 860, 75' long

ROAD NO.	BUILDER	DATE	BLDR. NO.	ENGINE & DRIVE	BODY TYPE	LGTH.	WT.	DISPOSITION	REMARKS
M-206 -207	Brill	1931	22937	Brill-WH 535hp GE	RPO-Bag.	77½'	67½t	M-206 wrecked	Nee CCC&St.L M-1214, 1215. Model 860
M-400 -405	Brill	1928	22544	Brill-WH 250hp GE	7win RPO Bag. 40p	75½'	62t	M-400 to Alaska 116; M-405 to Can. Gulf & Term.	Nee NYCRR M-201-206. M-403 to W&OD 52. M-404 weighed 63t
M-406 -408	Osgd Bdly EMC	1928	9375 227-29	2-Wint. 106A 220hp GE	7win RPO Bag. 39p	76'	74t	—	Nee NYCRR M-207-209
M-409	Brill	1928	22871	2-HS 275hp GE	6win RPO Bag. 39p	76'	80t	—	Nee NYCRR M-210
M-450 -451	Budd	1950	5001-02	2-GM6-280 275hp DH	RDC-1 89p	85'	59t	To Penn Central 50, 51	—
M-452	Budd	1950	5005	2-GM6-280 275hp DH	RDC-1 89p	85'	59t	To Penn Central 52	—
M-453	Budd	1950	5203	2-GM6-280 275hp DH	RDC-1 89p	85'	59t	To Penn Central 53	—
M-454 -456	Budd	1951	5403-05	2-GM6-280 275hp DH	RDC-1 89p	85'	59t	To Penn Central 54-56	—
M-457 -459	Budd	1951	5411-13	2-GM6-280 275hp DH	RDC-1 89p	85'	59t	To Penn Central 57-59	—
M-460 -462	Budd	1952	5508-10	2-GM6-280 275hp DH	RDC-1 89p	85'	59t	To Penn Central 60-62	—
M-463 -464	Budd	1952	5601-02	2-GM6-280 275hp DH	RDC-1 89p	85'	59t	To Penn Central 63, 64	—
M-465	Budd	1953	5807	2-GM6-280 275hp DH	RDC-1 89p	85'	59t	To Penn Central 65	—
M-480	Budd	1951	5420	2-GM6-280 275hp DH	RDC-2 Bag. 70p	85'	57t	To Penn Central 80	—
M-497	Budd	1953	5705	2-GM6-280 275hp DH	RDC-3 RPO Bag. 48p	85'	59t	To Penn Central 98	Equip. with jet engine in demo. at 183.8 mph
M-498 -499	Budd	1950	5109-10	2-GM6-280 275hp DH	RDC-3 RPO Bag. 48p	85'	59t	M-498 wrecked prior to 1964. M-499 to PC 99	—
X8015	Brill	1931	22871	HS 300hp GE	Rail detect.	73½'	—	—	Nee NYCRR X8015, re-eng. Cat. D375 D, 1955
X8016	Brill Co. Shops	1928 1955	22545	2-Brill-WH 250hp GE	Clearance	73'	80t	—	Ex M-10

Trailers

MT 1	Brill	1925	22129	—	16win 58p	41'	21½t	To Sou. Ga. Ry.	Nee NYCRR 01

In addition, trailers MT2-MT6 were rblt. from coaches in Co. Shops, 1929, and tlrs. MT7-MT9 and MT200 were rblt. from Mich. Elec. interurban cars 805, 801, 803, 811, 1929.

Michigan Electric steel interurban car 803 was rebuilt into NYC doodlebug trailer MT9. Here it is at Fort Wayne, IN, on June 18, 1939.
M. D. McCarter Collection

Cars of Predecessor or Underlyer Companies
(Not surviving until general renumbering ca. 1937)

C.C.C. & St. L. (Big Four Route)

ROAD NO.	BUILDER	DATE	BLDR. NO.	ENGINE & DRIVE	BODY TYPE	LGTH.	WT.	DISPOSITION	REMARKS
123	Brill Service	1922	21487	Midwest 68hp GM	10win Bag. 35p	42½'	14½t	—	Ex-Service Demo.
M-1200	Brill Service	1923	22182	Midwest 68hp GM	10win Bag. 26p	42½'	15t	To East Jor. & Sou. M-1200, then Alb. & Nor., same no.	—
M-1201	St. Louis Sykes	1925	1346	Sterl. 175hp GM	RPO-Bag.	52'	27t	—	Hood in front
M-1203	St. Louis Sykes	1925	1357	Sterl. 175hp GM	RPO-Bag.	52'	27t	—	Hood in front
M-1204	St. Louis Sykes	1925	1355	Sterl. 175hp GM	RPO-Bag.	52'	27t	—	Hood in front
M-1206	St. Louis Sykes	1925	1355	Sterl. 175hp GM	RPO-Bag.	52'	27t	—	Hood in front
M-1209	Unit Laconia	1919	100	Unit 60hp steam	12win Bag. 40p	49'	—	Rblt. tlr. 1928	Ex-demo, acq. 1923
MT-1202, 1205, 07	St. Louis Sykes	1925	1356	Trail.	16win 60p	49'	—	—	—

Evansville, Indianapolis & Terre Haute

ROAD NO.	BUILDER	DATE	BLDR. NO.	ENGINE & DRIVE	BODY TYPE	LGTH.	WT.	DISPOSITION	REMARKS
M-1, M-3	St. Louis Sykes	1924	1355	Sterl. 175hp GM	RPO-Bag.	52'	47t	—	Hood in front
MT-2, MT-4	St. Louis Sykes	1924	1356	Trail.	16win 60p	49'	—	—	—

Cincinnati Northern

ROAD NO.	BUILDER	DATE	BLDR. NO.	ENGINE & DRIVE	BODY TYPE	LGTH.	WT.	DISPOSITION	REMARKS
M-100	St. Louis EMC	1925	1364 215	Wint. 120 275hp GE	RPO-Bag.	57½'	47t	Ret. by 1937. Wrecked (?)	—

New Haven

Perhaps the acme in the development of the Budd RDC was the ROGER WILLIAMS train, shown here running as the MURRAY HILL from Boston to New York City at Larchmont, NY, on May 30, 1957. *George E. Votava*

THE NEW HAVEN Railroad, operator of one of the most intense passenger services in the United States, dabbled in railcars as early as 1897 with a steam-driven model and worked up to a large fleet of Budd RDC cars which outlasted the railroad itself under the NYNH&H name. As the decade of the 1980s opened, railcars were still to be seen in former New Haven territory.

The rail motorcar story opened with conversion of an open platform, wooden diner into the New Haven's first self-propelled unit with a steam engine built by the Schenectady Locomotive Works in 1897. It ran from Dedham, Mass., to Islington Jct. until 1904.

Perhaps because the first car proved to be none too reliable, the New Haven did not have another rail motor until 1922, when three bulldog-nose Mack AC cars were bought. An unusual

hydraulic transmission-drive car built by Osgood Bradley and Waterbury came next, and then 10 Sykes gas-mechanical cars were purchased.

Sykes cars generally had a reputation for unreliability, but the New Haven thought otherwise and managed to operate the Sykes cars for years. The Sykes cars were dubbed *Seagulls* on the New Haven and were given a prominent place in the road's passenger advertising.

The *Seagulls* had hood fronts, and a year after the Sykes cars came, the New Haven bought 10 more of the same design gas-mechanical cars, including the hood fronts, only these were built by Brill. Shortly afterwards, however, in 1925, the New Haven started purchasing its fleet of 15 Brill Tyipe 250 gas-electrics. Three of them came used, from the New York, Ontario & Western.

With many Railroads trying daring new designs in the mid-1930s, the New Haven jumped aboard the bandwagon with its *Comet* streamliner, built by Goodyear Zeppelin. At the same time the New Haven rebuilt two coaches into railcars with a Besler steam power unit. The *Comet* was a success, but the steam unit was not.

After World War II, the New Haven was hit hard by rising costs and declining patronage, particularly on its commuter runs out of Boston. In 1952 President Frederick C. Dumaine, hoping that new equipment would rejuvenate the business, purchased no less than 40 Budd RDC cars and used them to increase the number of trains on most routes.

Dumaine also consulted Mack about a smaller, lighter version of the RDC for branch lines and off-peak commuter service. He wanted a vehicle capable of

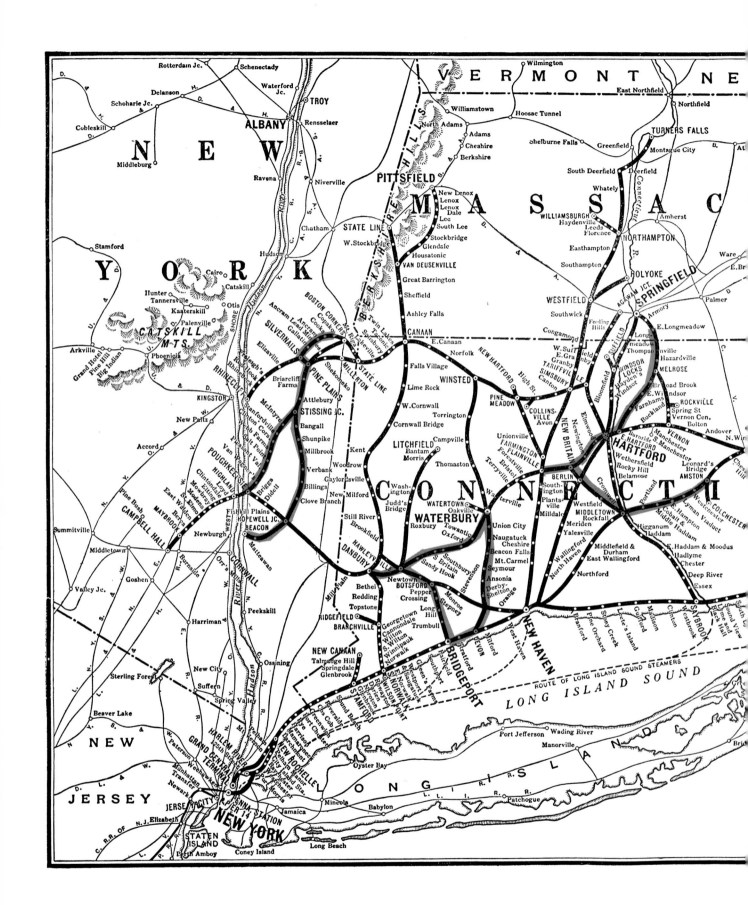

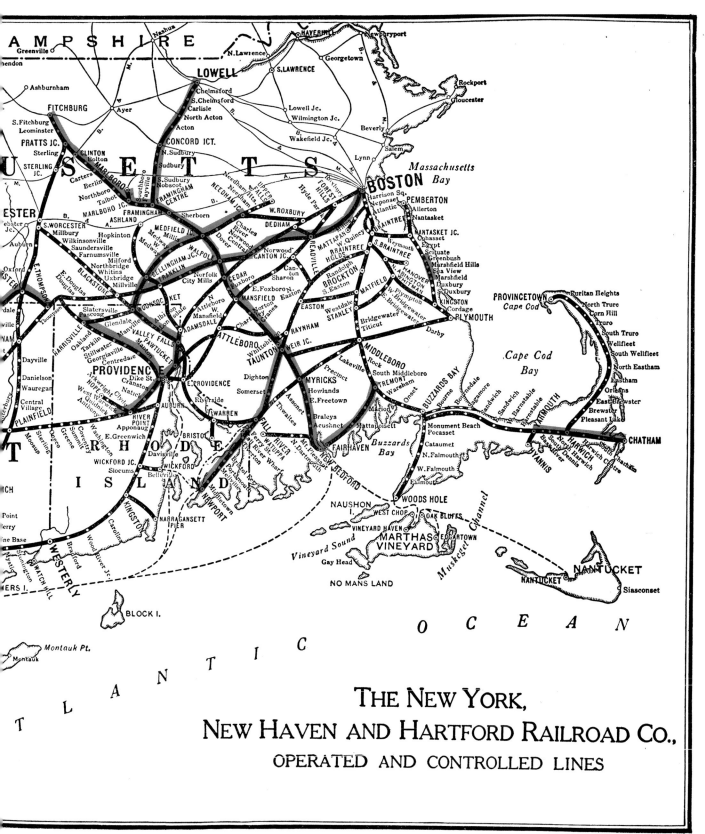

THE NEW YORK,
NEW HAVEN AND HARTFORD RAILROAD CO.,
OPERATED AND CONTROLLED LINES

Heavy gray lines indicate the doodlebug runs of the New Haven.

New Haven—Author's Collection

125

Ninety seated passengers could be accommodated in the New Haven's 9104, a 1926 Brill product.   *Author's Collection*

competing with the motor bus with its rider appeal.

The result was in fact a railbus based on the Mack Type C-50 city bus, dubbed Type FCD in honor of Dumaine. The prototype, car 10, went into service in 1952. The bus body was a single-end design, but in fact the 40-foot-long car could operate in either direction, and often did. Its first assignment was between Boston and Blackstone, Mass., and it later saw service between Buzzards Bay and Woods Hole on Cape Cod, and eventually ran a shuttle service between Fall River and Taunton, Mass.

Dumaine ordered an additional nine cars. They were delivered in 1954 and were slightly longer, had center doors and couplers and MU connections on one end only. But only one of the new cars entered revenue service due to a change in New Haven management which saw Dumaine replaced by Patrick McGinnis who did not like railbuses.

The one car which did see service was No. 12, known as the *Little Shoreliner* (the RDC cars were called *Shoreliners*). Car 12 made a weekday run from Worcester to Providence, later cut back to Woonsocket-

Providence. This lasted only until 1956.

The RDC cars, on the other hand, were quite successful and the orignal 40 were joined by six more in 1956 made up into one train called the *Roger Williams*. The end RDC cars had special streamlined front ends. The

New Haven was absorbed into the ill-fated Penn Central Railroad and after th PC's bankruptcy, many of the same RDC cars saw continued service on operations taken over by Amtrak or Boston's Massachusetts Bay Transportation Authority.

Hood-fronted Brill unit 1919 was a copy of the Sykes car. It is shown at Plymouth, MA.   *P. Kutta Collection*

Prototype Mack railbus 10 initially excited New Haven officials, who ordered nine more. They were delivered, but a new management made scant use of them. *M. D. McCarter Collection*

A real curiosity in the streamlined age was this Besler-powered steam train, built in the New Haven shops in 1935. It pauses at Bridgeport, CT, on Nov. 11, 1936 while a mechanic peers at something under the front fender shroud.

George E. Votava

Goodyear-Zeppelin's only effort in the railway field was the motor-trailer COMET train, built for the New Haven in 1935. Here it is at Boston's South Station on July 4, 1936.

George E. Votava

With the famed Buzzard's Bay lift bridge in the background, two of the New Haven's highly-successful RDC cars take some spot time from their runs to Hyannis and Woods Hole on July 17, 1952. Cars are 21 and 25.
George E. Votava

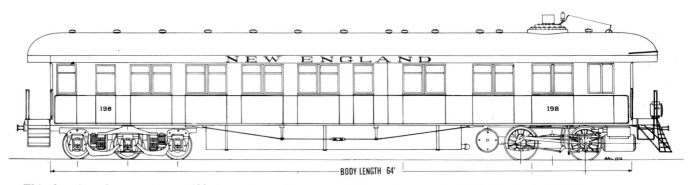

This drawing of composite car 198 shows the unit as converted to a steam motor by Schnectady in 1897.
A. A. Lawrence; Author's Collection

New York, New Haven & Hartford

ROAD NO.	BUILDER	DATE	BLDR. NO.	ENGINE & DRIVE	BODY TYPE	LGTH.	WT.	DISPOSITION	REMARKS
1098	Schnectady Wason	1897 1884	—	2cyl Alco Steam	17win Bag.-Pass.	64'	—	To Bellefonte Central, 1907	Orig. blt. as diner, motorized 1897
9000-02	Mack Osgd Bdly	1921	60003, 02, 04	Mack AC 68hp GM	7win Bag. 35p	34½'	12t	Scr. 1939	O-B bldr. no. 6630. 9001 re-eng. Knight 6
9003	Osgd Bdly Waterbury	1923	7195	Ricardo WB-GH	12win DE Bag. 60p	57½'	26½t	Rblt. tlr., 1933	Re-eng. Winston 110. Had matching tlr. blt. in Co. Shops
9004-13	St. Louis Sykes	1923	1328	Sterling 120hp GM	9win Bag. 45p	39½'	20½t	9009 rblt. Insp. car, 1931; others retired	9005, 09 had bag. sect. altered. All had hood fronts
9014-23	Brill	1924	22082	Sterling 120hp GM	10win Bag. 50p	51½'	25t	9015, 16, 19, 21, 23 rblt. tlr., 1933. 9020 wrecked 1926, rblt. Insp. car	Hood fronts removed on those rblt. to tlr. 9020 when rblt. re-eng. Winton 110.
9100 (9024)	Brill	1925	22076	Sterling 180hp GE	13win DE Bag. 65p	62'	41t	—	Del. as 9024, soon re-numbered
9101-05	Brill	1926	22329	Brill-WH 250hp GE	18win DE Bag. 90p	73'	54½t	All retired in 1940s and 1950s	—

ROAD NO.	BUILDER	DATE	BLDR. NO.	ENGINE & DRIVE	BODY TYPE	LGTH.	WT.	DISPOSITION	REMARKS
9106-11	Brill	1927	22358	Brill-WH 250hp GE	18win DE Bag. 90p	73'	54½t	All retired in 1940s and 1950s	—
9112	Brill	1926	22276	Brill-WH 250hp GE	18win DE Bag. 88p	73'	54t	—	Ex-NYO&W 803, acq. 12/30
9113	Brill	1925	22233	Brill-WH	12win	60'	47t	Rblt. Insp. car, 2/40	Ex-NYO&W 802, acq. 4/32
9914	Brill	1926	22277	Brill-WH 250hp GE	15win RPO Bag. 69p	73'	55t	Ret. 8/46	Ex-NYO&W 804, acq. 7/35
9200 9202	Goodyear Zeppelin	1935	—	WH-Beard 400hp DE	6win CE 48p	74'	126t (total)	—	Power unit cars "Comet." Had matching tlr. 9201
9210	Co. Shops	1935	—	Besler 2cyl. 550hp steam	16win Bag. 64p	83'	90½t	—	Rblt. from coach, had matching tlr. Last steam railcar built in USA
10	Mack	1952	1001	Mack-GE 200hp DE	11win C-50 bus, 45p	40'	20t	To Spain, 6/67	Type FCD; Clark trucks
11-19	Mack	1954	1002-10	Mack-GE 175hp DE	12win CE bus, 51p	43½'	25t	13-14 to Remington Arms, '61; 18-19 to Sperry Rail Svc., '58. 10-12, 14, 16, 17 to Spain, 6/63	Type FCD; St. Louis PCC trucks; dbl. end, MU control. Train door rear end
20-24	Budd	1952	5501-05	2-GM6-280 275hp DH	RDC-1 89p	85'	59t	20 wrecked, 21-24 to PC 66-69	21-23 ultimately became Amtrak 17-18
25-27	Budd	1952	5605-07	2-GM6-280 275hp DH	RDC-1 89p	85'	59t	To PC 70-72	—
28-30	Budd	1953	5706-08	2-GM6-280 275hp DH	RDC-1 89p	85'	59½t	28-29 to PC 73-74. 30 wrecked	PC 74 wrecked
31-42	Budd	1953	5709-20	2-GM6-280 275hp DH	RDC-1 89p	85'	59t	31-34 to PC 75-78; 35 wrecked; 36-42 to PC 36-42	34 became AMT 20; 36-39, AMT 10-13; 41, AMT 14; 31, 33 became MBTA 75, 77
43-48	Budd	1953	5801-06	2-GM6-280 275hp DH	RDC-1 89p	85'	59t	To PC 43-48	PC 45 to B&M, 1973, for parts. 44 became AMT 15; 48, AMT 16
120-21	Budd	1952	5608-09	2-GM6-280 275hp DH	RDC-2 Bag. 70p	85'	59½t	To PC 81, 82, then AMT 35, 36	—
125-27	Budd	1953	5702-04	2-GM6-280 275hp DH	RDC-3 RPO Bag. 48p	85'	61t	To PC 92-94. 126 became SEPTA (Reading) 9169	—
128-30	Budd	1953	5818-20	2-GM6-280 275hp DH	RDC-3 RPO Bag. 48p	85'	61t	To PC 95-97; 129 became SEPTA 9170	129 ultimately to Pittsburgh (PAT)
135-37	Budd	1953	5901-03	2-GM6-280 275hp DH	RDC-4 RPO-Bag.	74'	56½t	Cannibalized for parts	—
140-41	Budd	1956	—	2-GM6-280 275hp DH	RDC-1	—	—	To PC 83-84, then AMT	"Roger Williams" control units, streamlined nose
160-63	Budd	1956	—	2-GM6-280 275hp DH	RDC-1	—	—	To PC 85-88; 162 became AMT 29	"Roger Williams" coaches

Trailers

ROAD NO.	BUILDER	DATE	BLDR. NO.	ENGINE & DRIVE	BODY TYPE	LGTH.	WT.	DISPOSITION	REMARKS
9201	Goodyr.-Zep.	1935	—	—	8win 64p	58½'		—	"Comet" tlr.
9211	Co. Shops	1935	—	—	22win 88p	80'	66t	—	trailer for 9210, round end

In addition, motors 9003, 9015, 9016, 9019, 9021, 9023 rblt. to trailers in Co. Shops, 1933. All but 9003 had 16 win., seated 48. Tlr. 9003 had 16 win., bag. sect., 60p. All but 9016 ret. 4/52; 9016 ret. 2/43.

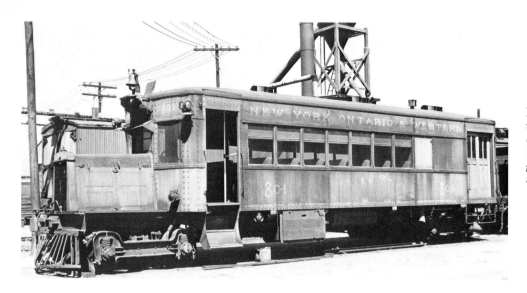

By the time this photo was taken of New York, Ontario & Western's Sykes car 801 in 1937, most of the paint was gone. It is shown in the yards at Middletown, NY.

George E. Votava

New York, Ontario & Western

ROAD NO.	BUILDER	DATE	BLDR. NO.	ENGINE & DRIVE	BODY TYPE	LGTH.	WT.	DISPOSITION	REMARKS
801	St. Louis Sykes	1925	1328A	Sterling 175hp GM	8win Bag. 38p	42'	12t	Ret. 1939	—
802	Brill	1925	22233	Brill 250hp GE	13win Bag. 52p	60'	47t	To New Haven 9113, 4/32	—
803	Brill	1926	22276	Brill 250hp GE	18win Bag. 88p	73'	54t	To New Haven 9112, 12/30	—
804	Brill	1926	22277	Brill 250hp GE	14win RPO Bag. 69p	73'	55t	To New Haven 9114, 7/35	—

One of the Susquehanna's handsome double-enders stops at the Broadway Station, Paterson, NJ, on September 24, 1940.

Stephen D. Maguire Collection

Budd RDC M-2 was brand-new when it was photographed at Rochelle Park, NJ, on the Susquehanna. It later was sold to the Jersey Central.

George E. Votava

New York, Susquehanna & Western

ROAD NO.	BUILDER	DATE	BLDR. NO.	ENGINE & DRIVE	BODY TYPE	LGTH.	WT.	DISPOSITION	REMARKS
1001-02	ACF	1940	1941	Wau.-Hess 225hp DM	19win	76'	37t	1001 burned	Both double end
1003	ACF	1940	2023	2-Wau.-Hess 225hp DM	15win 69p	75'	45t	Traded to Budd, 1950	Ex-IC 131 "Miss Lou," acq. 1943
1004	ACF	1940	2023	2-Wau.-Hess 225hp DM	16win 71p	75'	50t	Traded to Budd, 1950	Ex-IC 130 "Illini," acq. 1943
1005	ACF	1941	2109	2-Wau.-Hess 225hp DM	19win 73p	75'	49t	Traded to Budd, 1950	Ex-IC 140 "Land O'Corn" front unit, acq. 1947
1006	ACF	1941	2110	Wau.-Hess 225hp DM	19win 73p	75'	45t	Traded to Budd, 1950	Ex-IC 141 "Land O'Corn" rear unit, rblt. to operate separately
3001	Brill	1926	22270	Brill 250hp GE	13win Bag. 62p	62½'	38t	To U.Rys. Havana, 1949	Ex-B&M 1171, acq. 11/40
3002	Brill	1928	—	2-Brill 300hp GE	16win Bag. 73p	75'	77t	To U.Rys. Havana, 1949	Ex-Cumb. & Penn. 101, acq. 1943. Rblt. to tlr.
5012	Bethlehem EMC	1931	— 473	Wint. 146 300hp GE	11win Bag. 44p	73½'	88t	Ret. to Erie, 1944	Leased from Erie, 1940. Now at Ohio Ry. Museum
M-1 -2	Budd	1950	5006-07	2-GM6-280 275hp DH	RDC-1	85'	58t	To CNJ 558-559, 4/58	—
M-3 -4	Budd	1950	5107-08	2-GM6-280 275hp DH	RDC-1	85'	58t	To CNJ 560-561, 4/58	—

131

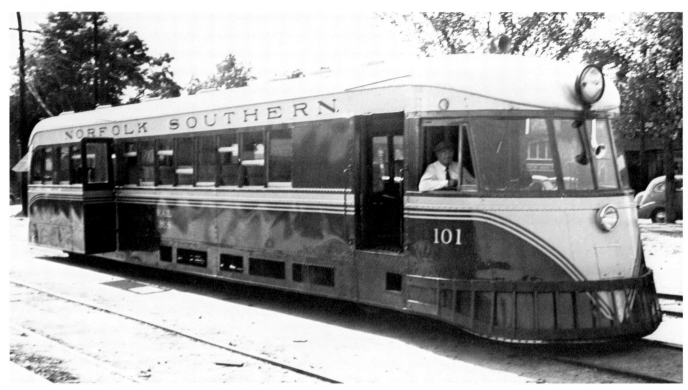

One of the earliest doodlebug streamlining efforts was Brill-built car 101 for the Norfolk Southern. This photo was taken in July, 1941, at Park Ave. Station, Norfolk.
Henry S. Libby Collection

Norfolk Southern

ROAD NO.	BUILDER	DATE	BLDR. NO.	ENGINE & DRIVE	BODY TYPE	LGTH.	WT.	DISPOSITION	REMARKS
90	McKeen	1909	—	McKeen 200hp GM	12win CE Bag. 64p	70'	39t	Scr. c.1942	Rblt. to electric car about 1923
101-02	Brill ACF	1933	23180	H-S 168hp GM	13win CE Bag. 53p	56½'	20½t	To Cuba	101 ''Carolinian,'' 102 ''Raleigh''
103-04	Brill ACF	1935	23227	H-S 180hp GM	13win CE Bag. 57p	56½'	21t	104 wrecked, 1944 103 to Cuba	103 ''Cavalier,'' 104 ''Princess Anne''
105-06	ACF	1935	1432	H-S 176hp GM	14win CE Bag. 57p	64'	26t	To Cuba	Ex-SAL 2024-2025, acq. 1944

Some of the cars sold to Cuba still in service.

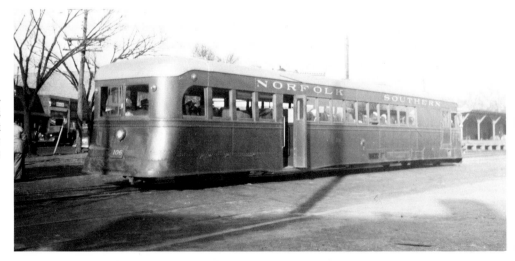

"Automotive" styling was evident in the rear-end treatment of ACF-built 106 of the Norfolk Southern. *E. T. Francis; A. E. Barker Collection*

Northern Pacific

In July of 1947 St. Louis-EMC-built B-23 putters along the Northern Pacific main line near Spokane, WA. The unit was still in the same baggage-RPO-passenger configuration as when built in 1929.   *W. C. Whittaker*

THE POLICIES of the Northern Pacific and its ultimate corporate partner, the Great Northern, with regard to rail motorcars were similar. Each dabbled superficially in the early types, bought a few of the lightweight cars of the early 1920s, and then invested heavily in the "standard" gas-electric cars of the middle-to-late 1920s.

About the only points of departure would be that the NP converted an old open-platform coach to a railcar, using the Oneida motorization package, and rebuilt several motors to trailers to be used behind motors.

Both NP and GN were noted for meticulous maintenance, although the "Big G" liked flashy, splashy paint jobs on both railcars and locomotives while the Northern Pacific projected a conservative but immaculate image.

NP Rail Motorcar Runs—1928

Route	Train No.	Mileage
Logan-Helena	235-236	74
Paradise-Spokane	305-306	186
Little Falls-Morris	29-30	87
Fargo-Edgeley	145-146	110
Staples-Oakes	111-112	151
Mandan-Mott	161-162	129
Billings-Bridger	209-210	44
Spokane-Coulee	315-316	125
Lewiston-Stites*	327-328	76
Pasco-Pendleton	349-350	54
Pasco-Walla Walla	351-2-3-4	64
Pasco-Attalia	349-350	12
Seattle-Bellingham	343-344	118
Tacoma-South Bend	591-592	111

*Camas Prairie Railroad

The NP used its cars on branches and secondary mainline runs throughout the system, including on the jointly (with the Union Pacific) owned Camas Prairie road in Washington and Idaho.

In later years, the NP was a modest user of Budd RDC cars, purchasing three units new and three used, including the two Western Pacific "Zephyrettes." All six were sold to Amtrak with three being quickly resold to the British Columbia Railway of Canada.

Car B-3 was Northern Pacific's first "standard era" motor, and was later converted to a shop switcher. *W. C. Whittaker*

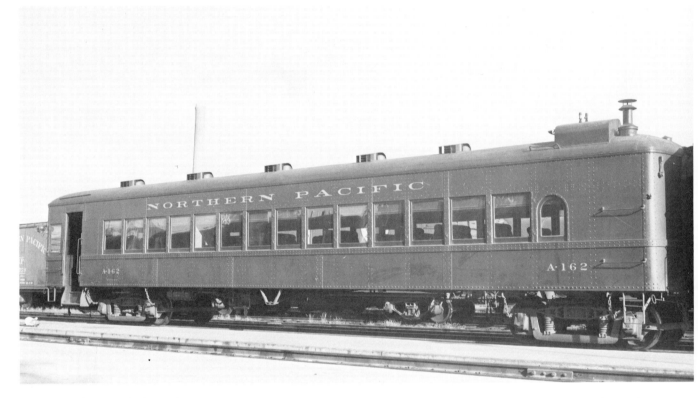

Motor B-10 was rebuilt to this trailer, A-162 (above) and is viewed at Mandan, ND, on May 28, 1958. Side details of NP car B-11 (right) show up clearly at Jamestown, ND, in May of 1958. *Both: W. C. Whittaker*

134

Car B-24, sans passenger accommodation, is at Staples, MN. It operated on trains 55 and 56 between Staples and Duluth-Superior. *James H. Harrison Collection*

Northern Pacific

ROAD NO.	BUILDER	DATE	BLDR. NO.	ENGINE & DRIVE	BODY TYPE	LGTH.	WT.	DISPOSITION	REMARKS
A-1	McKeen	1909	—	McKeen 200hp GM	10win CE Bag. 38p	55'	30t	Destroyed 6/22	—
B-1	Mack Cummings	1923	60008	Mack AC 68hp GM	7win Bag. 31p	34½'	10t	To Winnipeg Hydro, 1/29	Model AC, hood front
B-2	White Eckland	1922	6940	White 40hp GM	8win CE Bag. 57p	34'	12t	To Gen. Const. 2/29	—
B-3	St. Louis EMC	1925	1332 102	Wint. 106 175hp GE	12win Bag. 58p	59½'	39t	Rblt. to shop switcher, 6/56	To Northwest Steel Rolling Mills
B-4	Barn. & Smith Oneida	1890 1924	— —	2-Cont. 104hp GM	9win Bag. 32p	59'	40t	Ret. 3/34	Ex-coach 862, motorized by Oneida
B-5	St. Louis EMC	1925	1348B 105	Wint. 106 175hp GE	12win Bag. 42p	59½'	39t	Rblt. tlr. A-152, 1/44	—
B-6[1]	St. Louis EMC	1926	1348B 108	Wint. 106 175hp GE	12win RPO Bag. 47p	59½'	39t	Rblt. tlr. A-160, 3/39	—
B-6[2]	Std. Steel EMC	1929	328 344	Cat. D375 300hp DE	2win RPO Bag.	70'	55t	Ret. 5/56	Ex-Minn. & Int. M-1, acq. 1941
B-7	St. Louis EMC	1926	1348B 107	Wint. 106 175hp GE	12win RPO Bag. 47p	59½'	39t	To Gilmour & Pittsburgh B-7, 5/31	—
B-8	St. Louis EMC	1926	1352 109	Wint. 106 175hp GE	12win Bag. 32p	59½'	39t	Rblt. tlr. A-155, 4/56	—
B-9 -10	St. Louis EMC	1926	1352 111-12	Wint. 106 175hp GE	12win Bag. 32p	59½'	39t	Rblt. tlr. A-161, 162, 1946	B-9 seated 42
B-11	St. Louis EMC	1926	1397 153	Wint. 106A 220hp GE	5win RPO Bag. 52p	73'	45½t	Ret. 4/62	—
B-12	St. Louis EMC	1926	1396 152	Wint. 106A 220hp GE	7win RPO Bag. 22p	73'	46t	Ret. 9/56	—
B-13	St. Louis EMC	1926	1396 151	Wint. 106A 220hp GE	7win RPO Bag. 29p	73'	46t	Ret. 4/62	—
B-14	St. Louis EMC	1927	1437 224	Wint. 120 275hp GE	9win RPO Bag. 32p	74'	52t	Scr. 7/57	—

ROAD NO.	BUILDER	DATE	BLDR. NO.	ENGINE & DRIVE	BODY TYPE	LGTH.	WT.	DISPOSITION	REMARKS
B-15 -16	St. Louis EMC	1927	1438 225-6	Wint. 120 275hp GE	RPO-Bag.	74'	51t	Ret. 4/62, 12/61	B-15 re-eng. 1950, 275hp Cat. D375 D
B-17	Brill	1929	22697	H-S 275hp GE	11win Bag. 52p	77'	57½t	Ret. 10/45	—
B-18 -19	Std. Steel EMC	1929	328 345-6	Wint. 146 300hp GE	8win RPO Bag. 32p	77'	63t	Ret. 12/63, 12/61	—
B-20 -22	St. Louis EMC	1929	1512 410-12	Wint. 146 300hp GE	9win RPO Bag. 34p	77'	64½t	Ret. 12/61, 9/56, 12/61	B-20 weighed 63½t; B-21 had 7 win.
B-23	St. Louis EMC	1929	1513 413	Wint. 146 300hp GE	6win RPO Bag. 20p	77'	64t	Ret. 9/56	—
B-24 -25	St. Louis EMC	1930	1514 415-16	2-Wint. 146 300hp GE	RPO-Bag.	77'	83t	B-24 scr. 7/57; B-25 burned 8/32	—
B-26	St. Louis EMC	1930	1515 414	Wint. 146 300hp GE	10win RPO Bag. 44p	77'	63t	Scr. 10/59	—
B-30	Budd	1955	6001	2-GM6-280 275hp DH	RDC-2 Bag. 60p	85'	59t	To Amtrak 30, 1973	—
B-31	Budd	1950	5008	2-GM6-280 275hp DH	RDC-2 Bag. 60p	85'	59t	To Amtrak 31, 1973	Ex-West. Pacific 375, acq. 4/62
B-32	Budd	1950	5010	2-GM6-280 275hp DH	RDC-2 Bag. 60p	85'	59t	To Amtrak 32, 1973	Ex-West. Pacific 376, acq. 4/62
B-40	Budd	1955	6017	2-GM6-280 275hp DH	RDC-3 Bag. 48p	85'	59t	To Amtrak	Not used by Amtrak, resold to Brit. Col. Ry.
B-41	Budd	1956	6507	2-GM6-280 275hp DH	RDC-3 Bag. 48p	85'	59t	To Amtrak	Not used by Amtrak, resold to Brit. Col. Ry.
B-42	Budd	1952	5701	2-GM6-280 275hp DH	RDC-3 Bag. 48p	85'	59t	To Amtrak	Ex-Duluth, S. Shore & Atl. 1, acq. 3/63. Not used by Amtk., to B.C. Ry.

NOTE: Motors B-5, B-6[1], B-8, B-9, B-10, rblt. to tlrs. A-152, A-160, A-153, A-161, A-162 in Co. Shops in 1944, 1946, 1939, 1946, 1946. A-152, 153 were 11win 57p. A-160-162 were 15win Bag. 59p.

To show the infinite variety of passenger space found on the NP doodlebugs, here is the B-6 with seats for only about eight passengers, at Mandan, ND, in May of 1959.

W. C. Whittaker

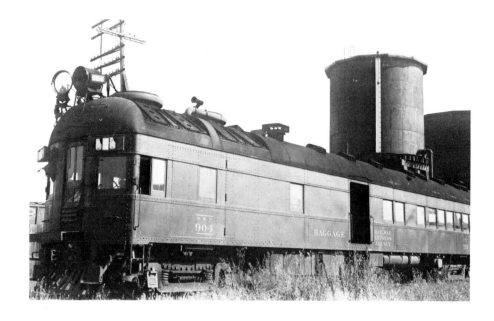

The NWP Brill units had quite a boomer career. Unit 904 was one of a pair that migrated from NWP to parent SP to the Pacific Electric. *Author's Collection*

Northwestern Pacific

ROAD NO.	BUILDER	DATE	BLDR. NO.	ENGINE & DRIVE	BODY TYPE	LGTH.	WT.	DISPOSITION	REMARKS
850	Co. Shops	1915	—	Thomas 4 60hp GM	16p	17½'	5½t	—	—
851	Co. Shops	1915	—	Overland 4 26hp GM	10p	9'	1t	—	—
900	Gen. Elec. Wason	1912	3735 12050	GE 16A5 175hp GE	17win Bag. 73p	72'	55t	To Bridge Ry. 01	Ex-Visalia Elec. 450, orig. Dan Patch 9. Re-eng. Sterling 225hp DE ca. 1920
901	Pullman EMC	1930	6297 435	Wint. 148 400hp GE	10win Bag. 34p	76½'	79t	To SP 12, 6/35, then SSW 18, 8/41	—
902	Pullman EMC	1930	6297 437	Wint. 148 400hp GE	10win Bag. 34p	76½'	79t	To SP 13, 6/35, then CM St.P. & P 5941[2], 8/41	—
903-04	Brill	1930	22789	2-HS 300hp GE	10win Bag. 34p	76½'	87t	To SP 14, 15, 1941, then Pac. Elec. 1648-49, 1943	—

The NWP's only General Electric car, No. 900, was sold to the Bridge Railway for maintenance service on the San-Francisco-Oakland Bay Bridge. *Author's Collection*

Panama Railroad

THE PANAMA RAILROAD is the world's oldest and shortest (47.6 miles) transcontinental railroad, and shares with the world's longest transcontinental railroad (in Soviet Russia) its five-foot gauge.

Intended as a short cut from the east coast to the west, particularly for those going to the California gold fields, the road was chartered in New York in 1849, and opened for traffic January 28, 1855. In May of 1904 the United States government, in anticipation of the building of the Panama Canal, bought control of the railroad.

During the construction of the canal the road was operated by the ISMU Canal Commission and since the canal pretty much followed the route of the railroad, it was necessary to almost completely rebuild it.

During the reconstruction period, the Commission acquired a fleet of at least four Stover railcars, which were used as inspection and official cars. The most elaborate of these, which had been the personal car of Gen. George W. Goethals, the officer in charge of building the canal, was turned over to the Panama Railroad when it resumed regular operation.

This car, which had been known as the "Yellow Peril," became car No. 1. It

Edwards-built car 6 and matching trailer 6A enter the Panama Railroad mainline from Balboa roundhouse, 1947. *James H. Harrison Collection*

was used primarily as an official car for the governor of the Canal Zone, but sometime during the 1920s it began to provide special trips to accommodate Panama Canal pilots.

A couple of the smaller Edwards

Panama Railroad

ROAD NO.	BUILDER	DATE	BLDR. NO.	ENGINE & DRIVE	BODY TYPE	LGTH.	WT.	DISPOSITION	REMARKS
1	Stover	1908	—	Stover GM	Hood front bus	—	—	Scr. 1932	Ex-Panama Canal Comm. 4, inspection car used in passenger service
2	Edwards	1927	—	Buda	7win Bag. 30p	32'	11t	Scr. 1938	—
3	Edwards	1928	—	Buda	8win Bag. 30p	32'	11t	—	Type 10, open rear platform
4	Edwards	1929	—	Buda	8win Bag. 30p	32'	12½t	Scr. 1948	Type 10, open rear platform
5	Edwards	1936	185	Buda	12win Bag. 46p	46'	21t	—	Type 20, open rear platform, streamlined front
6	Edwards	1939	—	2-Buda 630 125hp GM	12win Bag. 46p	50t	27½t	—	Type 20, open rear platform, streamlined front. Had matching tlr., 6-A
8	Stover	1908	—	Stover	Bus	—	—	—	Rebodied 1925. Ex-Panama C.C. 8 (?)

Trailers

ROAD NO.	BUILDER	DATE	BLDR. NO.	ENGINE & DRIVE	BODY TYPE	LGTH.	WT.	DISPOSITION	REMARKS
6A	Edwards	1939	—	—	56p	—	22½t	—	—

Type 10 cars were purchased to augment this service and the general public was allowed to ride, on a space-available basis. In 1935 a streamlined Edwards Type 20 car was acquired, and in 1938 another of this type arrived, along with a matching trailer. These cars were used largely for special parties, VIP groups and passengers from cruise ships calling at Panama. This service was continued until sometime in the 1950s.

In line with the turnover of the canal to the Republic of Panama, the railroad was nationalized and is now part of the Ferrocarril Nacional de Chiriqui, which now operates all of the railroads in Panama.

Here is a closeup of Panama Railroad trailer 6A at the Balboa roundhouse, taken in 1947.   *James H. Harrison Collection*

Pennsylvania Railroad

A S MIGHT BE expected, the "Standard Railroad of the World" operated one of the earliest examples of the self-propelled railcar. In July of 1861, Baldwin built a 4-4-0 tank engine in which the cab roof and engine frame were extended back to encompass a five-window open-platform coach body with a short four-wheel truck under the coach section.

Apparently the coal was carried in the forward part of the coach body, for the engine had no tender section.

This unit, numbered 217, was most likely used as an inspection car; it did not last long on company records and no mention can be found of it in revenue passenger service. The locomotive was soon rebuilt along conventional lines and the coach section wound up with a

large four-wheel caboose truck under it.

There is evidence that steam cars were built for lines that were, or became, subsidiaries of PRR including the Pittsburgh, Fort Wayne & Chicago and the Pittsburgh, Cincinnati, Chicago & St. Louis. These units had the steam boiler enclosed within the coach body. Again, records do not indicate where these cars were used in revenue ser-

This might have been the prototype for a whole fleet, but only the 4663 was modernized by the PRR with a streamlined front.   *James H. Harrison Collection*

Ultra-lightweight Budd railcar 4689 has its photo taken after being fitted with steel wheel two-axle trucks.

Arthur B. Johnson

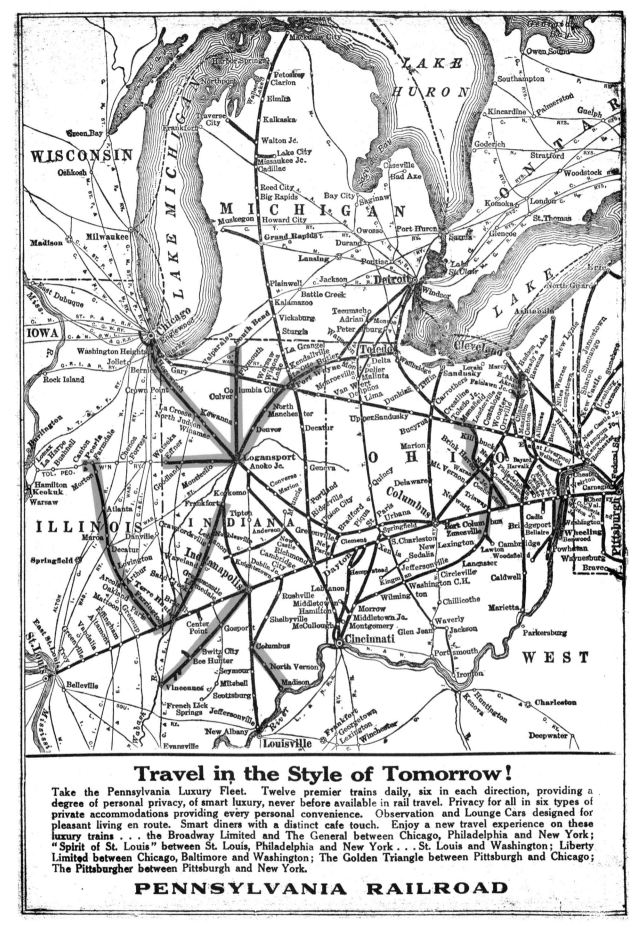

Travel in the Style of Tomorrow!

Take the Pennsylvania Luxury Fleet. Twelve premier trains daily, six in each direction, providing a degree of personal privacy, of smart luxury, never before available in rail travel. Privacy for all in six types of private accommodations providing every personal convenience. Observation and Lounge Cars designed for pleasant living en route. Smart diners with a distinct cafe touch. Enjoy a new travel experience on these luxury trains . . . the Broadway Limited and The General between Chicago, Philadelphia and New York; "Spirit of St. Louis" between St. Louis, Philadelphia and New York . . . St. Louis and Washington; Liberty Limited between Chicago, Baltimore and Washington; The Golden Triangle between Pittsburgh and Chicago; The Pittsburgher between Pittsburgh and New York.

PENNSYLVANIA RAILROAD

Heavy gray lines indicate the doodlebug runs on the Pennsylvania. Reproduced from THE OFFICIAL RAILWAY GUIDE® © 1939 NRPCo.

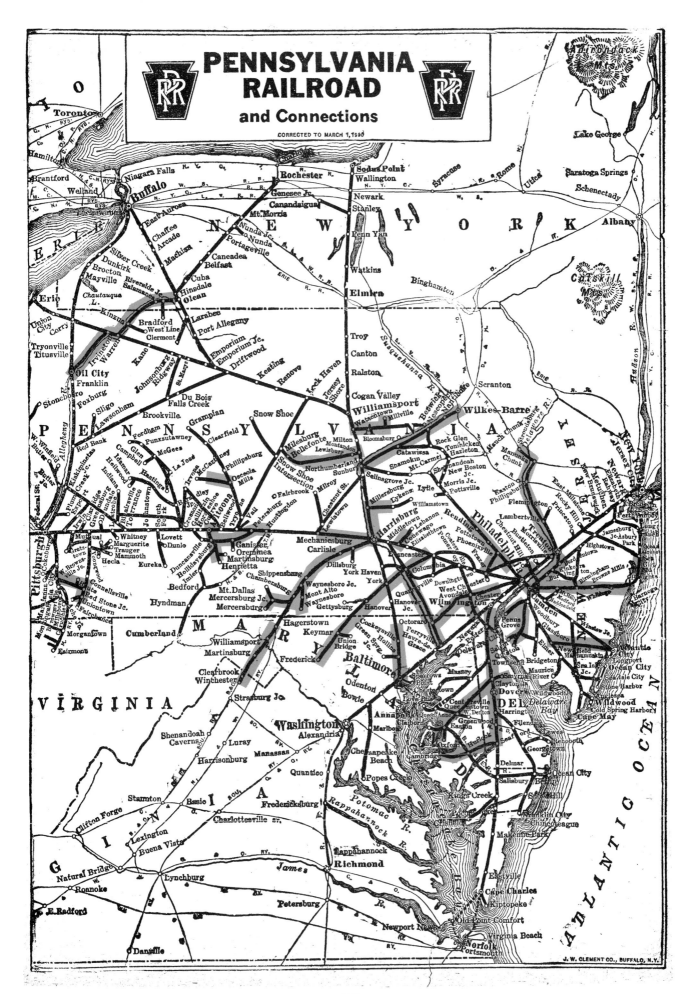

PENNSYLVANIA RAILROAD
and Connections

CORRECTED TO MARCH 1, 1930

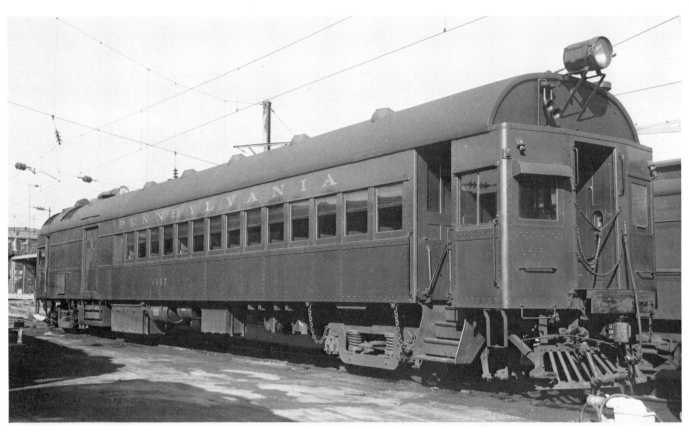

Combo car 4667 (Above) was typical of the heavy Pennsylvania Railroad railcars. This was one of five cars built by Brill in 1930. Motor 4657 (Below) is backing to the Calvert Street Station in Baltimore on June 15, 1946.

Author's Collection; C. A. Brown

vice; in all probability they did not last long.

After these early failures, the Pennsy adopted a very conservative policy toward the rail motorcar, buying only two of the early 20th century cars, a McKeen 70-foot unit and one of the small, four-wheel Fairbanks-Morse Model 24s.

From 1922 until 1930, however, the company acquired a rather sizable fleet of gas-mechanical, gas-electric and finally, oil-electric cars, to the number of about 50. These cars were used all over the system, from a rather unique all-railcar commuter service from Baltimore to Parkton, Md., to long rural runs, e.g., Terre Haute, Ind., to Peoria, Ill., 176 miles.

The PRR did have one motor train with a name: *The Bullet*, operating between Wilmington, Del., and Easton, Md. The usual consist was a Brill Model 660 pulling two P-54 coaches.

Although the motor cars covered many a run requiring Railway Post Office service, none of the PRR motor cars had an RPO compartment. The usual procedure was to use a P-54 class baggage-RPO car as a trailer.

Unlike most railroads, the Pennsy did not usually designate motor car runs as such in public timetables, though there were a few exceptions.

The Pennsylvania's final purchase of rail motorcars came in 1933 when two Budd-Michelin cars, with unique pneumatic rubber-tired trucks, were acquired. Despite being rebuilt with conventional trucks, the Budd cars were never successful. One of the oil-electric cars, number 4663, was rebuilt into a shovel-front streamliner perhaps as a prototype for a planned fleet of such units. It remained a one-of-a-kind.

Although the PRR never purchased a single Budd RDC car after World War II, its subsidiary, the Pennsylvania-Reading-Seashore lines, did buy 12 of them.

Like other railroads, the PRR phased out nearly all motorcar runs in the 1940s and 1950s, though one run, from Camden to Trenton, in New Jersey, held on until 1962. Since the PRR operated a sizable electrified territory, it was able to utilize a number of railcars as electric overhead tower cars after their days as passenger cars had ended.

Pullman and Brill collaborated on PRR 4658 and mates in the 4650 series.

Tom Gray

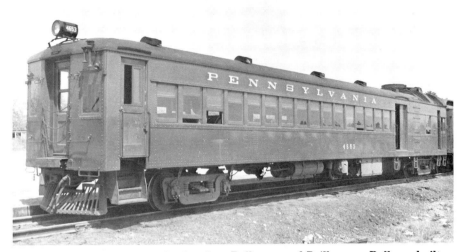

Somewhat lighter in weight than late Pullmans and Brills were Pullman-built 4650-62, of which 4653 (top) is seen at Toms River, NJ, in 1952. Pullman 4664 (below) wound up as a Penn Central M/W car, as shown at Trenton NJ in June of 1968.
Louia A. Marre; Richard S. Short

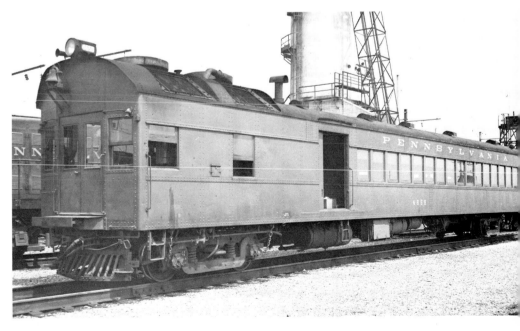

Pennsylvania Railroad

ROAD NO.	BUILDER	DATE	BLDR. NO.	ENGINE & DRIVE	BODY TYPE	LGTH.	WT.	DISPOSITION	REMARKS
4635-36	Brill	1926	22385	Brill-WH 250hp GE	13win DE Bag. 62p	62'	45t	4635 to PRSL 400; 4636 scr. 1948	Class GEW 250A, Model 250
4637-42	Brill	1927	22652	2-Brill-WH 175hp GE	16win DE Bag. 73p	76'	66t	4639 to tower car, 4641 sold 1959, others scrapped	Class GEW 350; 4640-42 dieselized 1943
4643	Brill Mack	1927	22653 161003	2-Mack AP 120hp GE	14win Bag. 77p	77'	57½t	Burned 11/34	Class GEW 240
4644-49	Pullman EMC	1928	6159 306-11	Wint. 120 275hp DE	16win DE Bag. 77p	76'	61t	4644 to tower car, 4648 wrecked 7/40	Class GEW 275; 4649 weighed 64½t
4650-62	Pullman Brill	1928	6202 22697	2-Wint. 110 175hp GE	16win DE Bag. 77p	76'	64½t	4651 to tower car, 4654 to PRSL 401	Class OEG 350; all but 4654 re-eng. w. 2-Cummins diesels 1941-43
4663-64	Pullman WH	1929	6219	WH-Beard 330hp OE	15win DE Bag. 72p	76'	71½t	4664 weighed 66½t, to tower car, 1952	Class OEW 330A; dieselized
4665	Pullman EMC	1929	6218 348	Wint. 148 400hp GE	15win Bag. 72p	76'	70½t	Scr. 1952	Class OEG 400
4666-70	Brill	1930	22848	Brill 660 415hp OE	15win DE Bag. 66p	77½'	69½t	4666, 4667 to museums	Class OEG 415; re-eng. Ham. diesel, 1942
4688	Budd	1933	—	Cummins 125hp OE	11win Bag. 30p	50'	12½t	To W&OD, 1943	Class OEG 125 then GEG 190. Re-eng. 1936 w/Lycoming 190hp Gas.
4689	Budd	1933	—	Cummins 125hp OE	12win 46p	50'	11t	To W&OD, 1943	Class OEG 125 then MPB 28. Goodyear pneu. railcar tires on 6-wh. trucks. Rblt. w/28hp aux. eng., 1936.
4701	McKeen	1910	—	McKeen 200hp GM	13win CE Bag. 80p	70'	34t	To Ill. Cent. (?)	—
4728	Brill	1925	22294	Wint. 110 175hp GM	13win Bag. 34p	55'	29t	Sold 1937	Class GM 175, Model 75
4729	Brill	1925	22255	Wint. 110 175hp GM	13win Bag. 41p	55'	29t	Scr. 1937	Class GM 175A
4731-33	Brill	1925	22249	Brill-WH 250hp GE	13win Bag. 62p	62'	45t	4732 rblt. tlr. 1944	Class GEW 250, Model 250
4734	Brill	1925	22201	Wint. 110 175hp GM	13win Bag. 51p	55'	27t	Scr. 1937	Class GM 175B, Model 75
4735	Brill	1925	22183	Wint. 110 175hp GM	13win Bag. 41p	55'	27t	Scr. 1937	Class GM 175C
4736-37	Brill	1924	22137	Sterling 115hp GM	10win Bag. 26p	43½'	20t	Scr. 1936; 4637 seated 38	Class GM 115, Model 65
4738	Brill Mack	1921	21368 60005	Mack AC 64hp GM	7win Bag. 35p	32½'	10t	To Art. & Jell., 1931, Buff. Creek & Gauley	Class GM 68A, Model AC. Ex-Lewis, Milt. & Watson, acq. 11/28. Now at Strasburg Museum
4739	Brill	1923	21915	Cont. 14H 100hp GM	9win CE Bag. 34p	44½'	16t	Scr. 1935	Class GM 100, Model 55
4740	Brill	1923	21916	Midwest 39 68hp GM	10win Bag. 30p	43½'	15t	To US Army, 1935	Class GM 68A; to Aberdeen Proving Ground
4741	Brill	1923	21917	Midwest 39 68hp GM	10win Bag. 40p	43½'	15t	To tower car, 1931	Class GM 68C, Model 55
4742-44	Brill Service	1922	21651	Midwest 39 68hp GM	10win Bag. 38p	43½'	15t	4744 to US Army, 1935, seated 30; 4743 seated 34	Class GM 68, 68B, 68A. Model 55
4965	Brill Sheffield	1909	16790	F-M 50hp GM	9win Bag. 35p	26'	12½t	—	—

Trailers

ROAD NO.	BUILDER	DATE	BLDR. NO.	ENGINE & DRIVE	BODY TYPE	LGTH.	WT.	DISPOSITION	REMARKS
4730	Brill	1925	22256	—	16win 72p	53'	21½t	—	Class P42
4732	Brill	1925	22249	—	20win 93p	62'	45t	—	Class P55; ex-motor 4732 rblt. 1944

Hand-me-down from co-parent Pennsylvania Railroad was PRSL 400, taken at Woodbury, NJ on July 27, 1946.   *C. A. Brown*

For some three decades the remaining South Jersey passenger service has been given by Budd RDC cars. Here is the PRSL M-407 at Atlantic City on May 29, 1966.
George E. Votava

Pennsylvania - Reading - Seashore Lines

ROAD NO.	BUILDER	DATE	BLDR. NO.	ENGINE & DRIVE	BODY TYPE	LGTH.	WT.	DISPOSITION	REMARKS
400	Brill	1925	22385	Brill-WH 250hp GE	13win Bag. 60p	60'	47t	—	Ex-PRR 4635
401	Pullman	1928	6202	WH-Beard 350hp OE	16win Bag. 74p	76'	65½t	To FC de Tunas S.A., Cuba	Ex-PRR 4654
M402-07	Budd	1950	5101-06	GMC 275hp DH	RDC-1	85'	—	To NJ Transit except M404, burned 2/50	—
M408-11	Budd	1951	5307-10	GMC 275hp DH	RDC-1	85'	—	To NJ Transit 5185-88	—
M412-13	Budd	1951	5041-02	GMC 275hp DH	RDC-1	85'	—	M412 burned 2/58; M413 to NJ Transit	—

Pere Marquette
(Merged into Chesapeake & Ohio)

ROAD NO.	BUILDER	DATE	BLDR. NO.	ENGINE & DRIVE	BODY TYPE	LGTH.	WT.	DISPOSITION	REMARKS
17	Gen. Elec. Wason	1913	3737 10250	GE-GM1C1 175hp GE	— Bag. 91p	70'	49t	Off roster by 1930	—

Reading

Reading car 73, running as train 910 from Lancaster to Reading, makes the stop at Lancaster Junction on March 6, 1937.
John J. Bowman Jr.

Reading RDC Runs—1961

Route	Train No.	Mileage
Philadelphia-Newark	2 rt	81
Philadelphia-Newtown	3 rt	26.3
Fox Chase-Newtown	3 rt	15.2
Philadelphia-Bethlehem	3 rt	56.6
Lansdale-Bethlehem	4 rt	32.2
Philadelphia-Pottsville	2 rt	93.6
Philadelphia-Reading	4 rt	58.8
Pottsville-Reading	3 rt	34.8

Side grilles identify Beth-
lehem-built motorcar for
the Reading. Car 4071
(above) is at Woodbury,
NJ, on July 27, 1946. High-
browed 4068 is an equally-
distinctive Brill product.
*C. A. Brown; Author's
Collection*

Reading had a group of
10 lightweight trailers,
all but one built by Brill.
The 86 is shown at Phil-
adelphia in June of
1951. As far as can be
determined these were
the only control trail-
ers ever used by a U.S.
railroad in railcar ser-
vice. *W. C. Whittaker*

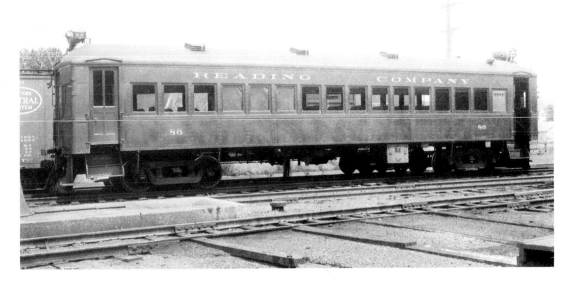

Reading Railroad

ROAD NO.	BUILDER	DATE	BLDR. NO.	ENGINE & DRIVE	BODY TYPE	LGTH.	WT.	DISPOSITION	REMARKS
65	Budd	1932	—	Cummins 125hp DE	11win 47p	50'	11½t	Scr. ca. 1943	6 wh. trucks, Michelin rubber tires
4066 (66)	Brill	1930	22843	2-HS 300hp GE	8win RPO Bag. 30p	75½'	81½t	Ret. 1948	—
4067-68 (67-68)	Brill	1929	22746	2-Brill-WH 250hp GE	8win RPO Bag. 30p	75½'	64t	4067 ret. 1957; 4068 ret. 1960	Re-eng. 2-Cum. 250hp D., 1946-7. 4068 weighed 78t, seated 47
4069 (69)	Brill	1929	22747	2-Brill-WH 250hp GE	8win RPO Bag. 30p	75½'	77t	Ret. 1957	Re-eng. 2-Cum. 250hp D., 4/47
4070 (70)	Bethlehem WH	1929	—	WH-Beard 300hp OE	7win RPO Bag. 26p	75'	69t	Ret. 1948	—
4071-72 (71-72)	Bethlehem Mack	1929	162004 -5	3-Mack AP 120hp GE	13win Bag. 71p	75½'	57½t	Ret. 1957	Re-eng. 3-Cum. HB15 D., 1946-7
4073 (73)	Brill	1929	22721	2-HS 350 300hp GE	8win RPO Bag. 30p	75½'	81t	Ret. 1949	—
4074 (74)	Bethlehem WH	1929	—	WH-Beard 300hp OE	7win RPO Bag. 41p	75½'	68½t	Ret. 1948	—
4075 (75)	Brill	1928	22655	Brill-WH 250hp GE	8win RPO Bag. 39p	75½'	68½t	Ret. 1946	—
4076 (75)	Mack Cummings	1928	162002	3-Mack AP 120hp GE	8win Bag. 39p	75½'	67½t	Scr. 11/45	—
4077-79 (77-79)	Brill	1927	22445	Brill-WH 250hp GE	8win RPO Bag. 32p	62'	52t	Ret. 1953, 1949, 1959	4078 weighed 49t, 4079 weighed 55t
4080 (80)	Brill	1925	22104	Brill-WH 250hp GE	13win Bag. 50p	62'	45t	Ret. 1953	—
98	Brill Service	1923	21869	Midwest 68hp GM	10win Bag. 31p	42½'	15½t	—	Model 55
99	Brill Service	1923	21675	Midwest 68hp GM	9win Bag. 30p	42½'	15½t	Rblt. work car, 2/31	Model 55
9151-52	Budd	1962	7011-12	2-GM6-280 300hp DH	RDC-1 89p	85'	59t	To SEPTA	—
9153-62	Budd	1962	7001-10	2-GM6-280 300hp DH	RDC-1 89p	85'	59t	To SEPTA	—
9163	Budd	1951	5410	2-GM6-280 275hp DH	RDC-1 89p	85'	59t	To SEPTA	Ex-Lehigh Valley 40, acq. 11/62
9164	Budd	1955	6104	2-GM6-280 275hp DH	RDC-1 89p	85'	59t	To SEPTA	Ex-Boston & Maine 6109, acq. 10/65
9165	Budd	1955	6008	2-GM6-280 275hp DH	RDC-2 Bag. 60p	85'	59½t	To SEPTA	Ex-Boston & Maine 6205, acq. 10/65. Snack bar in ex-bag. sect.
9166	Budd	1958	6819	2-GM6-280 275hp DH	RDC-3	85'	61t	To SEPTA	Ex-Boston & Maine 6305, acq. 8/66. Snack bar in ex-RPO/Bag. sect.

Trailers

ROAD NO.	BUILDER	DATE	BLDR. NO.	ENGINE & DRIVE	BODY TYPE	LGTH.	WT.	DISPOSITION	REMARKS
81	Brill	1927	22446	—	60p	51'	23t	Ret. 1953	Had MU controls
82	Cummings	1928	—	—	16win 73p	53½'	31t	—	Had MU controls
83	Brill	1928	22722	—	—	54'	30t	—	—
84	Brill	1928	22723	—	—	54'	30t	—	—
85-87	Brill	1928	22724	—	16win 73p	56½'	34t	—	Had MU controls
88-90	Brill	1930	22791	—	16win 73p	56½'	32½t	—	Had MU controls

The two Richmond, Fredericksburg & Potomac Brill cars are out to pasture in this photo, circa 1949.   *Gordon E. Lloyd*

Richmond, Fredericksburg & Potomac

ROAD NO.	BUILDER	DATE	BLDR. NO.	ENGINE & DRIVE	BODY TYPE	LGTH.	WT.	DISPOSITION	REMARKS
M-1	Brill	1927	22639	2-Brill 275hp GE	9win Bag. 41p	73'	67½t	Ret. 1949	—
M-2	Brill	1929	22757	2-HS 300hp GE	9win Bag. 41p	73'	73t	Ret. 1949	—

Trailers

| T-11 | Brill | 1927 | 22640 | — | 82p | 73' | 32½t | Ret. 1949 | — |
| T-12 | Brill | 1929 | 22758 | — | 100p | — | 41t | Ret. 1949 | — |

Frisco Car 2112 looks as if it has factory fresh paint in this scene at Enid, Okla., circa 1912. The SLSF was an enthusiastic user of rail motorcars in the earliest years, and General Electric was a favorite builder.
R. H. Carlson

Frisco

This was the Frisco's first standard-era gas-electric car, EMC-built 2120. It is pictured at Ardmore, OK, on October 18, 1940, ready to depart to Hope, AR, via Hugo, OK.
John B. Fink Collection

THE RELATIONSHIP of the Frisco, the Missouri Pacific, and the Gulf Coast lines was complex. The Gulf Coast Lines extended from New Orleans to Brownsville, Texas, and was assembled in the early part of the century by B. F. Yoakum, who was at the time chairman of the Rock Island Lines and the Frisco. His aim was to create a system of railroads extending from Chicago to Mexico City.

The Frisco appears to be the agency that actually operated the Gulf Coast Lines, and when the Frisco purchased a large group of General Electric gas-electric rail motorcars in 1910-11, seven were assigned to the GCL.

In 1913, the Frisco was forced into bankruptcy, carrying with it the Gulf Coast Lines. Apparently GCL operations did not change as a result, and the gas-electrics remained in service. The Interstate Commerce Commission, however, ordered the receivers of the Frisco to divest the GCL.

In 1923 the Frisco had recovered and felt secure enough to try and re-establish itself in the Louisiana-Texas area. There was one problem: the Frisco had no physical connection with the GCL since one important part of the Yoakum scheme, a line from Baton Rouge, La., to Memphis, had never been built.

To remedy this situation, the Frisco proposed to purchase the International-Great Northern Railroad, whose main line extended from Longview, in northern Texas, to Laredo, on the Mexican border. It also had a secondary main line from Houston, where it connected with the GCL, to the Dallas-Fort Worth area where it connected with the Frisco.

At that time the I-GN was independent, although at one time it had been a part of the Missouri Pacific and still maintained very close ties with that company. As it happened, the MP and I-GN were violently opposed to the Frisco's plans and immediately appealed to the ICC.

The ICC apparently felt that the Frisco had been maintaining de facto control over the GCL despite the ICC's earlier command to divest. Not only did the ICC deny the Frisco the right to acquire I-GN, but gave the MP permission to purchase both I-GN and the Gulf Coast Lines! This maneuver was accomplished by the MP first acquiring the GCL and having GCL in turn buy the I-GN.

SLSF Rail Motorcar Runs — 1933

Route	Train No.	Mileage
Oklahoma City-Quanah	409-410	183.6
Hugo-Hope-Ardmore	776-777	223
Tulsa-Enid-Vernon	609-610	329.9
Kansas City-Springfield via Bolivar	21-20	194.4
Arcadia-Cherryvale	179, 177-178	95.8
Jonesboro-Armorel	898-899	60.9
Poplar Bluff-Kennett	895-896	54
Sherman-Irving	817-818	65.1
Seymour-Mineral Wells	1-2	107.7

Over the years, the Frico had been very active in trying to expand. But for some rather dubious maneuvers during this period, it may well have become one of the dominant railroads in the country. The Frisco, for instance, was the original owner of the Atlantic & Pacific Railroad which had a land grant to build a line to the Pacific Coast. But after a brief liaison with the Santa Fe and a resulting bankruptcy, the Santa Fe ended up with this franchise and the Frisco lost any chance to get anywhere close to "Frisco."

The Gulf Coast Lines fiasco, and its problems with the ICC, was echoed in more recent times. After World War II, when the Central of Georgia came out of bankruptcy and its long affiliation with the Illinois Central terminated, the Frisco attempted to gain control of the road by purchasing its capital stock — again without formal ICC blessing. The result was that the C of G ultimately came under the control of the Southern Railroad.

At one time the Frisco controlled a rather strange group of short lines emanating from Brownsville, Texas. Apparently they were purchased in anticipation of the Gulf Coast Lines building into the tip of South Texas. These lines were the Brownsville Street and Interurban, the Brownsville & Matamoros Bridge Co. and the Rio Grande Ry.

The first two operated local service in the Brownsville area, with the S&IR using two of the very rare Barber gas cars, and the Bridge company had an open Fairbanks-Morse type 19 car. These three cars were numbered into the Frisco's fleet (2117-2119) but probably never got within 500 miles of the railroad.

The third line, which was to become in later (non-Frisco) years the Port Isabel & Rio Grande Valley, was a peculiar little narrow-gauge railway whose chief function seems to have been to haul water from the Brownsville area to a large Coast Guard station at Port Isabel.

It operated a weird-looking home-built gas car, but apparently for the short time it was controlled by the Frisco, it was independently managed since its equipment was never incorporated in the Frisco roster.

In the middle and late 1920s, a number of short lines were acquired. The Jonesboro, Lake City & Western, in Arkansas, had two used General Electric gas-electrics and a White railbus; the St. Louis, Kennett & South Eastern owned two Edwards cars, and the Butler county (among other items) had a demotorized Unit steam car.

The final line acquired was the Gulf, Texas & Western, in Texas. This line, which started pretty much nowhere, and ended in another nowhere, had a fleet of three Brill type 55 gas cars. It was the Frisco's intention to extend the line northward to connect with its line at Vernon, Texas, and extend southwards to its line in the Dallas-Fort Worth area.

But the depression of the 1930s ended any chance of this project being completed and the line was abandoned. With this string of bad luck in Texas, the Frisco sold its long branch from Fort Worth to Menard (219 miles) to the Santa Fe.

At one time or another the Frisco operated 21 of the General Electric gas-electrics, the greatest number operated by any railroad — although several that were assigned to the Gulf Coast Lines never operated on the Frisco itself.

Starting in 1925 a fleet of nine EMC-St. Louis and four Brill gas-electrics were purchased. In addition, one Brill gas-mechanical car and two Sykes gas-mechanical cars were acquired. These cars, plus an old wooden combo that had been modified with one of the Railway Motor Car's conversion kits, plus the second-hand equipment and the old GE cars made for a rather large fleet of rail motorcars in the period around 1930.

Several of the GE cars had been modified with what might be called a "motorman's cab" in the 1920s. The fleet was steadily diminished during the 1930s and 1940s and the last cars were scrapped in the mid-1950s as permission to terminate passenger service on the secondary lines was secured.

In 1922 the Frisco dabbled in lightweight motors, ordering one from White and one from Brill-Service. This is the latter unit shown minus trucks and power plant at the Brill factory.
Author's Collection

After a few years' experience with unwary autos and pedestrians, the Frisco painted bold zebra stripes on the fronts of its rail motors. Here is the 2110 at an unknown location.
Author's Collection

St. Louis-San Francisco Railway

ROAD NO.	BUILDER	DATE	BLDR. NO.	ENGINE & DRIVE	BODY TYPE	LGTH.	WT.	DISPOSITION	REMARKS
33	McKeen	1914	—	McKeen 200hp GM	10win CE Bag.-Pass.	55'	—	Ret. 3/30	Ex-Butler Co. 10; Orig. Jamestown, Chatq. & LE 1
600	Brill Service	1923	21749	Midw. 399 68hp GM	10win Bag. 32p	42½'	15t	Ret. 2/40	Ex-Gulf, Tex. & West. 600, acq. 7/30
601	Brill	1925	22122	Brill 55 68hp GM	10win Bag. 32p	42½'	15½t	Ret. 3/36	Ex-Gulf, Tex. & West 601, acq. 7/30
651	Brill	1924	21948	Brill 55 68hp GM	3win Bag.	42½'	14t	Ret. 10/35	Ex-Gulf, Tex. & West. 651, acq. 7/30
2100-03	Gen. Elec. Wason	1911	3711-14 10400	GE 16A1 175hp GE	15win CE Bag. 86p	70'	49½t	Scr. 3/34, 5/36, 11/43, 3/34	—
2104	Gen. Elec. Wason	1911	3715 10400	GE 16A1 175hp GE	15win CE Bag. 86p	71'	49½t	To Gulf Coast Lines, 1916; re-purchased 8/22; Scr. 5/36	Rblt. closed rear
2105[1]	Gen. Elec. Wason	1911	3716 10400	GE 16A1 175hp GE	15win CE Bag. 86p	72'	49½t	To GCL 500, 1916	—
2105[2]	Gen. Elec. Wason	1912	—	GE 16 175hp GE	15win CE Bag. 48p	70'	58t	Scr. 11/36	—
2106	Gen. Elec. Wason	1912	3723	GE 16A3 175hp GE	17win CE Bag. 91p	72'	51½t	Scr. 10/40	Ex-GCL, acq. 3/16
2107[1]	Gen. Elec. Wason	1912	3723	GE 16A3 175hp GE	17win CE Bag. 91p	72'	51½t	To NOT&M 501, 1916	—

ROAD NO.	BUILDER	DATE	BLDR. NO.	ENGINE & DRIVE	BODY TYPE	LGTH.	WT.	DISPOSITION	REMARKS
2107[2]	Gen. Elec. Wason	1911	3731 12200	GE 16C1 175hp GE	15win CE Bag. 91p	72'	52t	Re-no. 2110[2], 1927	Ex-Quanah, Acme & Pacific A-3, repurchased 1924; orig. SLSF 2113
2108-09	Gen. Elec. Wason	1912	3725-26 12200	GE 16A1 175hp GE	17win CE Bag. 91p	72'	51t	To GCL 502-3, 1916	2109 weighed 52t
2110[1]	Gen. Elec. Wason	1912	3728 12200	GE 16C1 175hp GE	17win CE Bag. 91p	72'	50t	To Hawkinsv., Fla. & Sou. 26, 12/22, then Mid. Vy. 8	—
2110[2]	Gen. Elec. Wason	1911	3731 12200	GE 16A1 175hp GE	15win CE Bag. 91p	72'	63t	Scr. 7/39	Ex-2107[2]; orig. 2113, then QA&P A-3
2111[1]	Gen. Elec. Wason	1912	3729 12200	GE 16C1 175hp GE	15win CE Bag. 91p	72'	50t	To Macon & B'ham 10	—
2111[2]	Gen. Elec. Wason	1913	3744 12226	GE 16C1 175hp GE	17win Bag. 91p	70'	62½t	Scr. 2/45	Ex-Jonesboro, Lake City & East. Ill.; orig. Chi., Peoria & St.L. 104, then Okmulgee Nor. 111, acq. 1923
2112-16	Gen. Elec. Wason	1912	3730-4 12200	GE 16C1 175hp GE	15win CE Bag. 91p	70'	52t	2113 to QA&P A-3, see 2107. 2115 to GCL 504, 1916	2116 to Macon & B'ham 12, 1916
2117[1]	Barber	1913	15	Knight 30hp GM	10win CE 40p	33'	—	Ret. 1914	4 wheel, wooden body
2117[2]	Gen. Elec. Wason	1911	3710	GE 16A1 175hp GE	12win CE Bag. 47p	59'	54t	Scr. 5/35	Ex-JLC&E 110, acq. 1925. Orig. Dan Patch 5, then Okm. Nor. 110
2118	Barber	1913	16	Knight 30hp GM	10win CE 40p	33'	—	Ret. by 1914	4 wheel, wooden body. Cannabalized to keep 2117[1] going
2119	Fair-Morse Sheffield	1911	—	Sheffield 30hp GM	Open 4-wh. 25p	22'	4½t	—	Ex-Brownsville & Matamoros Bridge & Ry.
2120	EMC St. Louis	1925	118 1360A	Wint. 106 175hp GE	12win Bag. 33p	57½'	40½t	Scr. 5/54	—
2121	EMC St. Louis	1925	126 1368A	Wint. 106 175hp GE	12win Bag. 49p	57½'	42½t	Scr. 10/51	—
2122	EMC St. Louis	1928	315 1474	2-Wint. 148 200hp GE	RPO-Bag.	74'	65½t	—	—
2123-24	EMC St. Louis	1928	313-14 1474	2-Wint. 148 200hp GE	RPO-Bag.	74'	65½t	2121 scr. 8/45; 2124 to Cassville & Exeter, 1953	Used on C&E only a short time; too heavy
2125-26	EMC St. Louis	1928	315-16 1474	2-Wint. 148 200hp GE	RPO-Bag.	74'	65½t	—	—
2127-28	EMC St. Louis	1928 1929	C20-21 1372	Wint. 106A 220hp GE	17win 62p	62'	44½t	Scr. 5/35, 5/54	Rblt. of Sykes gas-mech. cars 3010-11
2130-33	Brill	1926	22432	Brill-WH 250hp GE	13win Bag. 44p	61'	43t	Scr. 9/46, 4/44, 9/46, 6/48	—
2900	White Southland	1922	—	White 40hp GM	7win 7p	22½'	6t	—	Ex-JLC&E 101, acq. 11/25
3000	Brill Service	1922	21552	Midwest 68hp GM	10win Bag. 32p	42½'	15t	Scr. 8/35	—
3001	Barn. & Smith Ry. Motors	1902 1926	—	2-Cont. 104hp GM	12win Bag. 42p	51'	37t	Scr. 12/32	Ex-combo. car 181, wooden body
3002	Laconia Unit	1919	833	Unit.-Std. 60hp steam	11win Bag. 42p	50½'	26t	Rblt. tlr. 502, 2/30	Ex-Butler Co. 10
3010-11	St. Louis Sykes	1927	1372	Sterl. 275hp GM	17win 62p	62'	36½t	Rblt., re-no. 2127, 2128	

Trailers

ROAD NO.	BUILDER	DATE	BLDR. NO.	ENGINE & DRIVE	BODY TYPE	LGTH.	WT.	DISPOSITION	REMARKS
80	Edwards	1923	—	—	8win Bag.	26½'	9½t	Ret. 1932	Ex-St.L., Ken. & SE 80, acq. 9/27
81	Edwards	1923	—	—	32p	26½'	8½t	Ret. 1932	Ex-St.L., Ken. & SE 81, acq. 9/27

Cotton Belt

Known for its flirtation with experimental railbuses, the Cotton Belt also invested in standard, heavy-duty doodlebugs. Here is Pullman 16 pulling a converted General Electric motor at Dialville, TX, on May 6, 1949.
R. H. Carlson

	No. 401 Rail Motor Car	Miles from St. Louis.	November 5, 1939.	No. 402 Rail Motor Car	
Table 7—TYLER, JACKSONVILLE AND LUFKIN.					
....	*8 40 A M	685.8	lve.....+**Tyler**ठ .....arr.	5 15 P M	....
....	f8 56 "	691.8	..........Elkton..........	f4 52 "	....
....	f9 04 "	695.3	........Gresham..........	f4 45 "	....
....	9 09 "	697.5	...........Flint..........	4 40 "	....
....	9 20 "	702.5	.........Bullard........ठ	4 29 "	....
....	9 33 "	708.0	.......Mt. Selman........	4 17 "	....
....	f9 43 "	712.2	.........Pomona..........	f4 06 "	....
....	10 03 "	716.0	+....**Jacksonville**...ठ	3 54 "	....
....	f10 14 "	719.8	...........Craft..........	f3 37 "	....
....	10 24 "	724.1	.........Dialville........	3 28 "	....
....	10 42 "	731.5	+........ **Rusk** ....ठ	3 12 "	....
....	f10 50 "	736.0	........Broughton........	f2 59 "	....
....	f11 02 "	740.4	.........Redlawn.........	f2 48 "	....
....	11 11 "	743.6	+.........Alto......ठ	2 41 "	....
....	f11 19 "	747.4	..........Morrill.........	f2 32 "	....
....	f11 21 "	748.3	........Brunswick........	f2 30 "	....
....	11 31 "	753.4	.........Wildhurst........	2 21 "	....
..../	11 33 "	754.0	..........Forest.........	2 19 "	....
....	11 45 "	758.0	...........Wells.........ठ	2 09 "	....
....	11 56 A M	763.6	..........Pollok..........	1 59 "	....
....	12 08 P M	769.6	.........Clawson.........	1 47 "	....
....	– –	770.7	..........Durst..........	– –	....
....	12 17 "	773.5	..........Keltys.........	1 38 "	....
....	12 25 P M	775.4	arr.....+**Lufkin**ठ .....lve.	*1 30 P M	....

	103 Rail Motor Car	No. 101	Miles from St. Louis.	November 5, 1939.	No. 102	104 Rail Motor Car	
Table 10—MOUNT PLEASANT, TYLER, CORSICANA AND WACO.							
.....	.....	*6 35 A M	618.8	lve.+**Mt. Pleasant**ठ arr.	9 00 P M	.....	.....
.....	.....	f6 45 "	625.9	.........Harvard.........	f8 47 "	.....	.....
.....	.....	6 53 "	630.4	+........**Pittsburg**......ठ	8 39 "	.....	.....
.....	.....	f7 01 "	636.3	...........Pine..........	f8 28 "	.....	.....
.....	.....	f7 07 "	641.1	..........Smith.........	f8 21 "	.....	.....
.....	.....	f7 11 "	643.8	.........Bettie........ठ	f8 16 "	.....	.....
.....	.....	7 23 "	649.3	+.........Gilmer........ठ	8 06 "	.....	.....
.....	.....	7 32 "	656.2	.........Pritchett........	7 52 "	.....	.....
.....	.....	7 45 "	664.3	.........**Big Sandy**.......ठ	7 39 "	.....	.....
.....	.....	7 58 "	672.4	..........Winona........ठ	7 22 "	.....	.....
.....	P M	8 20 "	635.8	arr.....+**Tyler**ठ .....lve.	7 00 "	A M	.....
.....	*9 30	8 30 "	685.8	lve......**Tyler**......arr.	6 40 "	4 15	.....
.....	9 54	8 46 "	697.8	..........Chandler.........	6 19 "	f3 46	.....
.....	10 10	8 56 "	706.0	........Brownsboro........ठ	6 07 "	f3 28	.....
.....	– –	f9 01 "	709.3	.........Opelika.........	f6 01 "	– –	.....
.....	10 27	9 06 "	714.5	.........Murchison........ठ	5 55 "	f3 10	.....
.....	– –	– –	717.5	+...........Ash..........ठ	– –	– –	.....
.....	10 46	9 25 "	723.1	+.........**Athens**.........ठ	5 42 "	2 52	.....
.....	11 05	9 36 "	733.0	.........Malakoff.........ठ	5 28 "	f2 30	.....
.....	11 15	9 42 "	738.0	.........Trinidad........ठ	5 20 "	f2 17	.....
.....	11 33	9 53 "	746.4	+.........Kerens.........ठ	5 07 "	f1 59	.....
.....	11 45	10 01 "	752.3	..........Powell..........ठ	4 58 "	f1 47	.....
.....	11 59	10 15 A M	760.5	arr.+**Corsicana**ठ..lve.	4 45 P M	*1 30	.....
.....	P M	....	......	(*Texas Electric Ry.*)	....	A M	.....
.....	*11 40 A M	....	......	lve....**Corsicana**....arr.	4 30 P M	12 50	.....
.....	1 30 P M	....	......	.........**Dallas**.........	*2 40 P M	*11 00	.....
.....	....	....	......	ARRIVE] [LEAVE	....	P M	.....
.....	....	....	......	**Corsicana**	4 45	.....	.....

THERE WAS MORE than just a touch of novelty about the operation of rail motor cars on the St. Louis-Southwestern (Cotton Belt) railroad in the 1930s. The Southern Pacific subsidiary has always been a freight-oriented railroad, having few mainline passenger trains of note. But it provided the usual accommodation service on the branches.

The novelty came in the choice of equipment. In late 1933, the SSW inaugurated its "Eagle of the Rails," a railbus service between Jonesboro, Ark., and Dallas, Tex.

One of the railbuses was a converted Yellow Coach Z-250 highway coach. It had "rubber cushioned" steel wheels and seated 35. There were actually two such coaches on the roster, one used as a spare.

The other advertised railbus was a borrowed Daimler railbus of Austrian manufacture, featuring pneumatic tires mounted within a steel rim. The unit was 38½ feet long and had a pair of Daimler six-cylinder 80-hp gasoline engines with hydraulic transmission.

Though the Daimler bus was "capable of a maximum speed of 80

Here are sample doodlebug schedules for the Cotton Belt. Reproduced from THE OFFICIAL RAILWAY GUIDE® © **1939 NRPCo.**

miles per hour," the unit apparently lasted less than a year on the Cotton Belt. The through route was cut back from Texarkana, Tex., to Pine Bluff, Ark. and then eliminated altogether.

Other railcars on the Cotton Belt were more conventional and lasted a lot longer. Eight General Electric gas-electrics were purchased in 1914 (one of them, No. 15, was the "cover car" for *Interurbans Without Wires*) and were used on branch lines in Missouri, Arkansas and Texas. Two Brill Type 55 cars came in 1929, and all of these were superceded when a group of four Pullman-EMC cars were purchased from the Southern Pacific in 1941.

There was one other railcar oddity on the Cotton Belt. In 1929 the Cotton Belt purchased the Deering Southwestern Railway in Missouri and inherited Car No. 82, the only Cincinnati railcar ever built. It was sold to the Paris & Mt. Pleasant Railroad of Texas.

Meanwhile, the SSW's large Pullmans soldiered on through World War II and were finally scrapped in 1949, after all branch line passenger service had been abandoned.

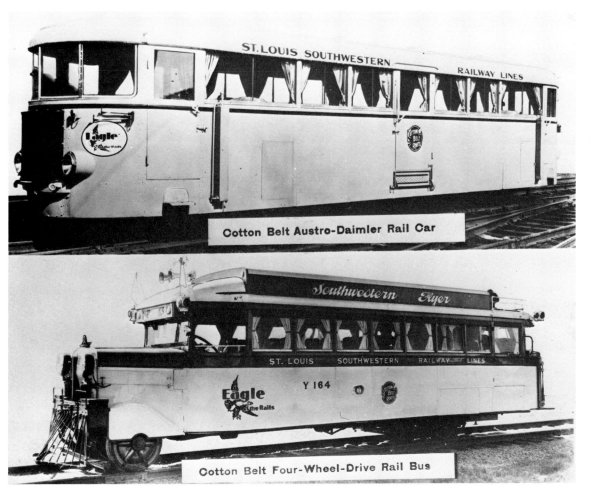

Cotton Belt Austro-Daimler Rail Car

Cotton Belt Four-Wheel-Drive Rail Bus

Austro - Daimler railcar (upper photo) was not actually on the Cotton Belt roster, and demonstrated for less than a year. Yellow railbus (lower photo) was dubbed "Eagle of the Rails" and although the railroad owned it, it did not endure for long.

Harold K. Vollrath Collection

St. Louis Southwestern

ROAD NO.	BUILDER	DATE	BLDR. NO.	ENGINE & DRIVE	BODY TYPE	LGTH.	WT.	DISPOSITION	REMARKS
10-17	Gen. Elec. Wason	1914	3768-75 14900	GE 16C7 175hp GE	17win Bag. 62p	70'	52t	10, 13 rblt. tlr. 51, 52, 1941	As tlrs. lengthened to 72'. Scr. 1949
15-17[2]	Pullman EMC	1930	6297 432-4	Winton GE	Bag.	76½'	79t	—	Ex-SP 3-5, rblt. from Bag.-Pass., acq. 8/41
18	Pullman EMC	1930	6297 435	Winton GE	9win Bag. 34p	76½'	79t	—	Ex-NWP 901, acq. 8/41
20-21	Brill	1929	22750- 51	Brill 55 68hp GM	8win Bag. 30p	43½'	14½t	M 21 to Ligonier Val, M 20 sold unknown pty.	—
22	Cincinnait	1922	2610	Intn'l GM	10win CE 40p	39½'	—	To Paris & Mt. Pleasant 22	Curved-side streetcar body; ex-Deering SW 82, re-no. 692 on P&MP
Y 164, Y (?)	Yellow FWD	1933	—	Yellow 150hp GM	8win bus 32p		13t	—	Hood front, ex-SW Transp. Co. motor coach. Type Z-250. Two buses, other number unknown

San Diego & Arizona Eastern

Where electric light rail vehicles run today, once roamed the doodlebug on the San Diego & Arizona Eastern. GE unit 43 is marked for Tijuana and Agua Caliente, Mexico.
R. P. Middlebrook; Randolph Brandt Collection

THE SAN DIEGO & EASTERN has been in the news lately by virtue of the new "Tijuana Trolley" light rail line built between San Diego and the Mexican Border. At one time, the route now traversed by the sleek new German-built trams was a doodlebug run, carrying tourists and commuters into Mexico to Tijuana and Agua Caliente.

The SD&AE was built by local San Diego interests to provide an independent rail outlet to the East. Its main line connected the Southern California metropolis with the Southern Pacific mainline at El Centro, in the Imperial Valley, via Mexico. Eventually the SP bought the SD&AE then sold it to a public agency in San Diego after a hurricane severed the through connection.

Steam-hauled passenger trains traditionally provided one through passenger service a day over the entire route, but beginning in 1911 General Electric rail motorcars provided local service to Tijuana.

A branch line was built from San Diego east to La Mesa and El Cajon, now populous suburbs but then tiny hamlets in the nearby hills, and a 25-foot, 10-ton rail motor was purchased from the Hewitt-Ludlow Auto Co. of San Francisco for this run.

The doodlebug runs were abolished in the 1930s, and now the El Cajon branch is due to become a second electric-powered light rail line.

This rare Hewitt-Ludlow car ran for a time on the SC&AE.
R. P. Middlebrook

San Diego & Arizona Eastern

ROAD NO.	BUILDER	DATE	BLDR. NO.	ENGINE & DRIVE	BODY TYPE	LGTH.	WT.	DISPOSITION	REMARKS
31	Hewitt-Ludlow	1917	—	Wisc. D 70hp OM	8win 32p	25'	10t	To Arcade & Attica	—
41	Gen. Elec. Wason	1913	3766 13700	GE-GM 16C1 175hp GE	17win Bag. 91p	70'	49t	Scr. 1939	Ex-Dan Patch 11, acq. 1916
42	Gen. Elec. Wason	1911	3767 13700	GE-GM 16C1 175hp GE	17win Bag.-Pass.	70'	49t	Scr. 1940	Ex-Dan Patch 12, acq. 1913
43	Gen. Elec. Wason	1911	3707	GE-GM 16A4 175hp GE	16win CE Bag. 69p	67'	45½t	Scr. 1939	Ex-BR&P 1001, acq. 1914

Seaboard Air Line

Table 36—SAVANNAH-MONTGOMERY.

.....	11	Mls.	*December* 15, 1939.	12
.....	A M	.....	(*Eastern time.*)	P M
.....	*8 00	0	lve. + **Savannah** ⊡ ♁ .arr.	8 00
.....	f8 22	9.7	.........Williams.........	f7 31
.....	f8 29	12.5	.........Ottawa.........	f7 25
.....	8 46	17.1	.... **Meldrim** ......♁	7 17
.....	8 59	23.7	.........Ellabelle.......♁	f7 05
.....	9 06	26.8	.... **Lanier** ....♁	f6 58
.....	9 17	31.8	........Pembroke......♁	6 48
.....	f9 24	35.0	.... Reka	f6 42
.....	9 32	38.9	........Groveland......♁	f6 35
.....	9 42	44.5	.... Daisy........♁	f6 26
.....	9 52	48.4	.... Claxton ....♁	6 19
.....	9 57	50.4	..........Hagan.........♁	f6 13
.....	10 02	52.9	.... Belleville ......♁	f6 07
.....	10 08	55.5	.... Manassas	6 02
.....	10 20	60.9	+ .... **Collins** ....♁	5 51
.. ..	10 35	68.0	.........Ohoopee.........	f5 37
.....	10 48	74.6	.... Lyons..........♁	5 26
.....	10 58	79.8	+ ...... **Vidalia** ⊡ ......♁	5 15
.....	f11 10	83.5	.... Higgston	f5 03
.....	11 23	89.8	.... Ailey ....♁	4 51
.....	11 28	91.6	......Mount Vernon......	4 45
.....	f11 36	94.6	........Ochwalkee........	f4 37
.....	11 41	96.4	.... Glenwood	4 33
.....	11 55	103.5	..........Alamo.........♁	4 19
.....	f12 02	107.2	.... Erick	f4 12
.....	12 15	113.6	+ .... **Helena** ....♁	3 57
.....	12 36	124.1	.... Milan ....♁	3 40
.....	f12 43	128.6	..........Calvin..........	f3 31
.....	12 50	132.6	.... Rhine.........♁	3 25
.....	1 05	139.0	+ ......**Abbeville**......♁	3 13
.....	1 23	148.2	+ ......Rochelle.......♁	2 58
.....	1 32	153.3	.... **Pitts** ....♁	2 49
.....	1 39	157.1	..........Seville.........♁	2 42
.....	f1 50	163.1	.... Penia	f2 28
.....	2 00	168.1	arr. + Cordele (E.T.) ⊡ ♁ .lve.	2 20
.....	*2 50	.....	lv. Cordele (E.T.)(G.S.W.& G) ar.	2 00
.....	4 30	.....	arr. **Albany.** " lve.	*12 30
.....	2 15	168.1	lve.. **Cordele** (*E.T.*)..arr.	2 10
.....	f2 26	174.2	..........Coney..........	f1 55
.....	f2 33	178.6	.........Flintside.........	f1 47
.....	2 38	180.7	.... Cobb ....♁	1 42
.....	2 45	185.1	.... De Soto..........	1 35
.....	2 51	186.5	.... Leslie.........♁	1 31
.....	f2 59	191.1	.... Huntington ......♁	f1 22
.....	3 18	198.6	arr. + Americus ⊡ (*E.T.*) lve.	1 05
.....	2 20	198.6	lve... **Americus** (*C.T.*) arr.	12 01
.....	f2 29	203.3	.... Newpoint	f11 52
.....	2 39	208.8	..........Plains.........♁	11 40
.....	2 56	218.8	.... Preston ....♁	11 19
.....	3 20	227.2	+ ...... **Richland**.......♁	11 05
.....	3 37	235.8	+ ...... Lumpkin ....♁	10 43
.....	3 49	243.3	.........Louvale.......♁	10 26
.....	3 57	247.5	..........Union..........♁	10 19
.....	4 09	254.4	.... Omaha ....♁	10 07
.....	f4 19	259.6	........McLendon........	f9 55
.....	4 29	264.3	.... Pittsview ....♁	9 47
.....	4 46	274.2	.... Rutherford .....♁	9 32
.....	4 58	281.1	.... **Hurtsboro**.....♁	9 19
.....	f5 16	287.8	.... Hannon ....♁	f9 06
.....	5 37	298.8	........Fort Davis......♁	8 45
.....	5 53	307.7	........Hardaway........	8 29
.....	f6 02	313.0	.... Chesson..........	f8 21
.....	6 11	317.7	.... Cecil.........♁	8 13
.....	6 22	323.4	.... Merry..........	8 03
.....	f6 33	328.3	.... Mitylene	f7 54
.....	7 00	337.6	ar. + **Montgomery** ⊡ ♁ lv.	*7 35
.....	P M	.....	(*Central time.*)	A M

Gas-Electric Motor Train. (Train 11)

Gas-Electric Motor Train. (Train 12)

Shovel-nose streamliner was either 2027 or 2028 OF THE Seaboard. It loads passengers at an unidentified location, circa 1940. *Author's Collection*

YOU COULD HAVE called it mid-west railroading Down South. The doodlebugs of the Seaboard would have been right at home on the Burlington or the Northwestern.

From Savannah, Ga., to Montgomery, Ala., was a run of 337 miles, and from Hamlet, N. C. to Savannah was 263 miles, but rail motorcars handled both in style.

Unlike many railroads, the Seaboard took a last fling at new railcars as late as the mid-1930s. In 1935 the road took delivery of three lightweight AC&F streamlined cars, all of which remained in operation into the 1970s on other lines.

One of the cars is especially famed. It was in 1981 the California Western's M-300, better known as the *Skunk*. It had two other owners after being sold by the Seaboard; the Aberdeen & Rockfish in North Carolina and the Salt Lake, Garfield & Western, a former electric inter-urban in Utah.

The other two cars went to the Norfolk Southern and then to Cuba where at least one was reported still in service, much rebuilt, on the government railways.

Two St. Louis-EMC cars built in 1935 had rounded fronts and had the distinction of being the last St. Louis-EMC doodlebugs ever built. One of them survived to the advent of Amtrak in 1971.

Counting three earlier Seaboard cars sold to the Sperry Rail Service, at least four and possibly more railcars were still running in 1981, perhaps some sort of a record for any one railroad's doodlebugs.

Seaboard's earliest railcar was General Electric unit 2000, shown at the Wason factory in 1915. *George E. Votava Collection*

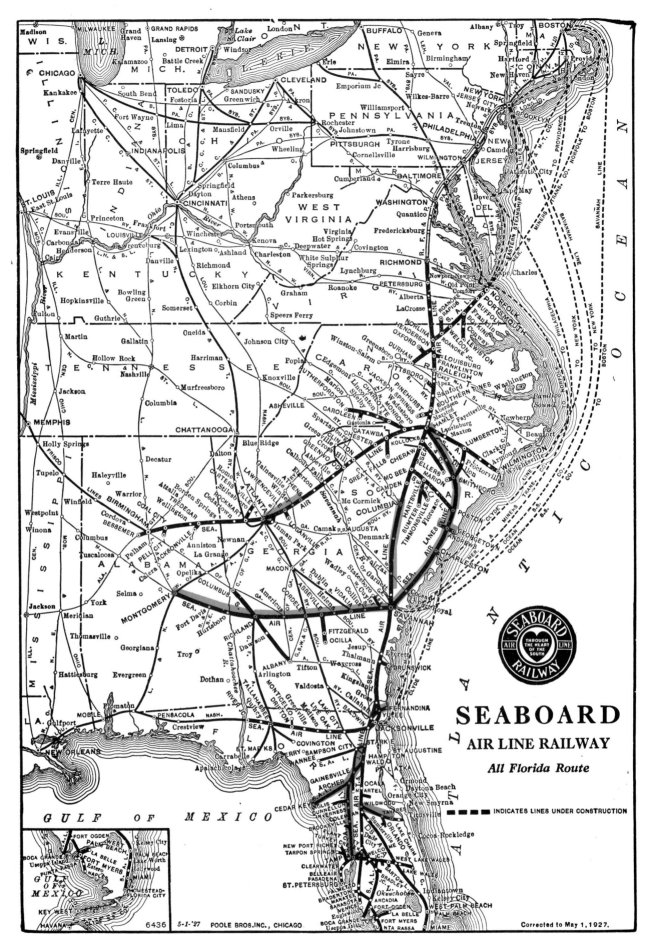

Heavy gray lines indicate the doodlebug runs on the Seaboard.

Author's Collection

Like a number of doodlebugs from various railroads, Seaboard 2003 eventually wound up as a Sperry Rail Service detector car.
A. E. Barker Collection

Seaboard Air Line

ROAD NO.	BUILDER	DATE	BLDR. NO.	ENGINE & DRIVE	BODY TYPE	LGTH.	WT.	DISPOSITION	REMARKS
2000-01	Gen. Elec. Wason	1917	3793-94	GE 16C10 175hp GE	14win Bag. 78p	70'	55t	Ret. 12/32, 5/23	2001 last GE gas-elec. car built
2002-03	St. Louis EMC	1925	1365 137-8	Wint. 106 175hp GE	8win Bag. 34p	59½'	55t	To Sperry Rail Svc. 133, 132, 4/43, 1/42	—
2012	Brill	1922	21559	Service 68hp GM	8win Bag. 30p	43'	14½t	Ret. by 1941	Model 55
2013-14	Brill	1927	22581	HS 275hp GE	2 door Bag.	75'	53t	Ret. by 1947	Dieselized
2015-16	Brill	1927	22580	HS 275hp GE	Mail-Bag.	75'	55t	Ret. by 1951, by 1947	Dieselized
2017	Brill	1927	22582	HS 275hp GE	Mail-Bag.	75'	55t	Rblt. tlr. 2045, 1943	—
2018-19	Brill	1927	22583	HS 275hp GE	Mail-Bag.	75'	59t	Ret. by 1947	—
2020-21	Brill	1927	22584	HS 275hp GE	Bag.	75'	58½t 53½t	Ret. by 1947	—
2022-23	St. Louis EMC	1928	1459 261-2	Wint. 120 275hp GE	8win Bag. 34p	74'	53t	To Sperry 134, 135, 1945	—
2024-26	ACF	1935	1432	HS 176hp GM	14win Bag. 52p	61½'	76t	2024-25 to Norf. Sou., 1944, then to Cuba	2026 to Ab. & Rock. 106, then SLG&W, then Calif. Western M-300
2027-28	St. Louis EMD	1936	1584 523-4	EMD 600hp DE	Mail-Bag.	72'	72t	2027 ret. 1957; 2028 to SCL 4900	Rounded front

Trailers

2041	Brill	1927	22586	—	Bag.	62'	—	Ret. 1953	—
2045	Co. Shops	1943	—	—	Bag.	75'	44t	Ret. 1958	Rebld. of Brill mtr. 2017
2050	Brill	1922	21560	—	10win 38p	34'	—	—	—
2051-54	Brill	1927	22585	—	22win 96p	75½'	39t	Ret. 1950s	2051, 52, 54, 55 rblt. to seat 54; 2053 to 62
2055-56	Brill Kuhlman	1927	22585 928	—	22win 96p	75½'	39t	Ret. 1953, 1950	Rblt. to seat 54
2057-59	Brill	1927	22585	—	22win 96p	75½'	39t	Ret. 1953, 1949, 1949	2057 bblt. to seat 62, others 54
2060-61	St. Louis EMC	1928	1460 263-4	—	96p, 58p	—	—	Ret. 1947, 1948	—

Southern Railway

THE SOUTHERN was never an extensive operator of rail motorcars, purchasing nine cars in all in two batches, one around 1911 and the other in 1939. Though a generation apart in design, the two batches of cars did have one thing in common: all the units had rounded noses.

It was to the Southern that the first two production models of the revolutionary General Electric gas electric cars went. These two cars, purchased in 1911, joined a lone McKeen car on the roster.

In 1939 six two-car railcar sets were obtained from St. Louis Car. The motor cars had the shovelnose look then popular on the new streamliners, and were powered by the Fairbanks-Morse opposed piston diesel engine, the first major application of this power plant to railroading.

These mini-streamliners were named *Golden Rod* for the Birmingham-Mobile run, the *Joe Wheeler* for Oakdale-

Chattanooga-Tuscumbia, the *Cracker* for Macon-Brunswick and the *Vulcan* for the Birmingham-Meridian schedule.

Two of the units were sold to short lines for use as locomotives, while the other units were cannibalized for parts.

Southern Railway motor 40 and its matching trailer—plus heavyweight coach and baggage—rest at Birmingham, AL, in June of 1941. This unit and sister 41 were dubbed VULCANS.   *Harold K. Vollrath Collectiion*

Southern Railway

ROAD NO.	BUILDER	DATE	BLDR. NO.	ENGINE & DRIVE	BODY TYPE	LGTH.	WT.	DISPOSITION	REMARKS
1[1]	Gen. Elec. Wason	1911	3701 9550	GE-GM 16A1 175hp GE	14win Bag. 52p	55'	41t	Gone by 1919	—
1[2]	St. Louis F-M	1939	1598	F-M OP 800hp DE	Bag.-Mail	81'	114t	Ret. 9/54	"Golden Rod." 6 wh. front truck inst. 1943-44
2[1]	Gen. Elec. Wason	1911	3702 12230	GE-GM 16A1 175hp GE	14win Bag. 52p	55'	41t	Gone by 1935	—
2[2]	St. Louis F-M	1939	1598	F-M OP 800hp DE	Bag.-Mail	81'	114t	To Ga. Nor. 2, 1944	"Joe Wheeler." 6 wh. front truck inst. 1943-44
3[1]	McKeen	1910	—	McKeen 200hp GM	Bag.-Pass.	—	—	Gone by 1915	—
3[2], 4	St. Louis F-M	1939	1598	F-M OP 800hp DE	Bag.-Mail	81'	114t	Ret. 8/54	"Cracker." 6 wh. front truck inst. 1943-44
40, 41	St. Louis F-M	1939	1598	F-M OP 800hp DE	Bag.-Mail	84'	114t	40 ret. 8/54; 41 to Ga. & Fla. 81, 9/54	Ala. Gt. Sou. "Vulcan." 6 wh. front truck inst. 1943-44

Trailers

MT 1[1]	Wason	1911	12232	—	16win 54p	42½'	—	—	—
MT 1[2]	St. Louis	1939	1599	—	21win 76p	73'	57½t	Ret. 1954	—
MT 2-4	St. Louis	1939	1599	—	21win 76p	73'	57t	MT2 to Ga. Nor. MT2, 1952	—
MT 40, 41	St. Louis —	1939 —	1599 —	— —	21win 76p —	73' —	57t 56t	Both to Ga. & Fla., 1954	—

Southern Pacific

Its knife-nose front surmounted by an enormous headlight, SP McKeen 61 is shopped at Sacramento. *Author's Collection*

THE KNIFE-NOSED McKeen railcar is usually regarded as purely a Union Pacific venture, and in many ways it was. However, according to rail historian John Labbe, its development was hastened by a situation that developed on the Southern Pacific.

When the SP built its line on the west side of Oregon's Wilamette Valley, it entered Portland on hilly Fourth Street, which soon became one of the most important (and congested) streets in the business district.

The Portland city council became distressed over the smoky steam trains and passed an ordinance forbidding steam locomotives on that thoroughfare. The SP, not wanting to lose its valuable Fourth Street entry to the city, proposed using self-propelled railcars.

Coincidentally, in 1908, William McKeen was perfecting his internal combustion railcar at the UP shops in Omaha. The very first production model, four-wheeled number 1, was sent to Portland to inaugurate the modernized Fourth Street service.

Unfortunately Car 1 could not make the grades on the Fourth Street line, so

it was returned to Omaha after operating for a short time between Ontario and Vale, Oregon.

Following the debacle of number 1, a whole series of cars kept coming from Omaha. Each one in turn failed to make the grade, literally and figuratively, and after number 8, which was pretty much the final refinement of the

The standard doodlebug era on the Southern Pacific was exemplified by car 7, shown here at Sacramento, CA, circa 1931.
Tom Gray Collection

161

Over its long SP career, McKeen 45 had its baggage and RPO sections removed and then reinstalled.

Author's Collection

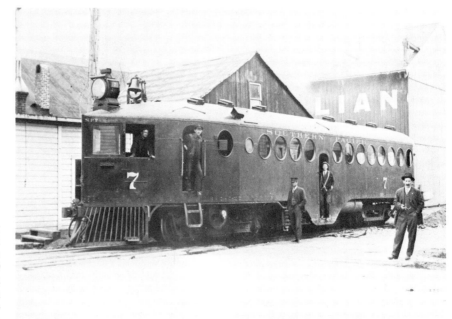

Motor 7 was typical of the earlier, shorter McKeens. The unit was photographed (right) at Marshfield, OR, circa 1910. Town is known today as Coos Bay. McKeen 39 tows shorty McKeen trailer 16 (below) at Sacramento. Southern Pacific had 10 such trailers, half of them starting out as four-wheelers. *James H. Harrison Collection*

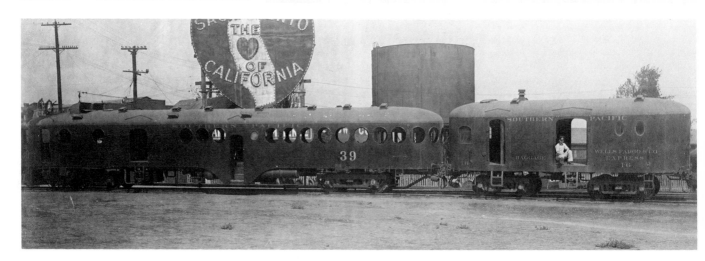

The Southern Pacific purchased but a single RDC car, and used it on the Oakland-Sacramento run. Here is the SP-10 at Crockett, CA, on July 24, 1954. It was later used between Willets and Eureka on the N.W.P. and survived until Amtrak.
W. C. Whittaker Collection

McKeen design, proved inadequate, the SP threw in the sponge and decided to electrify its West Side lines.

At this time the Southern Pacific was a part of the Harriman lines syndicate which also included the Union Pacific, so a good part of the McKeen output was sold to the SP for branch lline use. In the years from 1908 to 1911 the SP acquired 39 McKeen Motors plus 10 trailers. The Texas & New Orleans got 5 McKeen cars at a later date.

In 1913, the Harriman empire was broken up and the SP was cut loose from the UP. Perhaps significantly, the SP was not to buy another railcar until 1929.

Meanwhile the McKeen cars were flung over the whole system, but as early examples of the art of internal combustion power for the rails, they gave considerable trouble. A few were converted into trailers by 1918 and by the early 1920s others were headed into the scrapline.

Some McKeen cars continued as branch line accommodation trains, but the automobile killed this business and as the trains were phased out, so were the cars. Suddenly in 1929 the SP purchased 12 new gas-electric railcars, a very unexpected development considering the evaporation of the short haul passenger business.

Indeed, this purchase proved to be a fiasco, and most cars operated for just

four or five years; only one such run, from Bowie to Globe, in Arizona, lasted through World War II.

In one final twist of irony, it was one of the early McKeen cars which outlasted almost all of the new, large 1929-1930 gas-electric cars. After trying a gas-electric on the Sacramento-Placerville line, the SP decided that the mountain topography would be more suited to the gas-mechanical McKeen design and it was a McKeen car which closed out service on this branch in 1939.

Under the suburban SP electric wires at Alameda, Pullman-EMC unit SP 4 rests between assignments.
James H. Harrison Collection

163

Southern Pacific

ROAD NO.	BUILDER	DATE	BLDR. NO.	ENGINE & DRIVE	BODY TYPE	LGTH.	WT.	DISPOSITION	REMARKS
CP 1	McKeen	1908	20	McKeen 200hp GM	12win CE 72p	55'	32t	Ret. 7/20	Orig. no. 20
SP 3	McKeen	1908	23	McKeen 200hp GM	12win CE 71p	55'	30½t	Ret. 7/20	Orig. no. 23
SP 5	McKeen	1908	24	McKeen 200hp GM	12win CE 71p	55'	31t	Ret. 7/20	Orig. no. 24
SP 7	McKeen	1908	25	McKeen 200hp GM	12win CE 71p	55'	30½t	Ret. 7/20	Orig. no. 25
SP 9	McKeen	1908	26	McKeen 200hp GM	12win CE 72p	55'	30½t	Ret. 7/20	Orig. no. 26
SP 11	McKeen	1908	27	McKeen 200hp GM	12win CE 71p	55'	30½t	Burned 10/22	Orig. no. 27
SP 13	McKeen	1908	28	McKeen 200hp GM	12win CE 71p	55'	30½t	Ret. 7/20	Orig. no. 28
CP 15	McKeen	1908	29	McKeen 200hp GM	12win CE 71p	55'	30½t	Scr. 2/23	Orig. no. 29
CP 17	McKeen	1908	30	McKeen 200hp GM	12win CE 71p	55'	30½t	Ret. 7/20	Orig. no. 30
SP 19	McKeen	1909	33	McKeen 200hp GM	12win CE 69p	55½'	31t	Ret. 7/20	Used for a time as tlr., Mare Island Navy Yard, 1918-19
SP 21	McKeen	1909	34	McKeen 200hp GM	12win CE 69p	55½'	31t	Ret. 7/20	—
SP 23	McKeen	1909	35	McKeen 200hp GM	12win CE 70p	55½'	32t	Ret. 7/20	—
SP 25	McKeen	1909	36	McKeen 200hp GM	12win CE 69p	55½'	32t	Scr. 6/26	—
SP 27	McKeen	1909	37	McKeen 200hp GM	12win CE Bag. 62p	70'	37t	Rblt. Co. Shops 1917; Scr. 4/36	Orig. 55½' long
SP 29	McKeen	1909	38	McKeen 200hp GM	12win CE 69p	70'	36½t	Rblt. Co. Shops 1917 to RPO-Bag. 39p. Scr. 12/36	RPO sect. removed 3/19, re-inst. 5/20. Orig. 55½' long
SP 31	McKeen	1909	44	McKeen 200hp GM	12win CE 69p	70'	37t	Rblt. Co. Shops 1917 to RPO-Bag. 62p. Scr. 4/36	RPO sect. removed 10/18. Orig. 55½' long
SP 33	McKeen	1909	45	McKeen 200hp GM	12win CE 69p	55½'	30t	Ret. 7/20	Used for a time as tlr., Mare Island Navy Yard
SP 35	McKeen	1910	46	McKeen 200hp GM	12win CE 69p	55½'	31t	Ret. 7/20	Used for a time as tlr., Mare Island Navy Yard
SP 37	McKeen	1910	71	McKeen 200hp GM	12win CE RPO, 62p	70'	35t	Ret. 1/34	RPO removed 9/19
SP 39	McKeen	1910	72	McKeen 200hp GM	12win CE RPO, 62p	70'	35t	Ret. 8/36	RPO removed twice
SP 41	McKeen	1909	62	McKeen 200hp GM	12win CE 62p	55½'	30½t	Ret. 8/38	Bag. sect. inst. 4/12, 47p. Leased to Tonopah & Goldfield, 1932
SP 43	McKeen	1910	92	McKeen 200hp GM	12win CE RPO, 62p	70'	35t	Ret. 1/34	RPO removed 1/19, leased to T&G 12/31
SP 45	McKeen	1910	93	McKeen 200hp GM	12win CE RPO, 62p	70'	35t	Ret. 1/39	Both Bag. & RPO removed and reinstalled
SP 47, 49	McKeen	1911	94, 95	McKeen 200hp GM	12win CE RPO, 62p	70'	35t	Ret. 7/35, 8/36	RPO removed both cars
FC de S 50	McKeen	1909	50	McKeen 200hp GM	12win CE 71p	55½'	30t	Scr. 1936	Ex-FC de Sonora, acq. 1911

ROAD NO.	BUILDER	DATE	BLDR. NO.	ENGINE & DRIVE	BODY TYPE	LGTH.	WT.	DISPOSITION	REMARKS
SP 51, 53	McKeen	1911	96, 97	McKeen 200hp GM	12win RPO Bag. 62p	70'	35t	Ret. 8/36, 1/34	RPO removed car 51, 5/19
CP 55	McKeen	1911	98	McKeen 200hp GM	12win CE Bag. 70p	70'	36t	Ret. 1/34	—
CP 57, 59	McKeen	1911	99, 100	McKeen 200hp GM	12win CE Bag. 62p	70'	36t 35t	57 ret. 1/34; 59 burned 1/21	RPO removed both cars
SP 61	McKeen	1911	101	McKeen 200hp GM	12win CE Bag. 62p	70'	35t	Ret. 1/39	RPO removed both cars, 6/20
O&C 63	McKeen	1910	64	McKeen 200hp GM	12win CE 69p	55½'	30½t	To Dallas Lbr., 4/23	Orig. O&C 42
O&C 65	McKeen	1910	79	McKeen 200hp GM	12win CE 86p	70'	35t	Ret. 1/35	Rear pilot & whistle inst. 8/20
SP 67	McKeen	1909	48	McKeen 200hp GM	12win CE 75p	70'	30t	Ret. 8/29	Ex-Salem Falls, C. & West. 1, acq. 7/15
AE 69, 71	McKeen	1909	48, 49	McKeen 200hp GM	12win CE 75p	55½'	30t	Ret. 8/29	Ex-Ariz. East. 1, 2, acq. 11/24
AE 73	McKeen	1911	88	McKeen 200hp GM	12win CE Bag, 78p	70'	36t	Ret. 8/29	Ex-AE 3, acq. 11/24
AE 75	McKeen	1910	69	McKeen 200hp GM	12win CE Bag. 51p	55½'	30½t	Ret. 8/29	Ex-AE 4

Non-McKeen Cars

ROAD NO.	BUILDER	DATE	BLDR. NO.	ENGINE & DRIVE	BODY TYPE	LGTH.	WT.	DISPOSITION	REMARKS
SP 1	Mack Cummings	1929	162003	3-Mack AP 120hp GE	16win Bag. 77p	77'	66t	Conv. to M/W serv., 1943	—
SP 2	Brill	1929	22715	2-HS 300hp GE	12win DE Bag. 59p	73'	77t	Conv. to M/W serv., 1943	—
SP 3-5	Pullman EMC	1930	6279 432-34	Wint. 148D 400hp GE	10win DE Bag. 34p	73½'	79t	To SSW 15-17, 8/41	—
SP 6	Pullman EMC	1930	6279 436	Wint. 148D 400hp GE	10win DE Bag. 34p	73½'	79t	To CM St.P. & P 5940, 8/41	—
SP 7-10	Brill	1930	22788	2-HS 350 300hp GE	16win DE 54p	73'	83½t	Scr. 12/45 exc. SP 9, to M/W serv., 1945	—
SP 10²	Budd	1953	5917	2-GM 628 275hp DH	RDC-1	85'	56½t	To Ore. Pac. & East. 7/71	Leased to NWP, 5/59; damaged and rblt. with small bag. sect. in rear, sing. end
SP 11	Brill	1930	22788	2-HS 350 300hp GE	16win DE 54p	73'	83½t	Scr. 12/45	Leased to NWP, 1941

NOTE: Northwestern Pacific cars 901-904 were assigned SP numbers 12-15 for accounting purposes only. Never used on the SP.

McKeen Trailers

ROAD NO.	BUILDER	DATE	BLDR. NO.	ENGINE & DRIVE	BODY TYPE	LGTH.	WT.	DISPOSITION	REMARKS
SP 2	McKeen	1908	T 10	—	RPO-Bag.	31'	9½t	Scr. 1/20	Orig. T-10, 4 wheel originally
SP 4	McKeen	1908	T 11	—	RPO-Bag.	31'	9½t	Scr. 6/18	Orig. T-11, 4 wheel originally
CP 6	McKeen	1908	T 12	—	RPO-Bag.	31'	9½t	Scr. 6/18	Orig. T-12, 4 wheel originally
SP 8	McKeen	1908	T 13	—	RPO-Bag.	31'	12½t	To Mar. & Phoenix–Ariz. East. 8	Orig. T-13, 4 wheel originally
SP 10	McKeen	1908	T 14	—	RPO-Bag.	31'	12½t	To Mar. & Phoenix–Ariz. East. 10	Orig. T-14, 4 wheel originally
SP 12	McKeen	1908	T 15	—	RPO-Bag.	31'	12½t	To OSL 6/11	Orig. T-15
SP 14	McKeen	1909	T 14	—	Bag.	31'	12½t	Scr. 3/39	May have been second T-14. RPO removed
SP 16	McKeen	1909	T 16	—	RPO-Bag.	31'	12½t	To SF, Napa & Cal. 55, 2/27	Orig. T-16
SP 18	McKeen	1909	T 18	—	RPO-Bag.	31'	12½t	To FC de Sonora 50, 8/09	Orig. T-18
SP 20	McKeen	1909	T 20	—	Bag.	31'	12½t	Scr. 3/20	Orig. T-20. RPO removed

Two-thirds of the Spokane, Portland & Seattle's GE doodlebug fleet is represented in this photo. The location is the SP&S roundhouse at Vancouver, WA.

"Dutch" Hendrick Collection

Spokane, Portland & Seattle

ROAD NO.	BUILDER	DATE	BLDR. NO.	ENGINE & DRIVE	BODY TYPE	LGTH.	WT.	DISPOSITION	REMARKS
1101	Gen. Elec. Wason	1915	3785	GE 16C5 175hp GE	13win Bag. 68p	71'	52t	Conv. to M/W, 4/40	In 1929 rblt. by Brill, ord. 22736, with Brill GE engine, flat front
1102	Gen. Elec. Wason	1912	3720	GE 16B 175hp GE	15win Bag. 68p	67'	45t	To Warren & OV, 1929	Ex-Dan Patch 8
1103	Mack Cummings	1922	60007	Mack AC 68hp GM	Railbus Bag. 32p	35'	10t	To SE Port. Lbr., 1934	—

It was the good old summertime somewhere on the Texas & New Orleans system, 1915.

Richard Reynolds

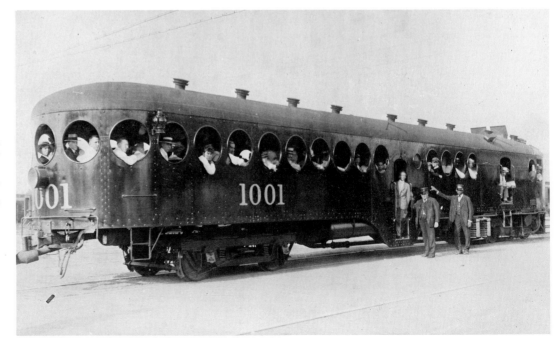

166

Texas & New Orleans

Even though lettered for the parent Southern Pacific, motor 1027 belongs to the Texas & New Orleans. In this 1932 photo it is lugging two heavyweight coaches.
James H. Harrison Collection

IN STUDYING the history of the Southern Pacific, one cannot help but remark on the high degree of corporate independence the subsidiary Texas & New Orleans enjoyed until fairly recent times.

The T&NO had its own president, based at Houston, and in general any communication with SP headquarters at San Francisco was done through the office of the Chairman of the Board in New York City.

In their policies toward rail motorcars, the SP and T&NO were as different as any two railroads in the country, and are treated separately in this volume.

The T&NO's first railcars were five McKeen cars, but they were acquired several years after the large SP fleet and cannot be considered as a legacy of the Edward Harriman administration. Except for some second-hand equipment picked up when the San Antonio

& Aransas Pass and the Texas Midland Railways were merged into the company, the T&NO did not acquire any railcars until 1929 when a fleet of RPO-Baggage units arrived.

These cars, which hauled standard passenger coaches as trailers, took over most of the T&NO's non mainline passenger service. They worked out nicely, and endured until these runs were eliminated in the late 1940s and early 1950s.

As can be seen from this contemporary 1932 map, most of the mileage of the T&NO had doodlebug runs. Such runs are indicated by heavy lines.

Railway Age

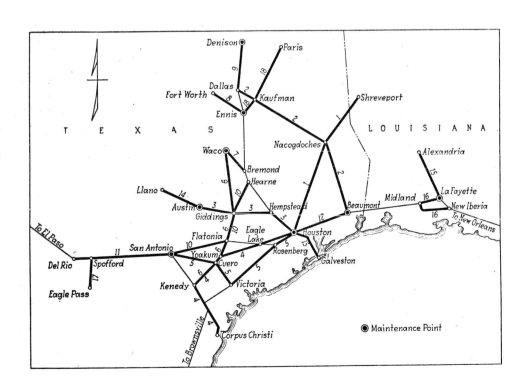

Texas & New Orleans

ROAD NO.	BUILDER	DATE	BLDR. NO.	ENGINE & DRIVE	BODY TYPE	LGTH.	WT.	DISPOSITION	REMARKS
ML&T 1001-02	McKeen	1913	—	McKeen 200hp GM	14win CE Bag. 38p	70'	38½t	1001 scr. 1920, 1002 scr. 1935	—
GH&SA 1003	McKeen	1913	—	McKeen 200hp GM	14win CE Bag. 38p	70'	38½t	Scr. 1939	—
GH&SA 1004	McKeen	1914	—	McKeen 200hp GM	14win CE Bag. 38p	70'	38½t	Scr. 1931	—
H&TC 1005	McKeen	1914	—	McKeen 200hp GM	14win CE Bag. 38p	70'	38½t	Scr. 1929	—
SA&AP 1006	FWD Boston	1923	—	Wisc. 40hp GM	4win CE Bag. 26p	24'	10½t	Scr. 1930	4 wheel, small hood; Ex-San. Ant. & Aransas Pass 500.
SA&AP 1007	McKeen Unit	1910 1924	— —	Unit-Std. 300hp steam	16win CE Bag. 58p	70'	48t	Scr. 1930	Body ex-ATSF M-103; Ex-San. Ant. & Aransas Pass 501
TM 1008-09	Gen. Elec. Wason	1912	3752-53 12715	GE 16C1 175hp GE	14win CE Bag. 100p	70'	48t	Scr. 1939	Ex-Texas Midland 5001-2
T&NO 1010-11	EMC Bethlehem	1929	350-51	Wint. 146 300hp GE	RPO-Bag.	72½'	59t	Scr. 12/45	—
T&NO 1012	EMC Pullman	1929	352 6226	Wint. 146 300hp GE	RPO-Bag.	73'	59½t	Scr. 12/45	—
T&NO 1013	Std. Steel WH	1929	362	Sterl. TT6 300hp GE	RPO-Bag.	72'	61t	Scr. 1950	—
T&NO 1014-15	Std. Steel WH	1930	362	Sterl. TT6 300hp GE	RPO-Bag.	76'	63t	Scr. 1945	—
T&NO 1025-30	EMC Pullman	1930	426-31 6295	Wint. 148D 400hp GE	RPO-Bag.	76'	70t	1029 burned 2/37; others scr. ca. 1947-51	—

Texas & Pacific

ROAD NO.	BUILDER	DATE	BLDR. NO.	ENGINE & DRIVE	BODY TYPE	LGTH.	WT.	DISPOSITION	REMARKS
100	Budd	1933	—	2-Am. LaFr. 240hp GE	Mail-Bag.	68½'	40t	—	Returned to bldr. (as was tlr. 150)

Trailers

ROAD NO.	BUILDER	DATE	BLDR. NO.	ENGINE & DRIVE	BODY TYPE	LGTH.	WT.	DISPOSITION	REMARKS
150	Budd	1933	—	—	11win 76p	68'	12t	—	6-wheel rubber tired trucks

Was this the first stream-lined train in the U. S.? Budd's SILVER SLIPPER is on a test run on the Burlington at Berwyn, IL, in 1933. Michelin supplied the rubber tires for the trailer.

Author's Collection

Union Pacific

Airbrushing added an air of mystique to publicity photo of the first Union Pacific streamliner, the M-10000.

Union Pacific

T HE INTIMATE relationship between the Union Pacific and the McKeen Motor Car Co. was thoroughly covered in our first book, *Interurbans Without Wires*. The UP set William McKeen up in the business in a part of the Union Pacific Omaha shops, was half-owner during the years that the cars were produced, and ultimately became complete owner until the firm was dissolved in 1920.

It is not surprising, therefore, to find that the first 19 McKeen cars were nominally built for the UP. In actual practice, often if an order was received for a car from another railroad, it was filled with a new car from the Union Pacific roster.

The original fleet numbering scheme used by the UP was to give the car the same number as the McKeen builder's number. This led to some rather puzzling gaps in the number sequence. To compound the problem, cars that were later purchased second-hand were given the numbers of these missing cars.

At the keystone of the Edward Harriman empire, the UP was a large and complex organization and the right hand did not always know what the left hand was doing. In 1911 Julius Kruttschnitt, then director of maintenance and operation for the UP (and later chairman of the board of the Southern Pacific) inquired as to why two McKeen cars built

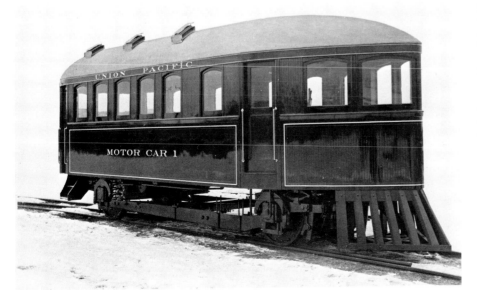

McKeen had publicity photos, too. Here's the very first windsplitter car , Union Pacific No. 1, on March 18, 1905.

Union Pacific

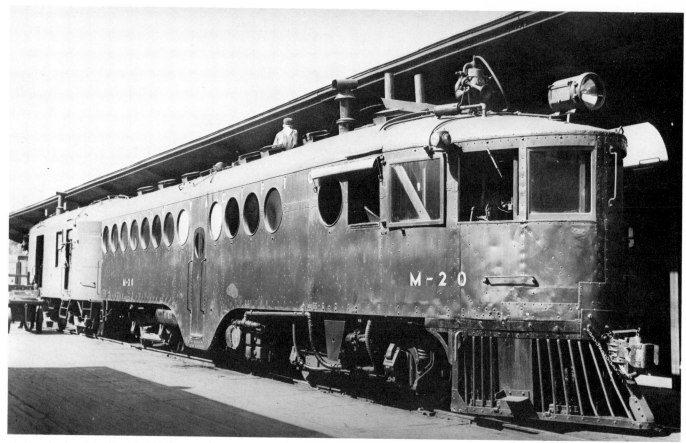

As late as July 5, 1941, the UP was running a pure McKeen combo—the M-20 and trailer T-52. Photo was taken at Ogden, UT; train was being readied for the Malad City, UT, branch run.

A. C. Phelps Collection

for the North Coast Lines, a subsidiary of the Oregon-Washington Railway & Navigation Co., were built with wedge-shaped fronts rather than the parabolic front standard on the Harriman lines.

A startled McKeen wrote to Kruttschnitt: "we built a wedge-shaped front end for the North Coast on their specifications, we not knowing at that time that they were a Harriman line interest."

The McKeens served the Union Pacific and associated lines very well—probably far better than their performance on other roads. Several ran through World War II with their original drives, and several others were converted to gas-electrics.

When it came to the second generation of rail motorcars, the UP built in its own shops what might be termed the ultimate McKeen. From what remained of the McKeen parts inventory, four unused sides were selected and were combined with the Hall-Scott gas engine, electrical components from GE, and trucks from Brill.

The cars, numbered M-29 and M-30, proved to be exceptionally reliable, became favorites of the company and eventually received such amenities as reclining seats, a feature not often seen in doodlebugs. The remaining motor-cars in the fleet were stock model EMCs and Brills.

Each division of the system, the UP, Oregon Short Line, Oregon-Washington Railway & Navigation Co., and the Los Angeles & Salt Lake, had its own numbering system, avoiding overlap, and although there was some transferring of equipment among the divisions, it was not extensive.

The UP division had by far the largest fleet, and a large proportion of the lines in Nebraska, Kansas and Colorado were served by railcars at one time or another. In contrast, the Los Angeles & Salt Lake had only two cars, and most of the time only one. One of the routes the LA&SL doodlebugs covered for a short line was the very obscure Montebello-to-Anaheim branch in Southern California.

The Union Pacific's only venture in the third generation of railcar was the famous *City of Salina*, one of the first streamlined trains. It spent its relatively short life (1934-1942) on the Kansas City-Salina run, later cut back to Topeka. It was retired just in time for the World War II scrap drives, thus it was unable to join its contemporary streamliners, the *Zephyrs* and the *Flying Yankee*, which were eventually presented to museums. Sadly, none of

the UP's early streamliners survived.

The last group of cars was retired in 1958 as the branch line runs they were protecting were eliminated. Oregon Short Line car M-66 was rebuilt in 1950 into detector car DC-2, and Oregon-Washington Railway & Navigation car M-98 survived until 1961, and then was converted into a work car.

Car M-35 has been restored and is now at the Illinois Railway Museum. One other car might be mentioned. Originally Detroit & Mackinac car 201 or 202, it was purchased by the Teledetector Co. of Chicago and converted into a rail detector car. This firm was apparently planning to beacome a rival to the Sperry rail detector service, and two cars from the D&M were purchased. Only one car was converted, however, and was sold to the UP as its detector car DC-3.

The DC-3 is still in service, and after many rebuildings it now sports a rakish front end dominated by a massive plate glass windshield which makes it appear a bit like an airport control tower!

The St. Joseph & Grand Island Railroad was very closely associated with the Union Pacific, but was not officially made a part of the system until after its last railcar had been retired.

Glistening with its fresh coat of
varnish, brand-new car No. 5 is
rolled out of the McKeen shops
at Omaha on Jan. 12, 1906.
Union Pacific

**Detector car DC-3 was a boomer doodlebug from the Detroit & Mackinac. It is shown at Denver in October of 1977. Since
then, it has been rebuilt with an enormous plate glass windshield.**
Louis Saillard

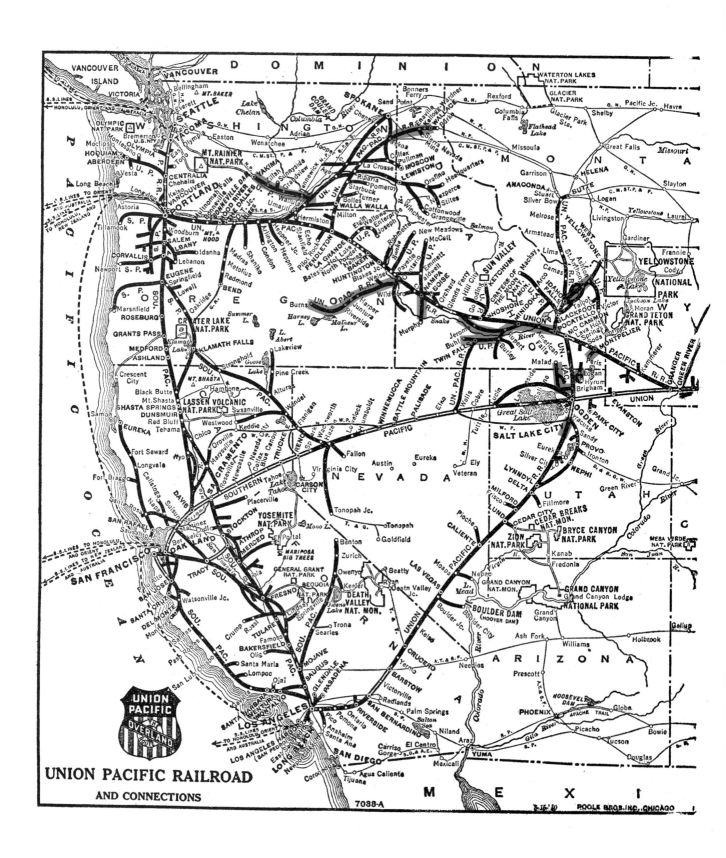

Heavy gray lines indicate the doodlebug runs on the Union Pacific. Reproduced from THE OFFICIAL RAILWAY GUIDE®
© 1937 NRPCo.

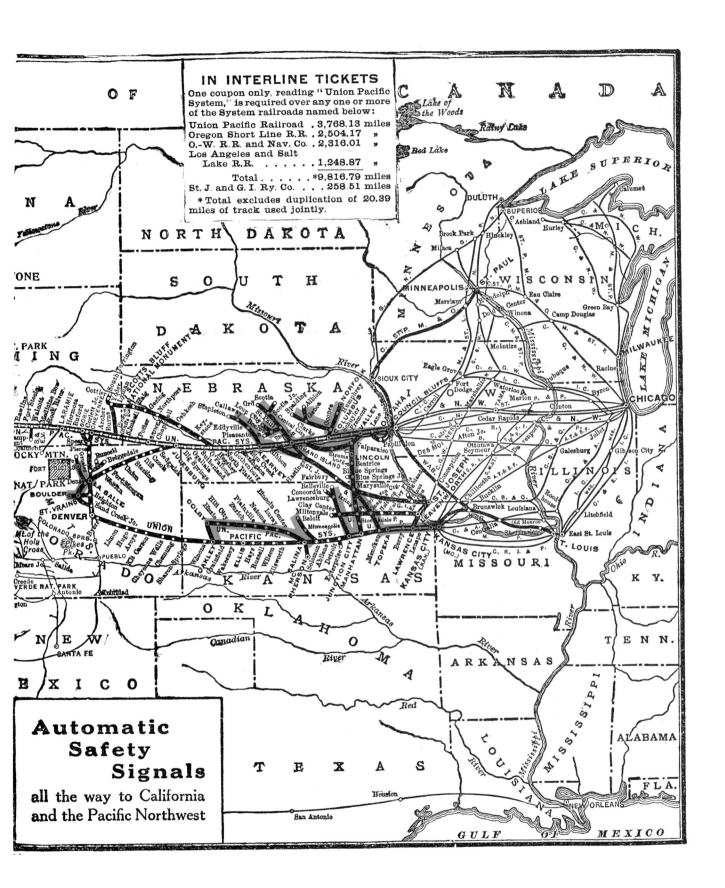

IN INTERLINE TICKETS

One coupon only, reading "Union Pacific System," is required over any one or more of the System railroads named below:

Union Pacific Railroad . 3,768.13 miles
Oregon Short Line R.R. . 2,504.17 »
O.-W. R.R. and Nav. Co. . 2,316.01 »
Los Angeles and Salt
   Lake R.R. . . . . . . 1,248.87 »

      Total . . . . . *9,816.79 miles
St. J. and G. I. Ry. Co. . . 258.51 miles

*Total excludes duplication of 20.39 miles of track used jointly.

Automatic Safety Signals

all the way to California and the Pacific Northwest

Now painted in streamliner yellow, Electro-Motive car M-32 hauls trailer T-11 through Twin Falls, ID, on July 5, 1952.
W. C. Whittaker Collection

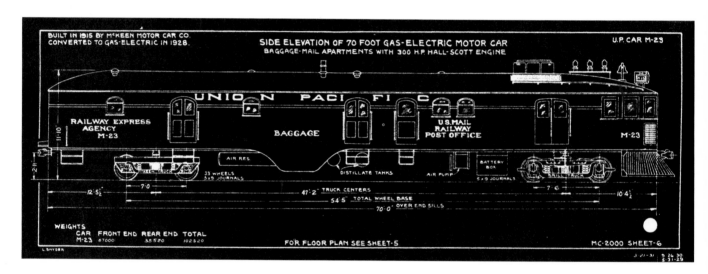

BUILT IN 1915 BY McKEEN MOTOR CAR CO.
CONVERTED TO GAS-ELECTRIC IN 1928.

SIDE ELEVATION OF 70 FOOT GAS-ELECTRIC MOTOR CAR
BAGGAGE-MAIL APARTMENTS WITH 300 H.P. HALL-SCOTT ENGINE

U.P. CAR M-23

UNION PACIFIC

RAILWAY EXPRESS
AGENCY
M-23

BAGGAGE

U.S. MAIL
RAILWAY
POST OFFICE

M-23

FOR FLOOR PLAN SEE SHEET-5

MC-2000 SHEET-6

Kansas was the heart of Doodlebug Country. Here is motor M-16 on UP rails at Beloit, KS, on October 22, 1948. This was the very last McKeen to operate on the UP.
A. C. Phelps

Union Pacific

ROAD NO.	BUILDER	DATE	BLDR. NO.	ENGINE & DRIVE	BODY TYPE	LGTH.	WT.	DISPOSITION	REMARKS
1	McKeen	1905	1	Riotti 100hp GM	6win wood 25p	31'	20t	Ret. 6/31	Burned, rblt. square end. 4-wheel car
2	McKeen	1905	2	Riotti 100hp GM	12win 57p	56½'	28t	Burned 1915	—
M-3 (3)	McKeen	1905	3	Riotti 100hp GM	10win Bag.-Pass.	55'	35t	To OSL M-62², 9/24	—
M-4¹ (4)	McKeen	1906	4	Riotti 100hp GM	10win Bag.-Pass.	55'	35t	Ret. 11/22	Eng. to M-27, demo. on Chi. & Alton
M-4²	McKeen	1911	107	McKeen 200hp GM	14win CE Bag. 38p	70'	40½t	Scr. 8/45	Ex-Gt. Western M-1, acq. 1928
5	McKeen	1906	5	Riotti 100hp GM	12win 38p	55'	35t	Ret. 4/16	—
M-5	McKeen	1910	89	McKeen 200hp GM	14win CE Bag. 38p	70'	39½t	Ret. 12/44	Ex-Gt. Western M-2, acq. 9/28
M-6 (6)	McKeen	1905	6	Riotti 100hp GM	12win CE 36p	55'	35t	Wrecked 1925	Rblt. 1926, body from Midl. Vly. 2, re-eng. McKeen 200hp GM, became 15win CE Bag. 38p, 70' 40t
M-7 (7)	McKeen	1906	7	Riotti 100hp GM	10win CE Pass.	55'	29t	Rblt. tlr. T-19, 1929	Used on Erie (no. 4000)
M-8	McKeen	1906	8	McKeen A 200hp GM	12win CE 49p	55'	30½t	Rblt. tlr. T-18, 1929	First car with McKeen eng.
M-9¹	McKeen	1906	9	McKeen A 200hp GM	12win CE 49p	55'	30½t	Ret. 11/22	Eng. to M-26. Square windows
M-9²	McKeen	1911	121	Samet 150hp GM	15win CE Bag. 38p	70'	39½t	Scr. 5/45	Ex-Saratoga & Encamp. Vy. M-1, acq. 1928
M-10	McKeen	1907	10	McKeen A 200hp GM	12win CE 54p	55'	34t	Ret. 4/34	Dist. fuel, heated by eng. water
M-11	McKeen	1907	11	McKeen A 200hp GM	12win CE Bag. 16p	55'	38½t	Ret. 7/42	Re-eng. Sterl. 180hp GE, 5/25; eng. to M-21, 1942
M-12	McKeen	1907	12	McKeen A 200hp GM	12win CE 50p	55'	35½t	Ret. 6/40	Dist. fuel
M-13	McKeen	1907	13	McKeen A 200hp GM	12win CE Bag. 34p	55'	35t	Burned 6/36	Dist. fuel
14	McKeen	1907	14	McKeen A 200hp GM	12win CE	55'	35t	To Ill. Cent. 111	Probably not used on U.P.
M-14	McKeen	1910	59	McKeen A 200hp GM	13win CE Bag. 38p	70'	39½t	Burned 8/35	Ex-St. Jos. & Grand Isl. 112, acq. 1917
M-15	McKeen	1911	116	McKeen A 200hp GM	17win CE Bag. 38p	70'	40½t	Ret. 1944	Ex-OSL M-62, acq. 10/17. Dist. fuel, later butane
M-16	McKeen	1911	117	McKeen A 200hp GM	16 win CE Bag. 50p	70'	43½t	Ret. 9/52	Ex-OSL M-63, acq. 10/17. Re-eng. 225hp Wint. 106A GE, 1926
M-17	McKeen	1907	17	McKeen A 200hp GM	12win CE 50p	55'	40t	Ret. 6/40	Dist. fuel, square rear windows
M-18	McKeen	1911	118	McKeen A 200hp GM	10win CE Bag. 38p	70'	41t	—	Ex-OSL M-65, acq. 1917
M-19	McKeen	1908	19	McKeen A 200hp GM	12win CE 48p	55'	40t	—	Dist. fuel, square rear windows
M-20	McKeen	1909	31	McKeen A 200hp GM	12win CE 50p	55'	35½t	Ret. 12/44	Dist. fuel, square rear windows
M-21	McKeen	1909	54	McKeen A 200hp GM	12win CE Bag. 50p	70'	40t	Ret. 1/48	Re-eng. 180hp Sterl. GE, 7/42; eng. from M-11

ROAD NO.	BUILDER	DATE	BLDR. NO.	ENGINE & DRIVE	BODY TYPE	LGTH.	WT.	DISPOSITION	REMARKS
M-22	McKeen	1909	55	McKeen A 200hp GM	12win CE Bag. 38p	70'	40t	Ret. 5/45	Dist. fuel
M-23	McKeen	1915	148	McKeen C 200hp GM	4win RPO Bag.	70'	40t	Rblt. by Brill, 1/29, ord. no. 22678	Re-eng. 300hp HS-GE, weight 51t
M-24	McKeen	1917	153	McKeen C 200hp GM	6win RPO Bag.	70'	40t	Rblt. by Brill, 1/29, ord. no. 22678	Re-eng 300hp HS-GE, weight 51t
M-25	McKeen	1910	104	McKeen A 200hp GM	15win CE Bag. 52p	70'	41t	Ret. 1944	Ex-ATSF M-102, acq. 1922
M-26	McKeen	1911	122	McKeen A 200hp GM	15win CE Bag. 48p	70'	38t	To LA&SL M-101, 1925	Blt. for Peoples Elec., Muskogee, OK, not del. Rblt. 6/23 with eng. from M-9[1]
M-27	McKeen	1913	137	McKeen A 200hp GM	12win CE 50p	55'	35t	Ret. 9/34	Ex-Minn. Nor. ''Minneapolis,'' eng. from M-4[1]
M-28	McKeen	1913	136	McKeen A	12win CE	55'	35t	Ret. 7/42	Ex-Minn. Nor. ''Anoka,'' acq. 1923
M-29 -30	Co. Shops	1927	—	HS 300hp GE	14win CE Bag. 44p	64'	46t 50t	—	Bodies from unused McKeen parts
M-31 -34	EMC St. Louis	1927	181-84 1412	Wint. 106A 225hp GE	19win 70p	72'	49½t	Ret. 6/48, 5/54, 5/54, 9/58	M-31, 33, 34 re-eng. from OSL M-65, 67, 68, 1933. 275hp Wint. 120
M-35	EMC St. Louis	1927	185 1412	Wint. 120D 275hp GE	19win 70p	72'	51½t	Ret. 8/58	Don. to Ill. Ry. Museum
M-36 -39	EMC Pullman	1928	322-25 6178	Wint. 120D 275hp GE	20win 74p	71'	55½t	Ret. 9/58 exc. M-37, scr. 8/51	M-36, 37 rbt. with 55 reclining seats, 8/32. M-39 seating reduced to 40
M-40 -41	Brill	1928	22677	HS 300hp GE	13win Bag. 44p	73'	56t	Ret. 9/58	M-41 don. to Stapleton, NB but scr. 1961
M-10000	EMC Pullman	1934	508 6424	Wint. 600hp DE	Power RPO Bag.	72½'	84½t	Scr. 2/42	''City of Salina'' Artic. Power Car; RPO elim. 1936

Trailers

10400	Pullman	1934	6424	—	16win 56p	58'	—	Scr. 2/42	''City of Salina'' chair car
10401	Pullman	1934	6424	—	14win 52p	71'	—	Scr. 2/42	''City of Salina'' obs.-buffet
T-1	McKeen	1905	T-1	—	Bag.	31'	13t	—	Orig. 4 wheel
T-2-4	McKeen	1906	T-2-4	—	Bag.	31'	14½t	Ret. 1934	T-3 weighed 12½t, T-4 14t
T-5-7	McKeen	1907	T-5-7	—	Bag.	31t	12½t	Ret. 9/34	T-6 weighed 13t, T-7 12t
T-8	McKeen	1908	T-8	—	Bag.	31'	14t	Ret. 9/34	—
T-10-17	Pullman	1928	6179	—	RPO-Bag.	71'	38½t	Ret. 1934	—
T-18, 19	Co. Shops	1929	—	—	13win 49p	50t	25½t	Ret. 1934	Rblt. from M-8, M-7. Bag. sect.
499	McKeen	1907	—	—	20win 78p	70'	—	—	Train doors

Oregon-Washington Ry. & Navigation Co.

ROAD NO.	BUILDER	DATE	BLDR. NO.	ENGINE & DRIVE	BODY TYPE	LGTH.	WT.	DISPOSITION	REMARKS
M-76 (600)	McKeen	1909	61	McKeen 200hp GM	9win CE Bag. 36p	55'	33t	Ret. 7/42	Ex-Ore. Ry. & Nav. 1
M-77 (601)	McKeen	1910	63	McKeen 200hp GM	11win CE Bag. 36p	55'	33t	Ret. 4/40	Ex-Ore. Ry. & Nav. 2
M-78 (602)	McKeen	1910	68	McKeen 200hp GM	11win CE Bag. 36p	55'	33t	Ret. 9/34	Ex-North Coast A-1
M-79 (603)	McKeen	1910	66	McKeen 200hp GM	11win CE Bag. 39p	55'	33t	Ret. 9/34	Ex-North Coast A-2
M-80 (604)	McKeen	1910	78	McKeen 200hp GM	15win CE Bag. 44p	70'	37t	Ret. 6/36	Ex-Ore. Ry. & Nav. 3

ROAD NO.	BUILDER	DATE	BLDR. NO.	ENGINE & DRIVE	BODY TYPE	LGTH.	WT.	DISPOSITION	REMARKS
M-81 (605)	McKeen	1911	119	McKeen 200hp GM	14win CE Bag. 44p	70'	39½t	Ret. 6/36	—
M-82 (606)	McKeen	1911	120	McKeen 200hp GM	13win CE Bag. 44p	70'	37t	Ret. 8/40	—
M-83 (607)	McKeen	1913	106	McKeen 200hp GM	13win CE Bag. 52p	70'	37t	Ret. 7/42	—
M-98	EMC St. Louis	1928	242 1454	Wint. 120 275hp GE	7win RPO Bag. 20p	72'	52½t	Ret. 1961	To work service, 1949
M-99	EMC St. Louis	1927	190 1414	Wint. 120 275hp GE	13win Bag. 36p	72'	48t	Ret. 1946	Pass. sect. eliminated

Oregon Short Line

ROAD NO.	BUILDER	DATE	BLDR. NO.	ENGINE & DRIVE	BODY TYPE	LGTH.	WT.	DISPOSITION	REMARKS
M-60 (470)	McKeen	1909	51	McKeen A 200hp GM	10win RPO Bag.	70'	37½t	To Pac. & Idaho Nor., 1928	Reacq. from PIN, 8/30. Ret. 1944
M-61 (480)	McKeen	1909	52	McKeen A 200hp GM	10win RPO Bag.	70'	37½t	Ret. 12/42	—
M-62[1] (491)	McKeen	1911	116	McKeen A 200hp GM	16win CE Bag. 50p	70'	40½t	To UP M-15, 10/17	—
M-62[2]	McKeen	1905	3	Riotti 100hp GM	10win Bag.-Pass.	55'	35t	Rblt. tlr. T-52, 1924	Ex-UP M-3, acq. 9/24
M-63 (492)	McKeen	1911	117	McKeen A 200hp GM	16win CE Bag. 50p	70'	43½t	To UP M-16, 10/17	—
M-64 (490)	McKeen	1811	115	McKeen A 200hp GM	18win CE 70p	70'	37t	Ret. 8/37	—
M-65[1] (493)	McKeen	1911	118	McKeen A 200hp GM	13win CE Bag. 38p	70'	37t	To UP M-18, 10/17	—
M-65[2]	EMC	1927	186 1413	Wint. 120 275hp GE	7win RPO Bag. 24p	72'	50t	Scr. 5/48	Re-eng. with eng. from UP M-31, 11/32.
M-66 -68	EMC St. Louis	1927	187-9 1413	Wint. 120 275hp GE	7win RPO Bag. 24p	72'	50t	M-66 rblt. detector car DC-2, 1950	Re-eng. with eng. from UP M-33, 34, 4/33
M-69 -70	Brill	1930	22866	HS 300hp GE	19win 70p	73'	57t	Ret. 5/58	—

Trailers

ROAD NO.	BUILDER	DATE	BLDR. NO.	ENGINE & DRIVE	BODY TYPE	LGTH.	WT.	DISPOSITION	REMARKS
T-50-51	McKeen	1909	—	—	RPO-Bag.	31'	12½t	T-50 to Pac. & Ida. Nor., 1928	T-51 blt. 1911, ex-SP 12
T-52	McKeen	1905	3	—	RPO-Bag.	31½'	20½t	—	Was M-62[1], orig. UP M-3, rblt. Co. Shops
T-53-54	Pullman	1930	6380	—	RPO-Bag.	71'	38½t	—	—

St. Joseph & Grand Island

ROAD NO.	BUILDER	DATE	BLDR. NO.	ENGINE & DRIVE	BODY TYPE	LGTH.	WT.	DISPOSITION	REMARKS
110	McKeen	1909	42	McKeen A 200hp GM	10win CE Bag. 36p	55'	35t	Ret. 1934	—
111	McKeen	1909	57	McKeen A 200hp GM	15win CE Mail-50p	70'	40t	Ret. 1944	—
112-115	McKeen	1910	59, 70, 73, 74	McKeen A 200hp GM	13win CE Bag. 38p	70'	39½t	112 to UP M-14, 1917	113-115 all burned, in 1920, 1912, 1928

San Pedro, Los Angeles & Salt Lake

ROAD NO.	BUILDER	DATE	BLDR. NO.	ENGINE & DRIVE	BODY TYPE	LGTH.	WT.	DISPOSITION	REMARKS
100 (1)	McKeen	1910	75	McKeen A 200hp GM	14win CE Bag. 53p	70'	39t	Scr. 7/42	Square back
101	McKeen	1911	122	McKeen A 200hp GM	15win CE Bag. 48p	70'	38t	—	Ex-UP M-26, acq. 1925

The Wabash was not a big doodlebug operator, but did have a couple. Here is the 4001 at Springfield, IL, on May 29, 1948.
Author's Collection

Wabash

ROAD NO.	BUILDER	DATE	BLDR. NO.	ENGINE & DRIVE	BODY TYPE	LGTH.	WT.	DISPOSITION	REMARKS
4000	St. Louis EMC	1926	1387 140	Wint. 106 175hp GE	Bag.	59½'	38t	To M/W, 1937	—
4001	St. Louis EMC	1926	1388 139	Wint. 106 175hp GE	6win Bag. 27p	59½'	39t	To broker, 1956	—

Western Pacific

Budd RDC demonstrator pauses at Yuba City, CA, on the Western Pacific (right) before the WP bought its own units. One of the two WP Brill-Service cars of 1922 is shown (below) after sale to the Chicago & Illinois Midland, where it was used as an inspection car.
Ted Wurm Collection; Author's Collection

IN ITS ENTIRE history, the Western Pacific has operated only four rail motorcars. These four cars came in pairs—one lightweight pair for the 23-mile San Jose branch in 1923, and one heavy pair of RDC cars for all 917 miles of the mainline, Salt Lake City to Oakland, in 1950.

The WP's San Jose branch was not opened until September 1, 1921, and on June 14, 1923, passenger service was inaugurated between the East San Jose station to the main line at Niles with two Service Motor Truck Co. Model 55 cars.

Only one round trip per day was operated, to connect with the main line *Scenic Limited*. Patronage was never very heavy, and the service was discontinued on August 30, 1931. The cars were sold to Georgia Car & Locomotive Co., a dealer in used railroad equipment. One of the cars was sold to the Georgia Northern and the other to the Chicago & Illinois Midland, where it was rebuilt slightly and made into an inspection car.

Since the WP has so few branch lines, its purchase of two Budd RDC cars in 1950 came as somewhat of a surprise. They were in fact used to replace the company's secondary main line train operating the entire length of the railroad.

Dubbed the *Zephyrettes*, the two Budd cars shuttled back and forth on a thrice-weekly schedule between September 15, 1950, and October 1, 1960. They handled local and company passengers not allowed on the haughty *California Zephyr* streamliner.

After their demise on the WP, the cars were sold to the Northern Pacific and eventually to Amtrak for further use.

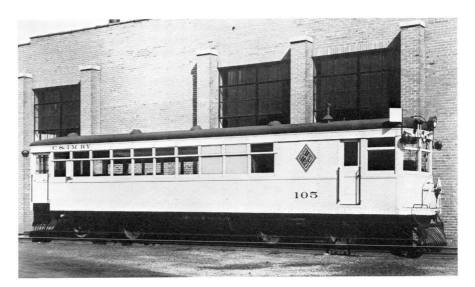

Western Pacific

ROAD NO.	BUILDER	DATE	BLDR. NO.	ENGINE & DRIVE	BODY TYPE	LGTH.	WT.	DISPOSITION	REMARKS
198-99	Brill Service	1922	21566	Midw. 399 68hp GM	10win Bag. 42p	43'	13t	To Ga., Car. & Loco., 1939	One car to Ga. Nor., 55, other to CI&M, 105
375-76	Budd	1950	5008, 5010	2 GMC 275hp GM	RDC-2	85'	—	To NP B-31, B-32, 4/62. To Amtrak 31, 32	"Zephyrettes"

Wheeling & Lake Erie's M-101 seems loaded with passengers at Brilliant, OH, in 1927. Additional capacity was provided by the wooden combine.
Harold K. Vollrath Collection

Wheeling & Lake Erie

ROAD NO.	BUILDER	DATE	BLDR. NO.	ENGINE & DRIVE	BODY TYPE	LGTH.	WT.	DISPOSITION	REMARKS
M101	Brill	1927	22439	Brill 250hp GE	12win Bag. 46p	60'	44t	Rblt. tlr., 1935. Scr. 6/42	Rblt. to 15 win, 54p, 1931
M102-03	Brill	1927	22438	Brill 250hp GE	10win RPO 44p	60'	46t	To Tonopah & Goldf., 1934-35	Both rblt. to 5 win, Mail-Bag. 18p, 1931

Index

Acknowledgments

PERHAPS THE GREATEST pleasure I have received as a result of having written the first book in this series, *Interurbans Without Wires*, has been the many warm and sincere letters telling me of the pleasure they have derived from that book.

Let me hasten to say that there certainly has been no diminution of help from the many whose contributions were listed in the first book, but for this volume I will list those of you whose material contributions came since that time, plus a few that were inadvertently left out of the acknowledgements in Special 66.

In this vein I would like to especially mention Bob Washbish of Culver City, CA, who provided many of the McKeen photos. Again, to all of you, my most sincere thanks!

The contributors:

Jim Bennett, Stuttgart, AR

C. A. Brown, New Haven RR Technical Assn., Sutton, MA

R. H. Carlson, Coombes, TX

Tom Dixon, Chesapeake & Ohio Historical Society, Alderson, WV

Charles Duckworth, Missouri Pacific RR, St. Louis

Tom Fetters, author, *Piedmont & Northern*

John Baskin Harper, Chicago, IL

Cornelius Hauk, Cincinnati, OH

L. C. Hutchinson, Boston & Maine Hist. Society, Wilmington, MA

Albin Lee, Albuquerque, NM

J. C. McDaniel, Carbon, TX

Don Marenzi, San Luis Obispo, Ca

Felix Refischneider, Fairton, NJ

Fred W. Schneider III, Lancaster, PA

Chuck Seibert, Camp Hill, PA

George Votava, New Hyde Park, NY

R. T. Wallis, Wheaton, IL

John H. Wickere, Minnesota Hist. Society, St. Paul

Van Wilkins, Shenandoah Jct, WV

Charles Winters, Kansas City, MO

Author's Note

THOSE OF US who took part in the production of our first book on this subject, *Interurbans Without Wires*, were extremely gratified and flattered with the way in which the book was so warmly received. It is our hope that *Doodlebug Country* will be welcomed in a like manner.

Our third book in the railcar series will explore the myriad short line railroads which operated rail motorcars. It will be the most difficult book of the series. We now have in our files the names of more than 500 lines that at one time or another operated doodlebugs. The problem is that in many cases we have no knowledge of exactly what the cars were. Often they were crude rebuildings of an automobile or truck, while others were of more elaborate design and adaptation. We would like to be able to document as completely as we can in this future volume these "question mark cars."

So I am asking for your help in identifying these obscure pieces of equipment. Not only do we need further information on data we now possess, even on some of the more prominent lines, such as the Akron, Canton & Youngstown, but we need photos of cars used on the out-of-the-way short lines. Inasmuch as many of the lines were abandoned 50 or 60 years ago we probably won't be able to completely cover the subject but, with your help, it won't be for lack of trying.

Further down the road—and as a natural conclusion to this series—will be a volume on the Budd Rail Diesel Car (RDC). By the time of its publication, the RDC story should be pretty well closed. Not only will American-built cars be covered, but also those built under license in Australia and cars built in other countries that seem to have been at least partially inspired by the RDC.

If you can help, please write to me directly at Troxel Models, 216 S. Western Ave., Los Angeles CA 90004. And if you're in Los Angeles by all means drop by for a chat.

—ED KEILTY